THE WALAYCHO CHORD BIBLE

(DGBEB Standard Tuning)

by

Tobe A. Richards

A Fretted Friends Publication for Cabot Books

Published by:
Cabot Books
Copyright © 2013 & 2016 by Cabot Books
All rights reserved.

First Edition October 2013
Second Edition March 2016

ISBN-13: 978-1-906207-47-2

No part of this publication may be reproduced in any form
or by any means without the prior consent of the publisher.

Cabot Books
3 Kenton Mews
Henleaze
Bristol
BS9 4LT
United Kingdom

Visit our online site at www.frettedfriendsmusic.com
e-mail: cabotbooks@blueyonder.co.uk

TABLE OF CONTENTS

Introduction...4-5

Fingering..5

Chord Theory & FAQs...6-7

Understanding Chord Boxes...8

Walaycho Fingerboard & Tuning Layout..9

Chords Covered in this Book...10

Slash Chords...11

Using a Capo or *Capo D'astra*..11

C Chords..12-16

C♯/D♭ Chords...17-21

D Chords...22-26

D♯/E♭ Chords...27-31

E Chords..32-36

F Chords..37-41

F♯/G♭ Chords...42-46

G Chords...47-51

G♯/A♭ Chords...52-56

A Chords...57-61

A♯/B♭ Chords...62-66

B Chords...67-71

Major Slash Chords..72-75

A Selection of Moveable Chord Shapes..................................76-79

The Charango Family Factfile & Tunings................................80-81

Alternative Chord Name Chart...82

Notes..83-85

Chord Window Blanks..86-110

INTRODUCTION

The Walaycho Chord Bible provides the musician with 1,728 chords in all keys, featuring 68 different chord types, with 3 variations of each standard chord. 144 major slash chords are also included, together with 48 moveable chord shape diagrams (providing access to a further 576 barré and standard moveable chords) making this the most comprehensive reference guide for the walaycho currently available. For many years now, guitarists have been able to pick up a songbook and instantly play the songs in front of them, either with the help of one of the many published guides, or through the chord boxes supplied with most popular music. With the help of this *Chord Bible*, beginners and experienced walaycho players alike will be able to take advantage of the many songbooks, fake books and musical compendiums by any artist you would care to name, from *The Beatles* to *Joan Baez*, from *Planxty* to *The Pogues* or *Springsteen* to *Simon & Garfunkel*. With 68 different chordal variations in all keys, virtually any song should be playable!

Having a good chordal knowledge should arguably be the bedrock in any fretted or keyboard musicians armoury. Whether you're playing rock, pop, folk, jazz, blues, country or other types of music, it's impossible to supply a suitable accompaniment to any vocal or solo instrumental music without providing a chordal or harmonic backing. The subtle nuance of an added ninth chord over a major chord is something that can't be captured simply by playing a melody line. In theory it is possible to approximate the harmonic intervals of any music using a limited palette of chords - probably around ten to twelve. But wherever possible it's best to use correct harmonies if they're available to you.

Having five courses of strings, the walaycho is obviously limited to five note chords, but by making acceptable compromises and omitting the least important parts of that chord, even the most complex musical structures are possible. For instance, in the case of an eleventh, the third is generally omitted without the character of the chord being adversely affected. Equally, the root or key note isn't always necessary to achieve an effective approximation of the full chord. The third is rarely missing from the majority of chords (other than elevenths) as it determines whether the key is major or minor - although this isn't a hard and fast rule, particularly in folk music where the root and fifth form the basis of most traditional music. These two intervals are generally the starting point for a number of open tunings of instruments as diverse as the guitar, the Irish bouzouki and the mountain dulcimer. The same interval is also used in a lot of heavy rock where a fifth chord is described as a *power chord*. Even though a power chord is technically neither major nor minor, it's more often used as an alternative for a major chord in most popular music.

One question which often pops up is *how many chords do I need to learn?* The smart answer is *'how long is a piece of string?'*, which is true, but it doesn't actually answer the question if you don't know where to start. My advice would be to begin with simple chord clusters like the popular G, C, D and Em progression and gradually work in new ones as you advance. If you intend playing within a rock format, it's probably sensible to learn the E, A, B sequence which is the staple of most guitarists and bassists. As a generalisation, jazz probably requires the greatest chordal knowledge of any form of music, so the learning curve will be longer if you're planning to pick up any songbook and instantly produce a recognisable version of your favourite *Duke Ellington* or *Steely Dan* number. The only truth as far as harmonic knowledge goes is you can never learn *too* much!

In this series of chord theory books, I've included a comprehensive selection of configurations of chords in all keys. As I mentioned previously, this will enable you to pick up virtually any songbook or fake book (topline melody and chord symbols) and look up the chord shape that's needed. Obviously, you'll come across the occasional song which doesn't conform to the normal harmonic intervals which you find in this, or any other chord theory publication, but with a little experimentation and experience, you'll be able to make a reasonable stab at it. For instance, most players would be more than a little bemused if they suddenly came across an instruction to play a *Gbmaj7add6/D*. Fortunately, this is fairly unusual, but from the knowledge you'll have learned, you'll be able to use a similar chord or work it out note by note. Put simply, if every theoretically possible chord shape were to be included in this or any other book, the result would resemble something akin to several volumes of the *Yellow Pages*!

FINGERING

Always a tricky subject and one which seems to generate a lot of discussion and differing opinions as to which method is correct. Personally, I take the view that it's a largely fruitless exercise, as the number of variables involved make a definitive answer unlikely. So what I've decided to do in this book is to choose fingering positions which feel comfortable to me. Some chord shapes will dictate the fingering used, but others will be down to personal preference. If you can practise your two and three finger chords using different fingers, it will make your playing a lot more fluid when you change to another chord shape. But if you develop habits which limit you to one playing position, it isn't the end of the world either, if you can make the transitions seamless.

The only rules, if you could loosely call them that, are:-

a) Don't abandon using your pinky or little finger if you're just beginning to play, as you'll eventually need it for some of the four finger chords which frequently crop up.

b) Try to avoid fretting with the thumb unless you're learning an instrument like the mountain dulcimer which requires a longer stretch. I know a number of players employ it on slimmer necked instruments, but I personally feel it leads to bad habits.

c) Keep your left hand fingernails short or fretting becomes a major problem. Obviously do the reverse if you're a lefty.

d) If you're a beginner and you're naturally left handed, don't get persuaded into buying a right handed instrument - it won't work! The learning curve will be steeper and you'll never get the fluidity you'd achieve with your natural hand. Most acoustic instruments can be adapted for a left hander apart from cutaway guitars and f-style mandolins etc., by reversing the nut and strings. For the non-reversible instruments, always go for a left handed model.

e) Learn to barré with other fingers apart from your index finger. This will prove invaluable with more complex chords and increase finger strength as well.

f) Don't be afraid to use fingerings further up the neck in combination with open strings as these will give you interesting new voicings and are generally quite popular in folk music. A number of these are provided in this book.

g) The walaycho should really be played with the fingers of your strumming and picking hand, but for all the pick or plectrum users out there, there's no reason why you shouldn't carry this technique over from the guitar. The only drawback being greater wear on the nylon strings if you're using a hard pick. The sound will also be brighter and generally louder.

CHORD THEORY & FAQs

Q *What is a chord?*
A It's a collection of three or more notes played simultaneously. The exceptions in this book are the fourths and fifths (power chords) which aren't in the strictest sense, true chords. For convenience sake, they are classed as such.

Q *What is a triad?*
A A chord containing three notes. For example, G Major, Bm, D+ or Asus4.

Q *What are intervals?*
A Intervals are the musical distance between notes in a musical scale. For instance in the scale of C Major, C is the 1st note, D is the 2nd note, E the 3rd and so on. So if you're playing the chord of C Major, your intervals will be 1–3–5 or C as the *first* note, E as the *third* note and G as the *perfect fifth*.

Q *What is a chromatic scale and which intervals does it contain?*
A: A chromatic scale encompasses all twelve notes in a musical scale, including the sharps and flats. It's also the basis for the naming of *every* chord in existence. See the staff diagram below to see the intervals:

Chromatic Scale in C

Root or 1st | Minor 2nd | Major 2nd | Minor 3rd | Major 3rd | Perfect 4th | Augmented 4th *or* Diminished 5th | Perfect 5th | Minor 6th | Major 6th | Minor 7th | Major 7th

Q *What is a seventh chord?*
A: In its most basic form, an additional note beyond the triad. Sevenths can be either major or flattened. For instance, returning to our old friend, the key of *C*, a *Cmaj7* has an added *B* on top of the *C–E–G* triad. The resultant chord has a mellow quality often found in jazz. Now if you take the B and flatten it by dropping the fourth note in your chord down to a B flat, you get a C7.

Q: *Then why isn't it called a C minor seventh?*
A: Technically this *is* a minor seventh note, but this would create a lot of confusion when naming chords, as you already have a minor interval option in your triad (in the key of C major, E flat), so it's always referred to as a 7th to differentiate between it and a major seventh.

Q: *What is an extension?*
A: A chord which goes beyond the scope of triads and sevenths. Basically, extensions are additional notes placed above the triad or seventh in a musical stave, fingerboard or keyboard. It's important to understand these are, for theoretical purposes, always placed above the seventh. Or in layman's terms, higher up the scale. The confusion comes when you start to realise a 9th is identical to a 2nd - in the scale of C – a D note.

Q: *So why is the ninth note the same as the second note?*
A: This takes a little grasping, but if you remember that if your note goes higher than the seventh it's a 9th, but if it's lower, it'll be a 2nd. An example of this would be Csus2, which contains the root

note of C, a 2nd or suspended D note and a G, the perfect 5th. You'll see this even more clearly if you look at the piano keyboard diagram below. Count from the C up to the following D beyond the 7th (B note). From the C to the second D is exactly nine whole notes.

Q: *Do any other extensions share a common note?*
A: Yes, other examples include the *11th*, which is also a *4th* and the *13th* which shares a note with the *6th*.

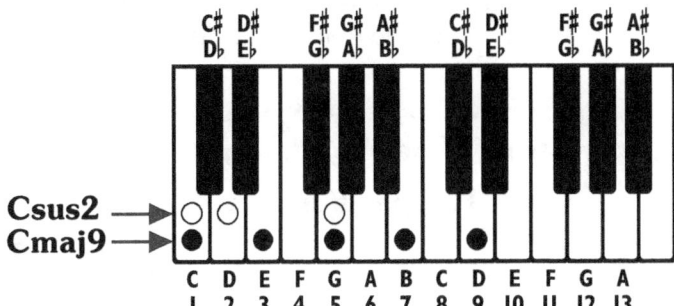

Q: *What are inversions?*
A: In the root version of a chord, the notes run in their correct order from lowest to highest. In the case of G major, it would be G–B–D. With an inversion of the same chord the notes would run in a different order. For example, the first inversion of G major would be B–D–G and the second, D–G–B. In general, triads sound more or less the same when they're inverted, but that's certainly not the case with sevenths and extensions which can sound quite different and occasionally discordant when the notes are jumbled up in certain configurations. Inversions can also produce different chords using the same basic notes. A good example of this would be *C6 (C-E-G-A)* which produces an *Am7 (A-C-E-G)* when it's inverted (both contain the notes of C–E–G–A, but in a different order). The major variations are in the tonal properties of the chords, making them sound quite different from one another.

Q: *Do elevenths and thirteenths have any particular properties?*
A: Yes. In most cases the 3rd is omitted from eleventh chords and the 11th from the majority of thirteenths as they're deemed unnecessary and arguably, create unwanted dissonance.

Q: *Some chords are called by different names in different music books. What should I do?*
A: The alternative chord name reference chart at the back of the book should help sort out the confusion.

Q: *What is a suspended chord?*
A: It's simpler to think of suspended chords as a stepping stone to a major or resolving chord. In effect the third has been left in a state of suspension by either raising it to a fourth (sus4) or lowering it to a second (sus2). Sevenths also provide versions of the suspended chord in the form of C7sus4 or C7sus2 (using the key of C as an example).

Q: *What is a diminished chord?*
A: A diminished chord has a dissonent quality to it where the third and fifth notes in a triad are flattened by a semi-tone. Again, using C as an example, C major (C-E-G) is altered to Cdim (C-E♭-G♭). A second version of a dimished chord is also used in many forms of music, the diminished seventh. This retains the elements of a standard diminished chord, adding a double flat in the seventh (C-E♭-G♭-B♭♭). A B♭♭ in this case is, to all intents and purposes, really an A note.

Q: *What is an augmented chord?*
A: An augmented chord basically performs the opposite task to a diminished one. Instead of lowering the fifth by a semitone, it raises it by the same interval. A C+ (augmented) chord contains the triad of C-E-G♯. The major root and third are retained and the fifth is sharpened.

7

UNDERSTANDING THE CHORD BOXES

The three diagrams below show the chord conventions illustrated in this guide. Most experienced fretted instrument players should be familiar with them. The suggested fingering positions are only meant as a general guide and will depend, in many instances, on hand size, finger length and flexibility, so feel free to experiment. The location of the black circles is unalterable, though, if you want to produce the correct voicing.

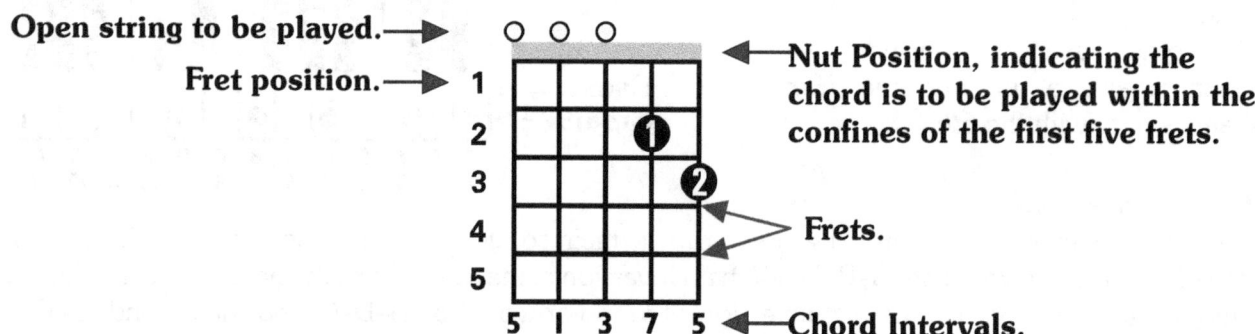

Open string to be played.

Fret position.

Nut Position, indicating the chord is to be played within the confines of the first five frets.

Frets.

Chord Intervals.

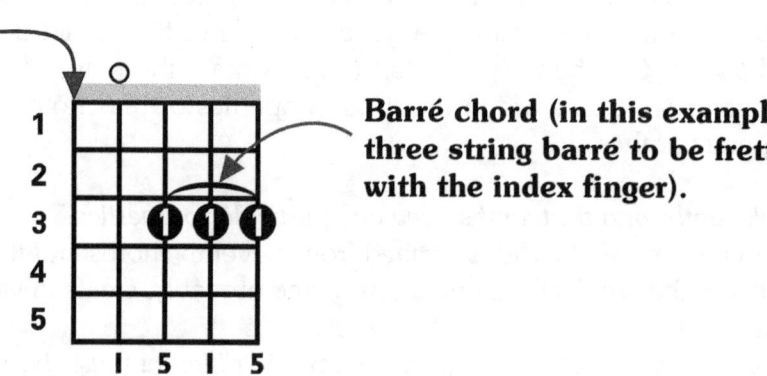

If there are no markers above or below the string, the string should not be played.

Barré chord (in this example, a three string barré to be fretted with the index finger).

Suggested fingering. In this case the 1st or index finger marker is displayed.

A damped string is represented by an 'X' on or above the string. This indicates the string shouldn't be played.

A two string barré to be played with the fourth finger.

Left to right: 5th, 4th, 3rd, 2nd and 1st courses of strings.

Whether a fretted instrument has single strings or pairs of strings, the chord boxes in this book, other chord dictionaries and songbooks treat it as a four stringed instrument. This convention is common to all double or triple course instruments such as the mandolin or tiple, making the diagrams a lot less confusing and free from unnecessary clutter.

WALAYCHO FINGERBOARD & TUNING LAYOUT

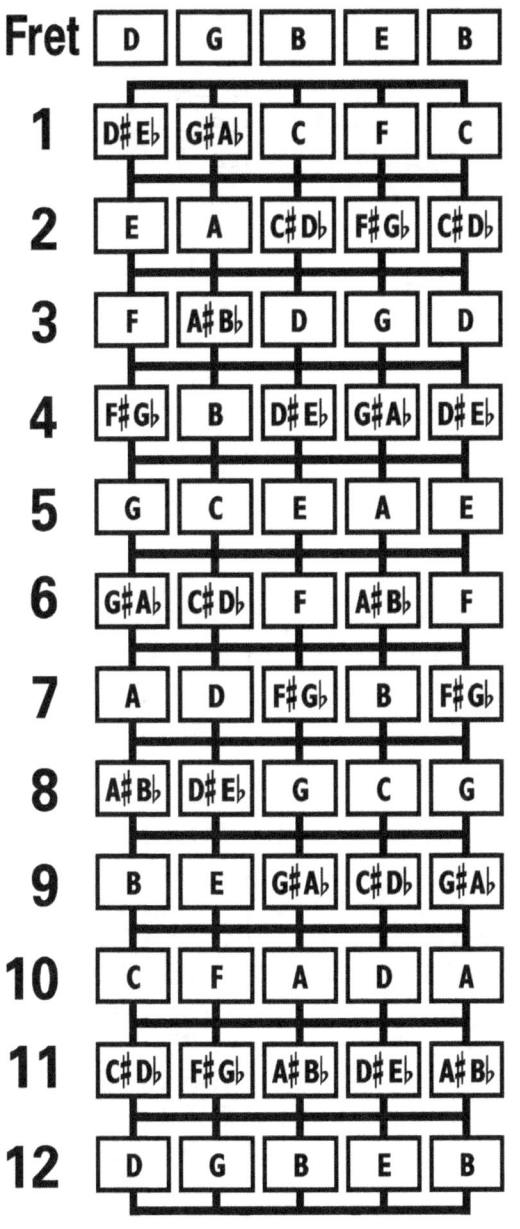

Fingerboard note layout

All matched pairs apart from the 5th and 6th strings which are an octave apart.

Optionally, some walaycho players like to use octave string pairs on the 4th and 5th courses.

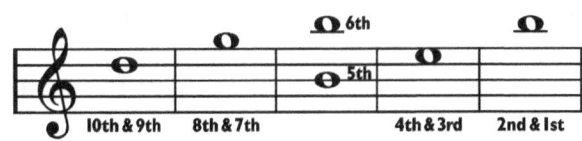

Walaycho Tuning in Standard Notation

To tune your walaycho accurately, it's best to use an electronic chromatic tuner, but if there isn't one available, you can tune it to a guitar or piano/electronic keyboard. The following tuning grid gives the correct fingering positions on the guitar fingerboard and piano keyboard.

Walaycho	Guitar	Piano
1st & 2nd string (B)	1st string (E) fretted at the 19th fret	2nd B above middle C
3rd & 4th string (E)	1st string (E) fretted at the 12th fret	2nd E above middle C
5th string (B)	1st string (E) fretted at the 19th fret	2nd B above middle C
6th low octave string (B)	1st string (E) fretted at the 7th fret	1st B above middle C
7th & 8th string (G)	1st string (E) fretted at the 15th fret	2nd G above middle C
9th & 10th string (D)	1st string (E) fretted at the 10th fret	2nd D above middle C

THE CHORDS COVERED IN THIS BOOK

Chord	Chord Name in Full	Harmonic Interval
C	Major	1–3–5
Cm	Minor	1–F3-5
C-5	Major Diminished Fifth	1–3–F5
C°	Diminished	1–F3–F5
C4	Fourth	1–4
C5	Fifth or Power Chord	1–5
Csus2	Suspended Second	1–2–5
Csus4	Suspended Fourth	1–4–5
Csus4add9	Suspended Fourth Added Ninth	1–4–5–9
C+	Augmented	1–3–S5
C6	Major Sixth	1–3–5–6
Cadd9	Major Added Ninth	1–3–5–9
Cadd11	Major Added Eleventh	1–3–5–11
Cm6	Minor Sixth	1–F3–5–6
Cm-6	Minor Diminished Sixth	1–F3–5–F6
Cmadd9	Minor Added Ninth	1–F3–5–9
C6add9	Major Sixth Added Ninth	1–3–5–6–9
Cm6add9	Minor Sixth Added Ninth	1–F3–5–6–9
C°7	Diminished Seventh	1–F3–F5–DF7
C7	Seventh	1–3–5–F7
C7sus2	Seventh Suspended Second	1–2–5–F7
C7sus4	Seventh Suspended Fourth	1–4–5–F7
C7-5	Seventh Diminished Fifth	1–3–F5–F7
C7+5	Seventh Augmented Fifth	1–3–S5–F7
C7-9	Seventh Minor Ninth	1–3–5–F7–F9
C7+9	Seventh Augmented Ninth	1–3–5–F7–S9
C7-5-9	Seventh Diminished Fifth Minor Ninth	1–3–F5–F7–F9
C7-5+9	Seventh Diminished Fifth Augmented Ninth	1–3–F5–F7–S9
C7+5-9	Seventh Augmented Fifth Minor Ninth	1–3–S5–F7–F9
C7+5+9	Seventh Augmented Fifth Augmented Ninth	1–3–S5–F7–S9
C7add11	Seventh Added Eleventh	1–3–5–F7–11
C7+11	Seventh Augmented Eleventh	1–3–5–F7–S11
C7add13	Seventh Added Thirteenth	1–3–5–F7–13
Cm7	Minor Seventh	1–F3–5–F7
Cm7-5	Minor Seventh Diminished Fifth	1–F3–F5–F7
Cm7-5-9	Minor Seventh Diminished Fifth Minor Ninth	1–F3–F5–F7–F9
Cm7-9	Minor Seventh Minor Ninth	1–F3–5–F7–F9
Cm7add11	Minor Seventh Added Eleventh	1–F3–5–F7–11
Cm(maj7)	Minor Major Seventh	1–F3–5–7
Cmaj7	Major Seventh	1–3–5–7
Cmaj7-5	Major Seventh Diminished Fifth	1–3–F5–7
Cmaj7+5	Major Seventh Augmented Fifth	1–3–S5–7
Cmaj7+11	Major Seventh Augmented Eleventh	1–3–5–7–S11
C9	Ninth	1–3–5–F7–9
C9sus4	Ninth Suspended Fourth	1–4–5–F7–9
C9-5	Ninth Diminished Fifth	1–3–F5–F7–9
C9+5	Ninth Augmented Fifth	1–3–S5–F7–9
C9+11	Ninth Augmented Eleventh	1–3–5–F7–9–S11
Cm9	Minor Ninth	1–F3–5–F7–9

Chord	Chord Name in Full	Harmonic Interval
Cm9-5	Minor Ninth Diminished Fifth	1–F3–F5–F7–9
Cm(maj9)	Minor Major Ninth	1–F3–5–7–9
Cmaj9	Major Ninth	1–3–5–7–9
Cmaj9-5	Major Ninth Diminished Fifth	1–3–F5–7–9
Cmaj9+5	Major Ninth Augmented Fifth	1–3–S5–7–9
Cmaj9add6	Major Ninth Added Sixth	1–3–5–6–7–9
Cmaj9+11	Major Ninth Augmented Eleventh	1–3–5–7–9–S11
C11	Eleventh	1–3–5–F7–9–11
C11-9	Eleventh Diminished Ninth	1–3–5–F7–F9–11
Cm11	Minor Eleventh	1–F3–5–F7–9–11
Cmaj11	Major Eleventh	1–3–5–7–9–11
C13	Thirteenth	1–3–5–F7–9–11–13
C13sus4	Thirteenth Suspended Fourth	1–4–5–F7–9–11–13
C13-5-9	Thirteenth Diminished Fifth Minor Ninth	1–3–F5–F7–F9–11–13
C13-9	Thirteenth Minor Ninth	1–3–5–F7–F9–11–13
C13+9	Thirteenth Augmented Ninth	1–3–5–F7–S9–11–13
C13+11	Thirteenth Augmented Eleventh	1–3–5–F7–9–S11–13
Cm13	Minor Thirteenth	1–F3–5–F7–9–11–13
Cmaj13	Major Thirteenth	1–3–5–7–9–11–13

Key: F = Flat   S = Sharp   DF = Double Flat

SLASH CHORDS

What is a slash chord? Put simply, they're standard chords with an added note in the bass. *So what differentiates a C chord from a C/G when the G is already part of that chord, in this case, the fifth?* Theoretically, nothing, but the difference is very apparent when you actually sound the chord. The G bass is emphasised to provide a different feel to the harmonics. Slashes are also commonly found when the music calls for a descending bassline. For example; C, C/B, C/A and C/G.

The note after the slash indicates the bass note being played. For instance C/D would be an instruction to play a C chord with a D bass.

Slash Note. Generally found on the 5th & 4th courses.

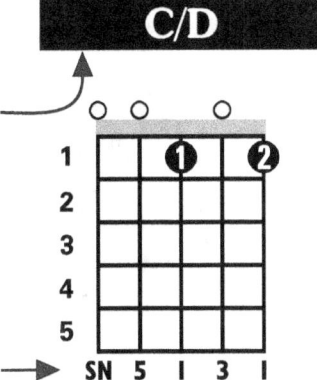

How do I play a slash chord that isn't listed in this book? Well, firstly, it would be an almost impossible task to cover every possible slash chord in existence, because the variations are potentially even greater than with standard chords. What you can do, within the confines of this guide, is to find the part of the chord before the slash in the main body of the book and then look for the nearest bass note on the fourth or fifth courses of strings . To find the right bass note, consult the fingerboard layout on *page 9*.

USING A CAPO (OR *CAPO D'ASTRA*)

Using a capo is a quick and *easy* way of changing key to suit a different vocal range or to join in with with other musicians playing in a different key. For the uniniated, a capo is a moveable bar that clamps onto the fingerboard of fretted instruments. It works in much the same way as using a finger barré to hold down the strings. They come in a variety of designs and prices, the simplest using a metal rod covered in rubber and sprung with elastic. For the walaycho look for a guitar capo.

C Chords

C	Cm	C7	Cm7
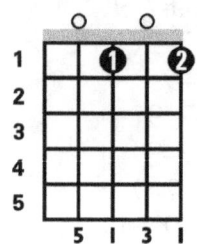	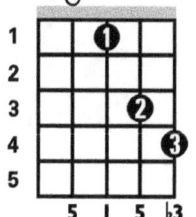	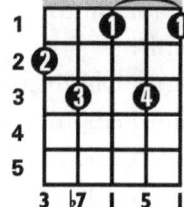	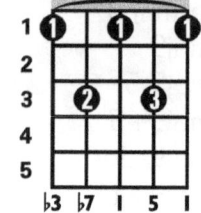
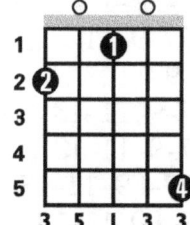	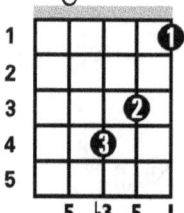	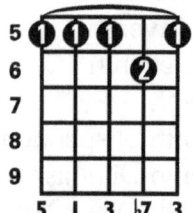	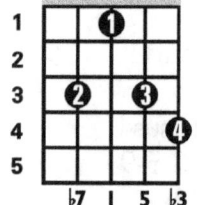
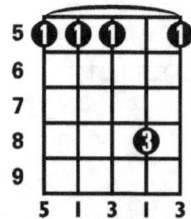	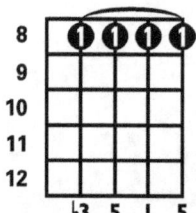	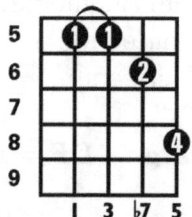	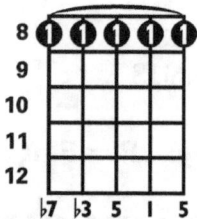

C5	C6	Cm6	Cmaj7
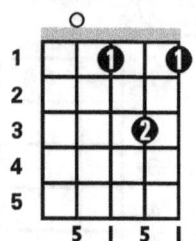	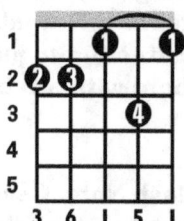	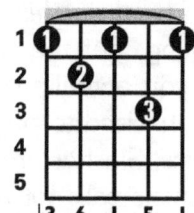	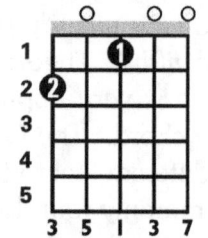
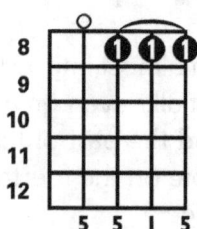	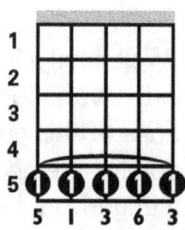	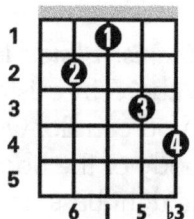	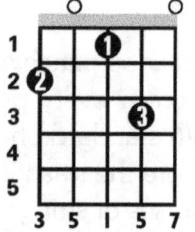
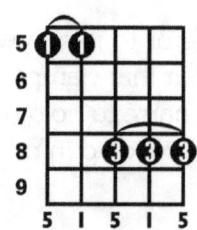	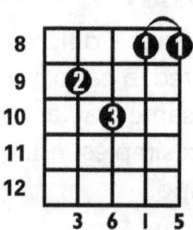	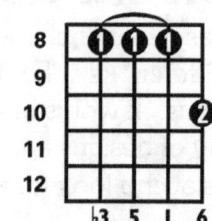	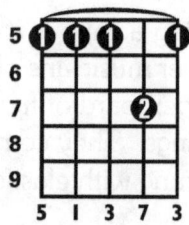

C Chords

C°
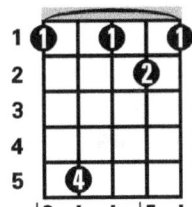
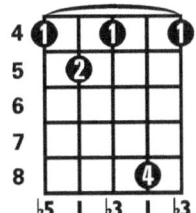
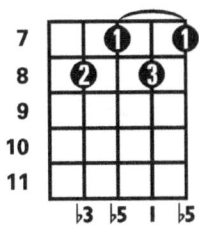

C°7
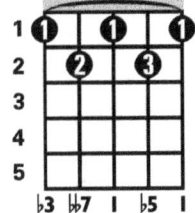
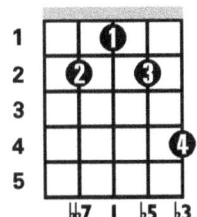
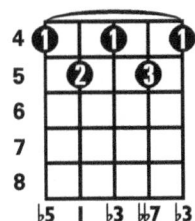

C-5
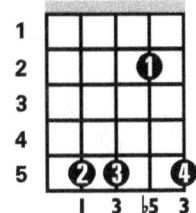
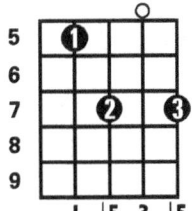
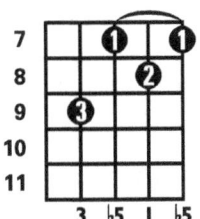

C+
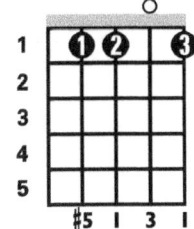
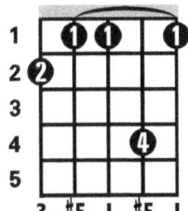
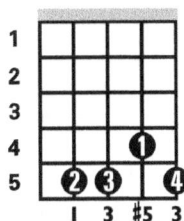

Csus2
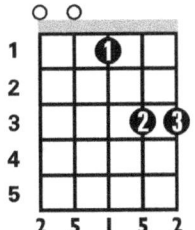
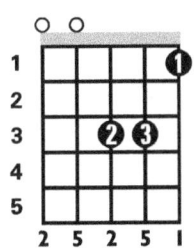
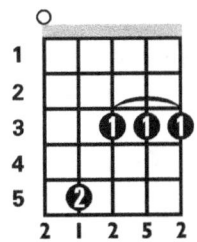

Csus4
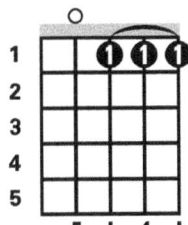
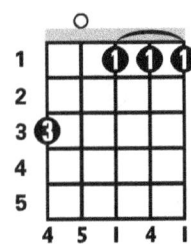
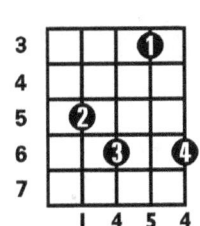

C7sus4
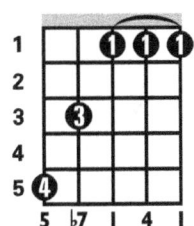
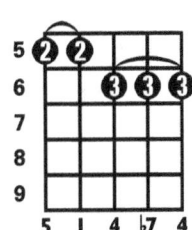
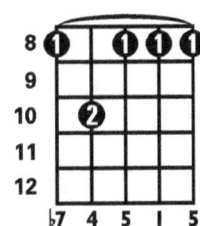

Cm7-5
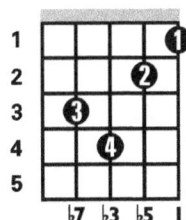
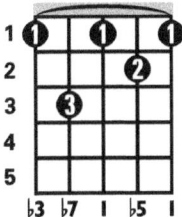
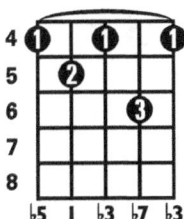

C Chords

Cadd9	Cmadd9	C6add9	Cm6add9
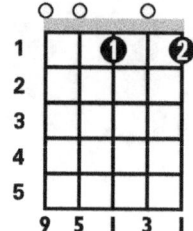	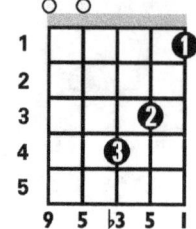	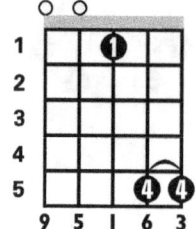	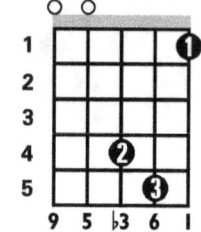
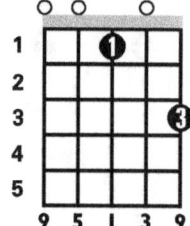	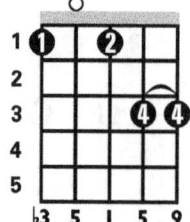	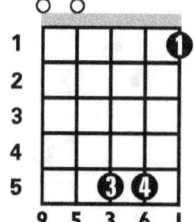	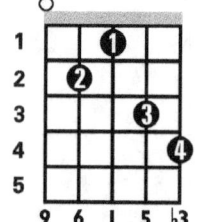
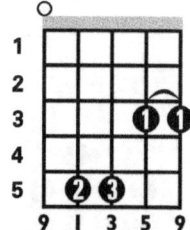	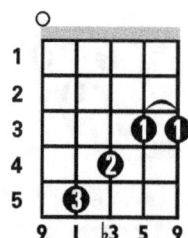	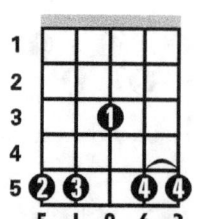	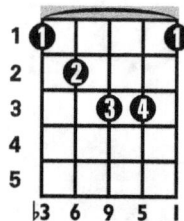

C7-5	C7+5	C7-9	C7+9
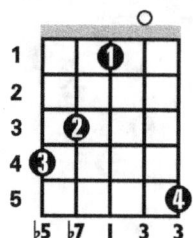	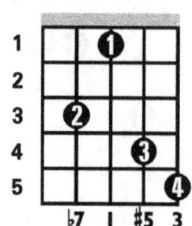	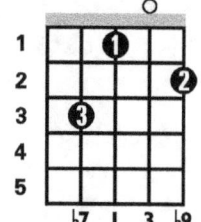	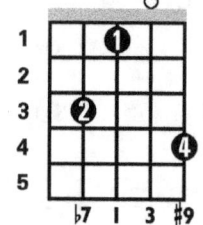
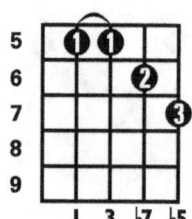	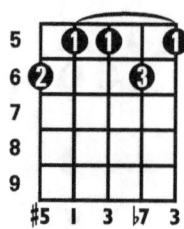	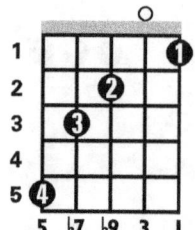	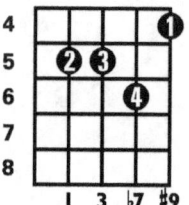
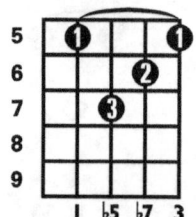	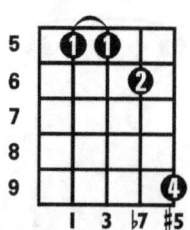	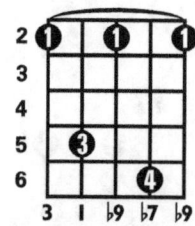	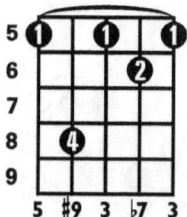

C Chords

Cm(maj7)
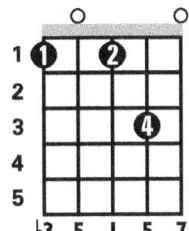
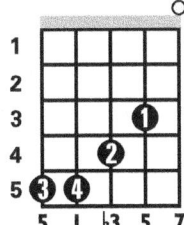
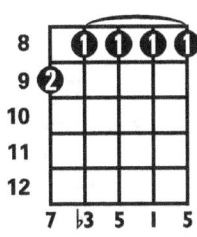

Cmaj7-5
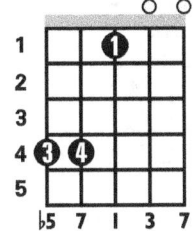
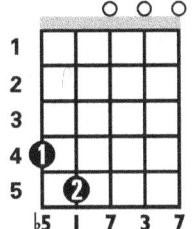
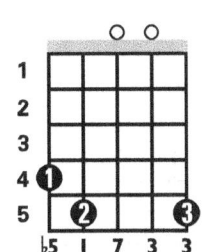

Cmaj7+5
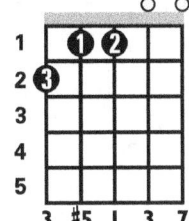
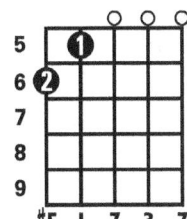
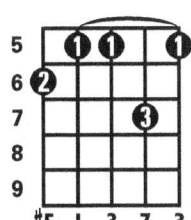

C9
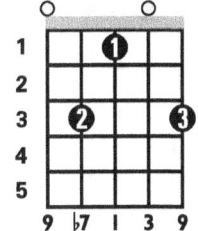
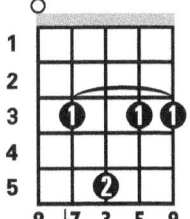
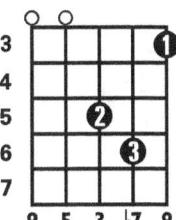

Cm9
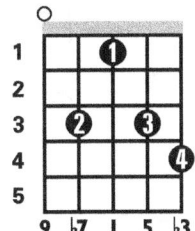
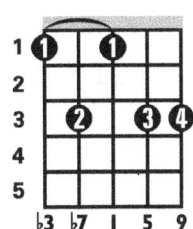
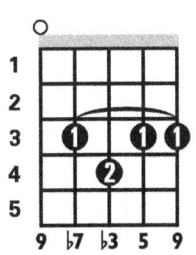

Cmaj9
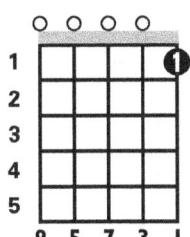
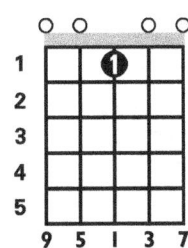
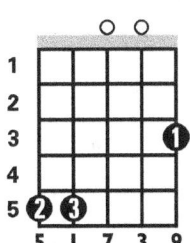

C11
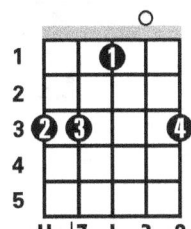
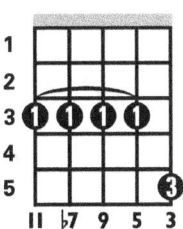
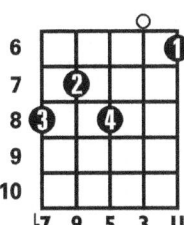

C13
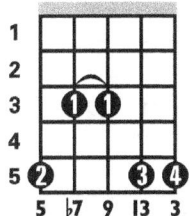
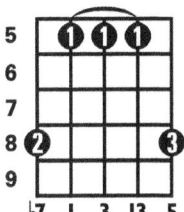
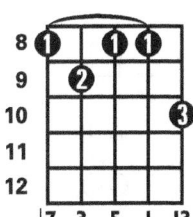

C Chords (Advanced)

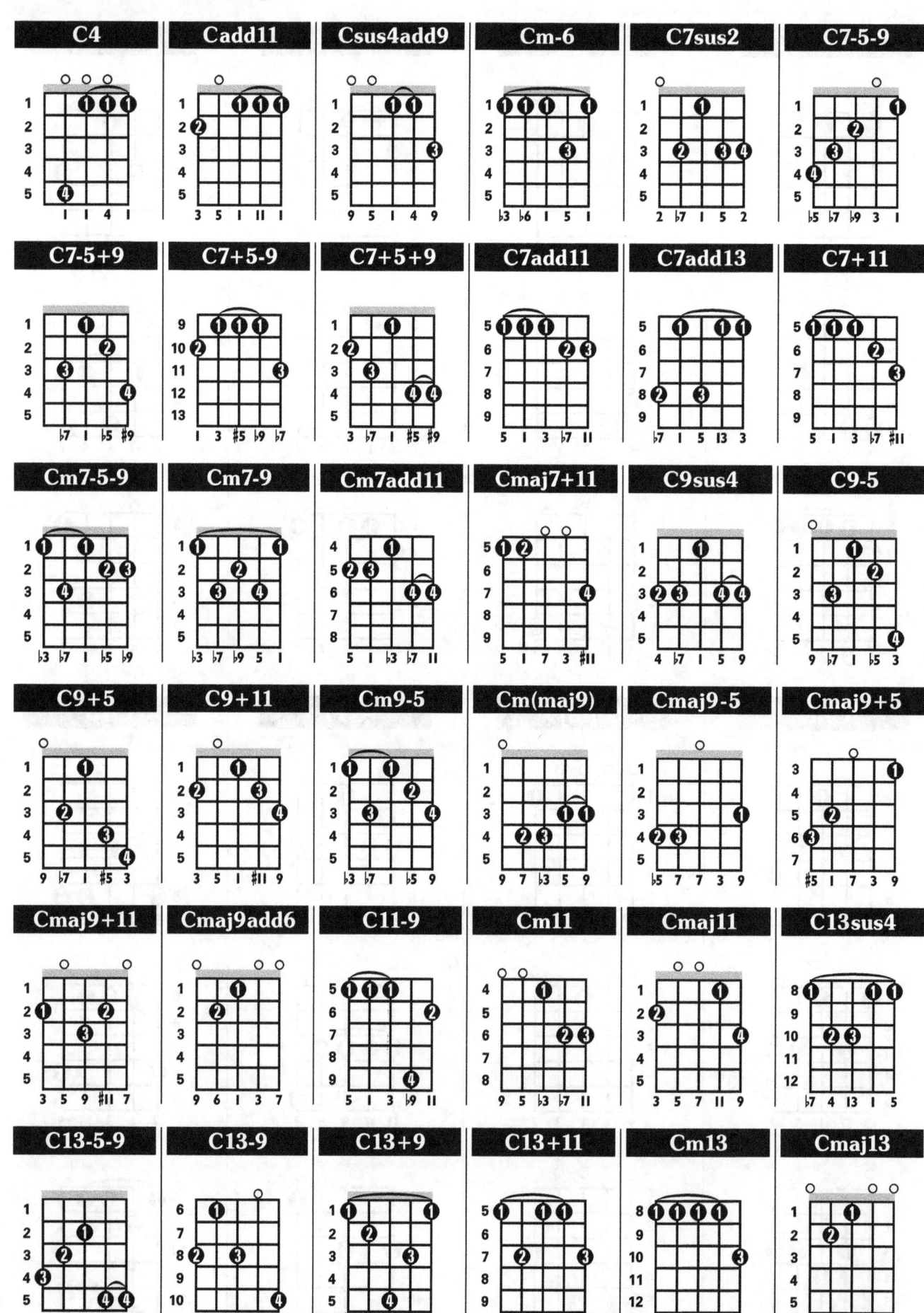

C#/ D♭ Chords

D♭	D♭m	D♭7	D♭m7
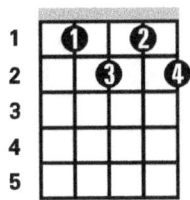	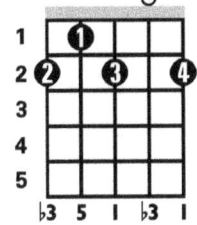	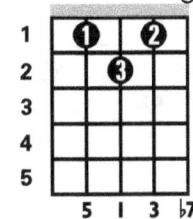	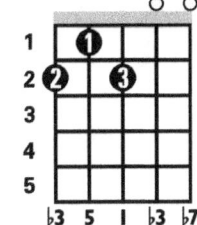
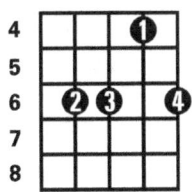	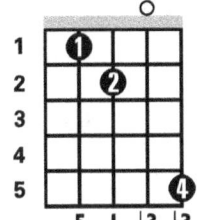	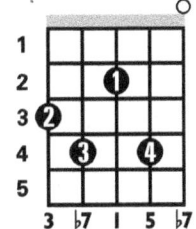	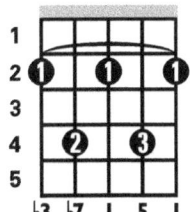
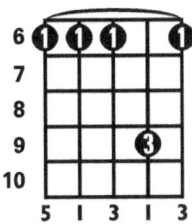	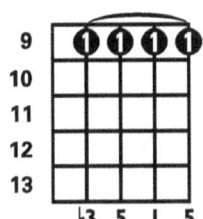	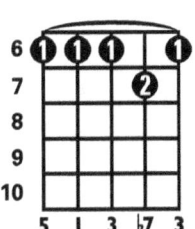	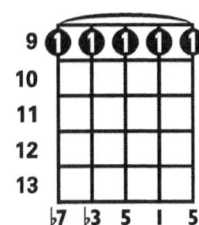

D♭5	D♭6	D♭m6	D♭maj7
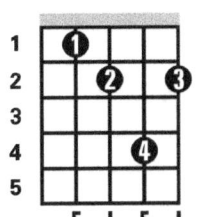	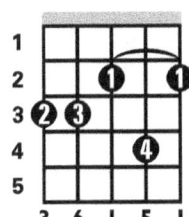	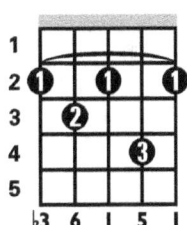	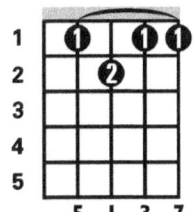
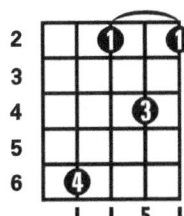	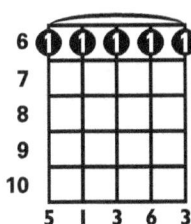	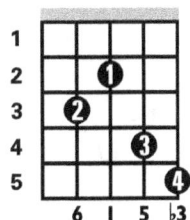	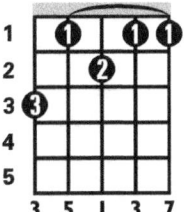
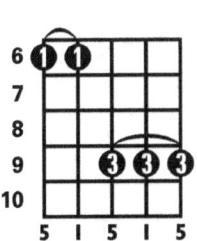	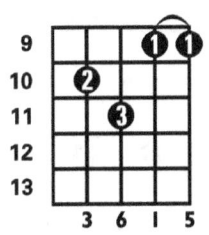	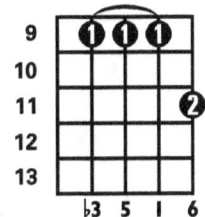	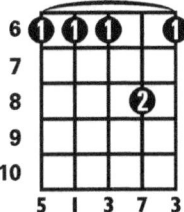

C#/ D♭ Chords

D♭°
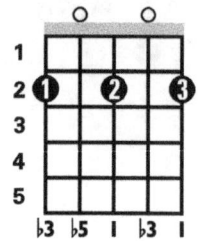

D♭°7
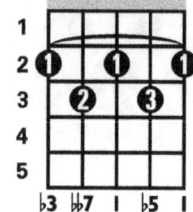

D♭-5
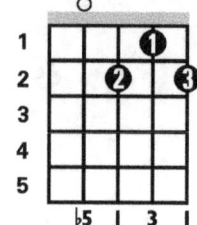

D♭+
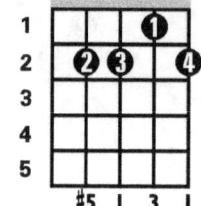

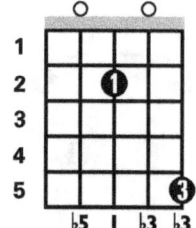
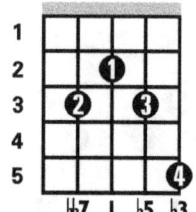
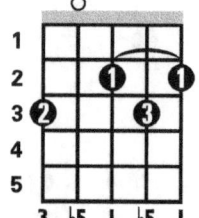
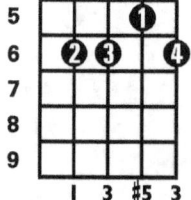

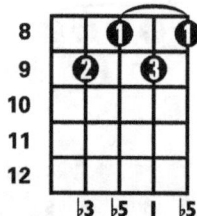
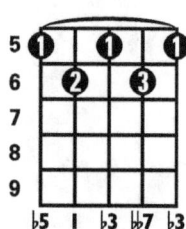
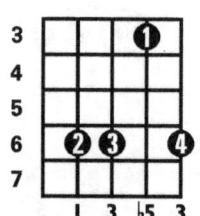
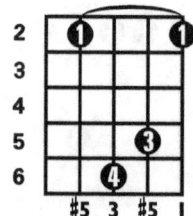

D♭sus2
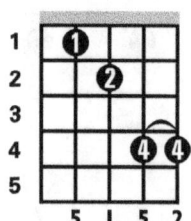

D♭sus4
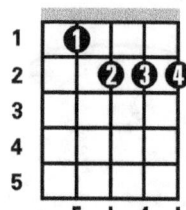

D♭7sus4
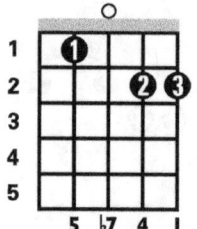

D♭m7-5
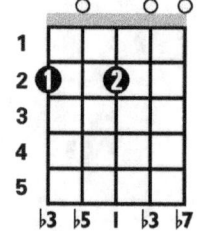

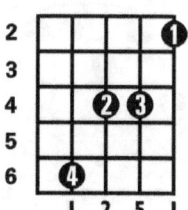
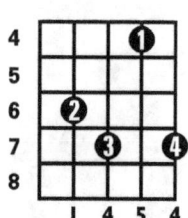
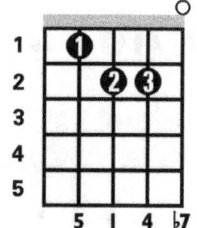
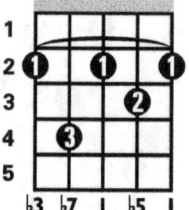

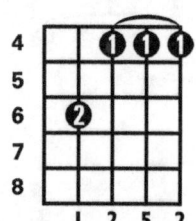
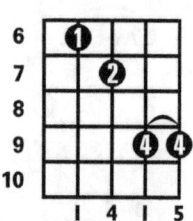
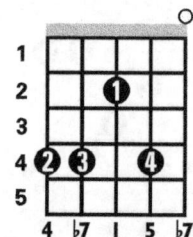
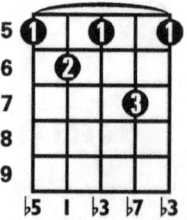

C#/D♭ Chords

D♭add9
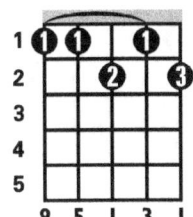
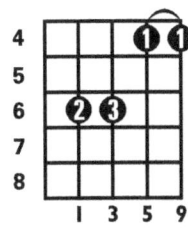
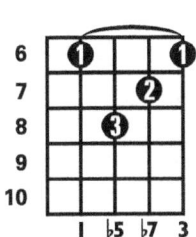

D♭madd9
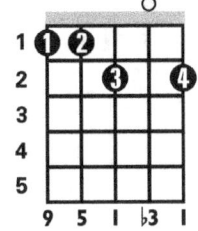
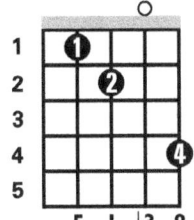
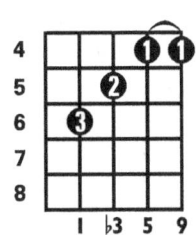

D♭6add9
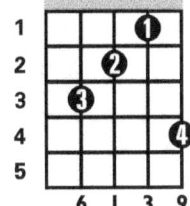
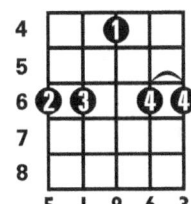
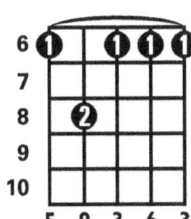

D♭m6add9
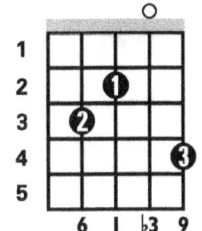
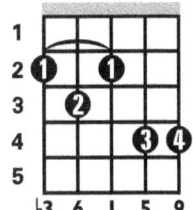
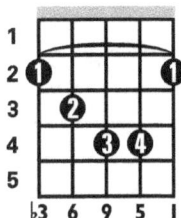

D♭7-5
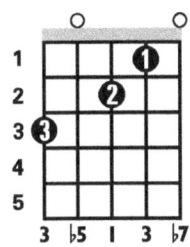
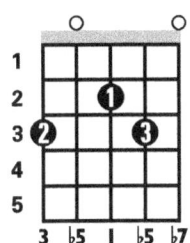
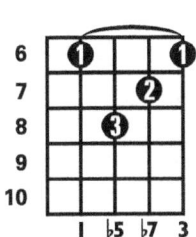

D♭7+5
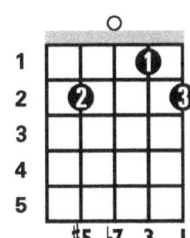
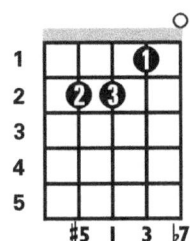
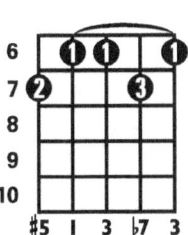

D♭7-9
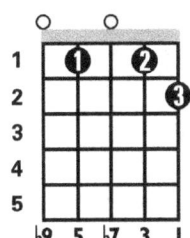
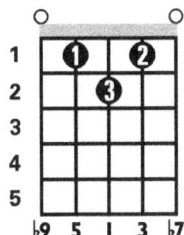
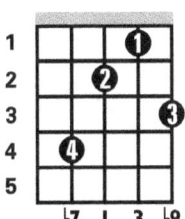

D♭7+9
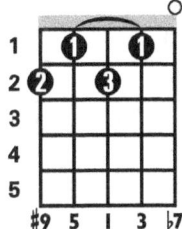
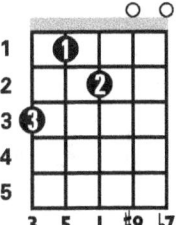
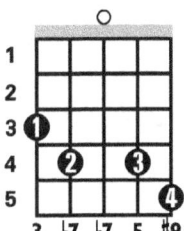

C#/ D♭ Chords

D♭m(maj7)
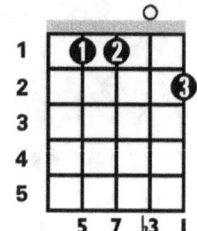
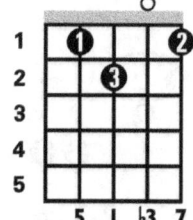
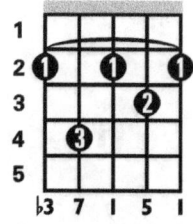

D♭maj7-5
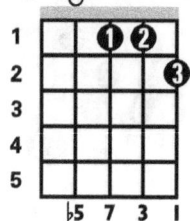
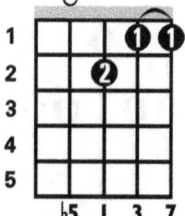
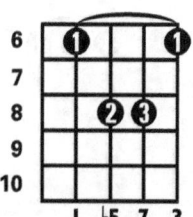

D♭maj7+5
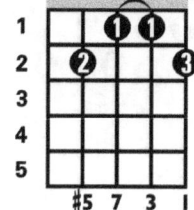
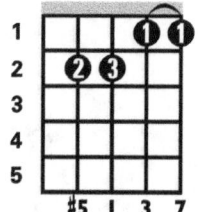
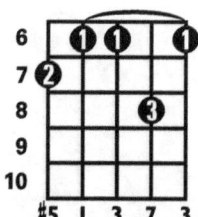

D♭9
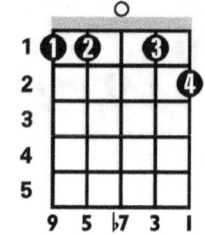
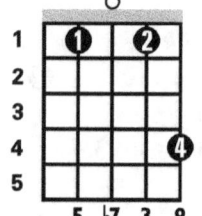
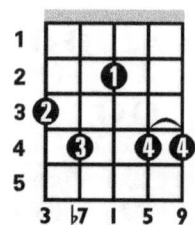

D♭m9
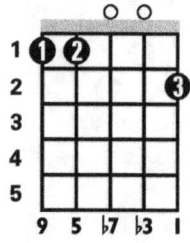
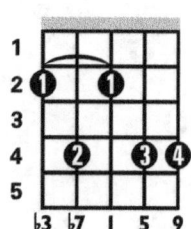
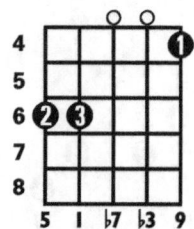

D♭maj9
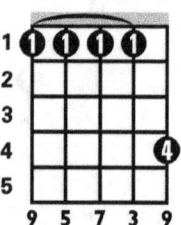
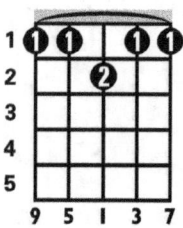
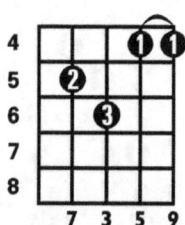

D♭11
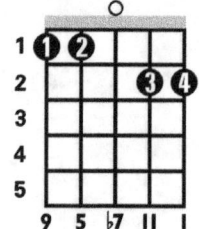
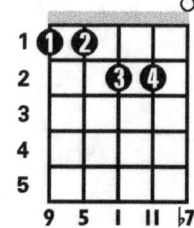
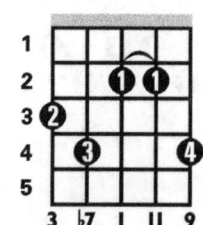

D♭13
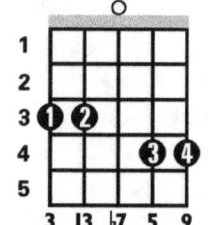
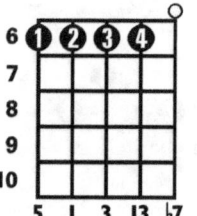
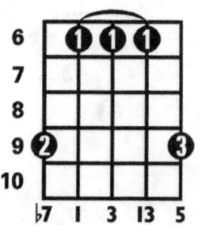

C#/ D♭ Chords (Advanced)

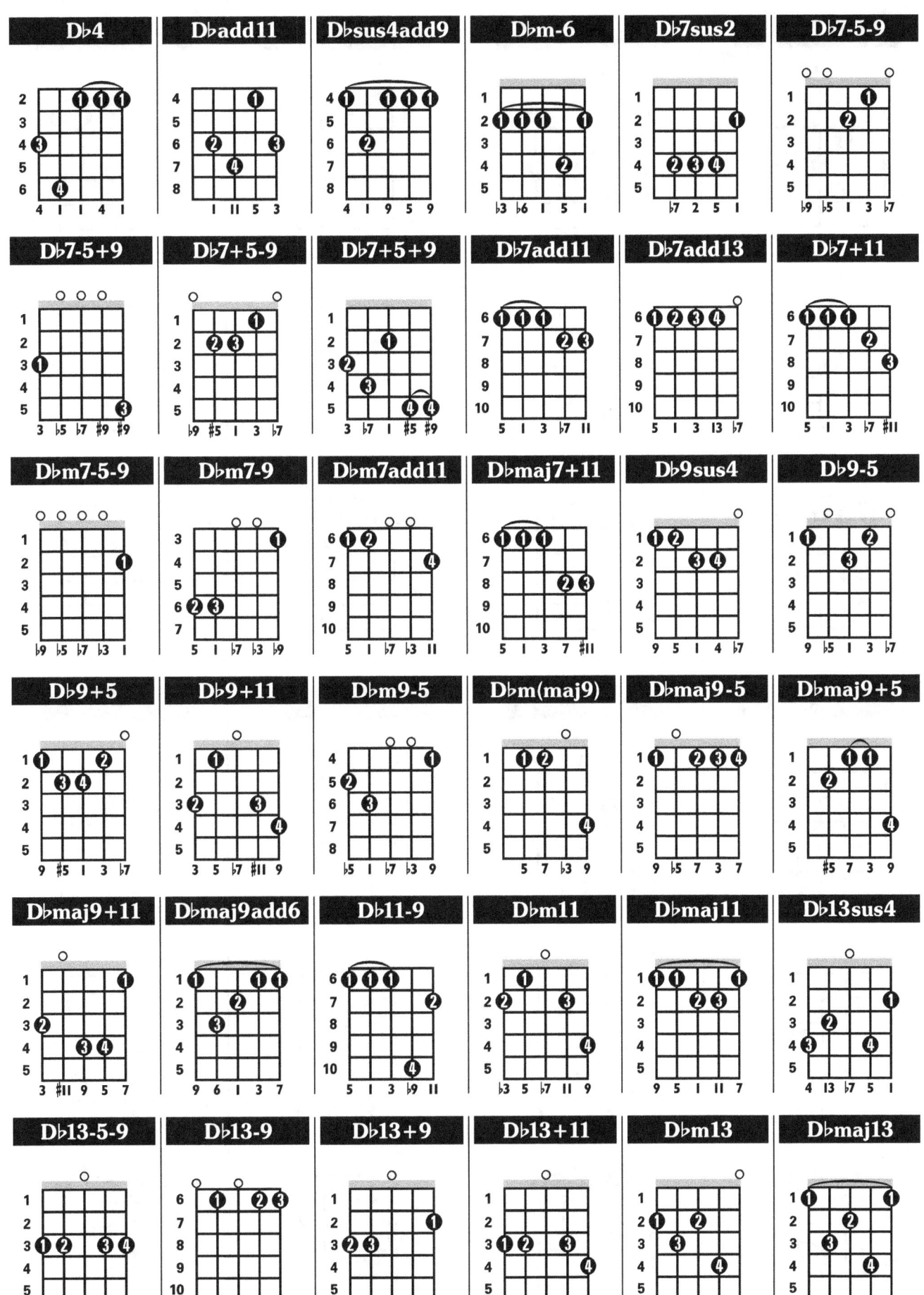

D Chords

D
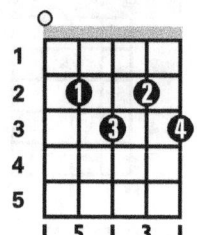
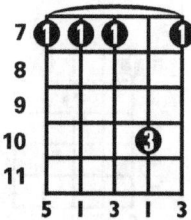
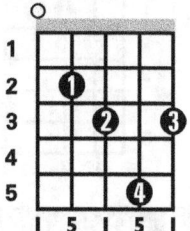

Dm
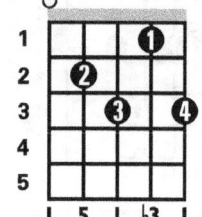
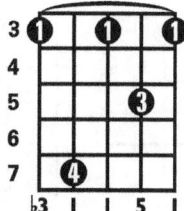
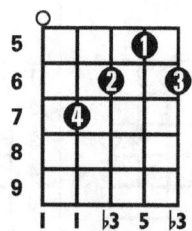

D7
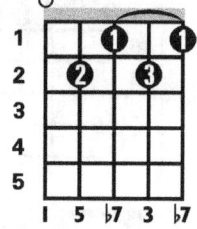
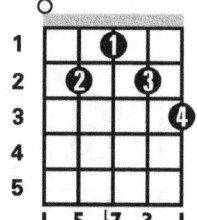
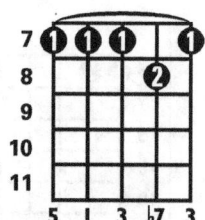

Dm7
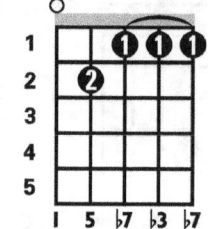
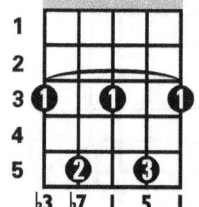
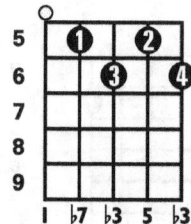

D5
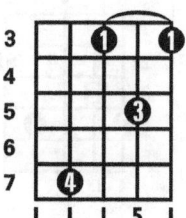
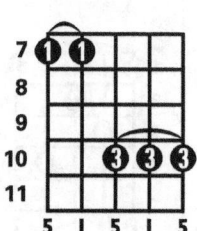

D6
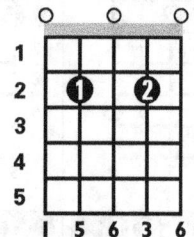
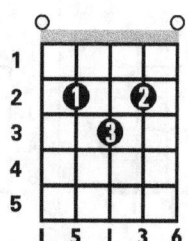
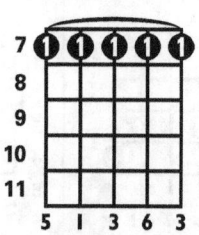

Dm6
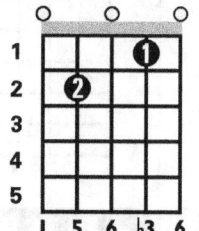
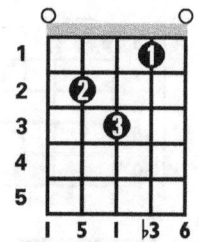
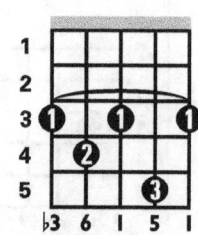

Dmaj7
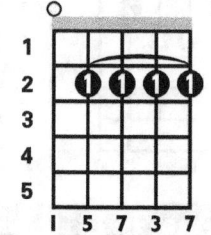
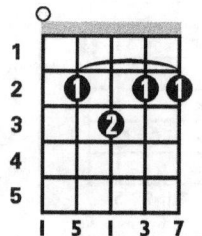
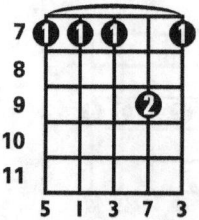

D Chords

D°
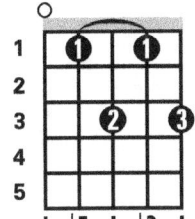
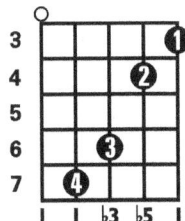
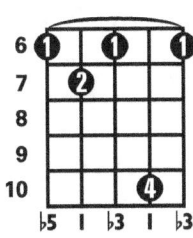

D°7
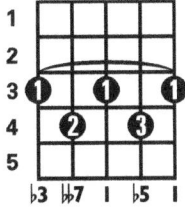
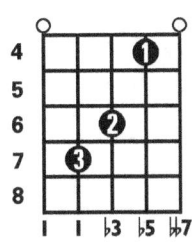

D-5
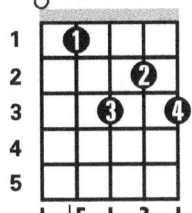
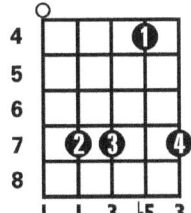
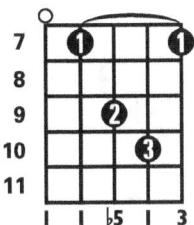

D+
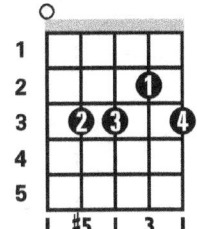
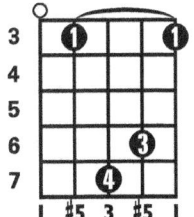
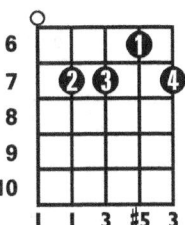

Dsus2
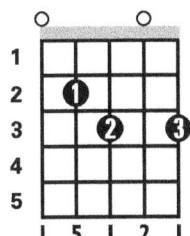
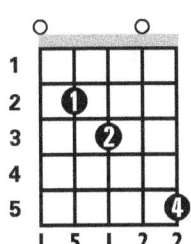
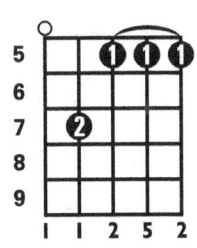

Dsus4
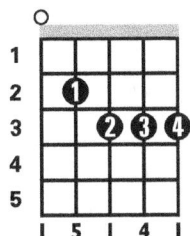
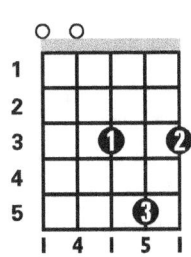
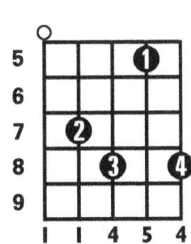

D7sus4
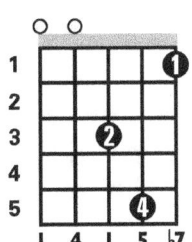
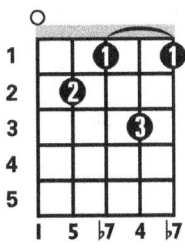
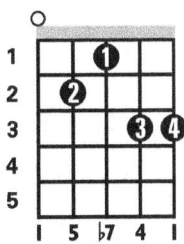

Dm7-5
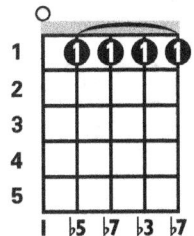
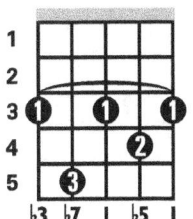
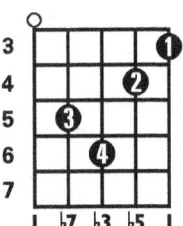

D Chords

Dadd9
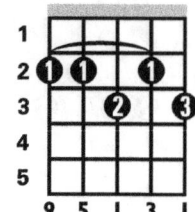
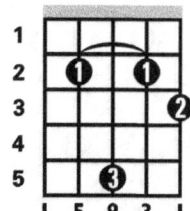
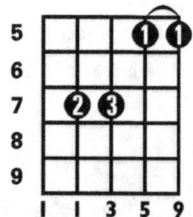

Dmadd9
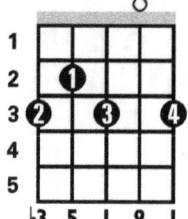
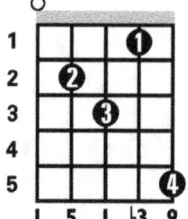
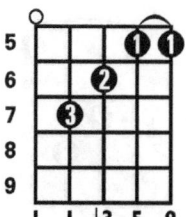

D6add9
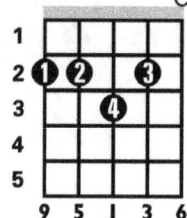
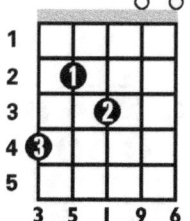
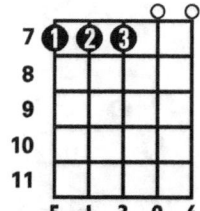

Dm6add9
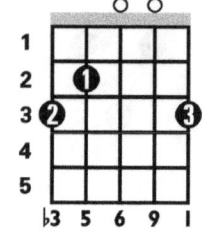
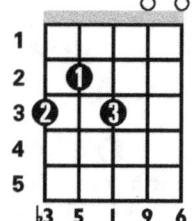
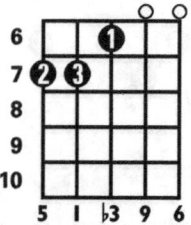

D7-5
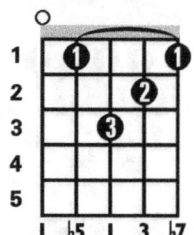
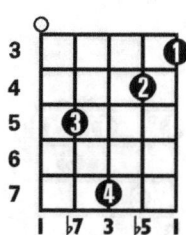
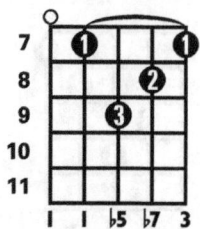

D7+5
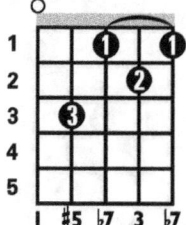
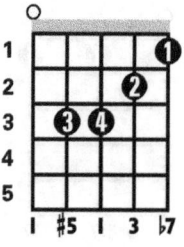
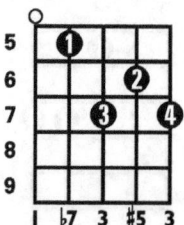

D7-9
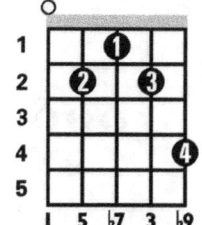
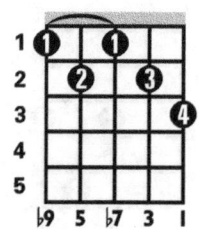
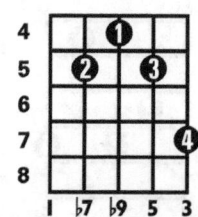

D7+9
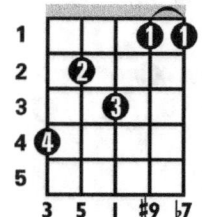
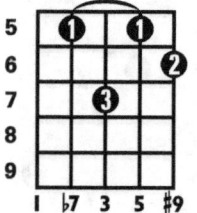
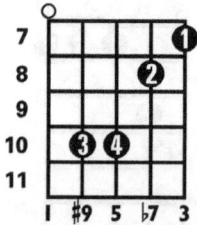

D Chords

Dm(maj7)
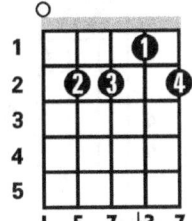
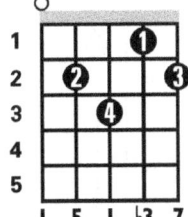
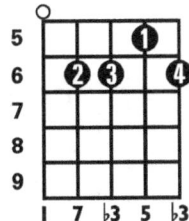

Dmaj7-5
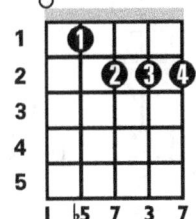
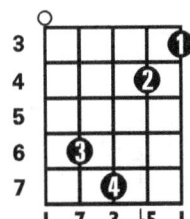
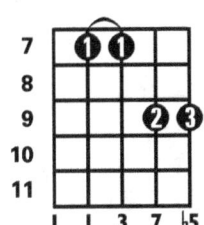

Dmaj7+5
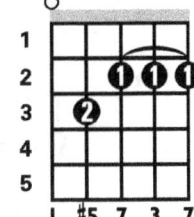
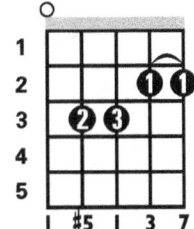
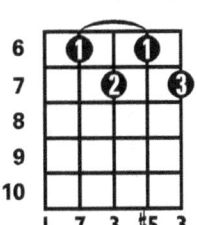

D9
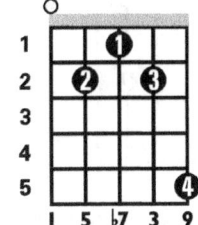
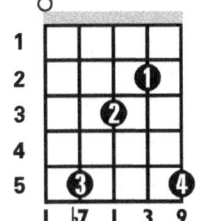
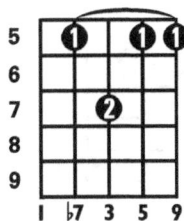

Dm9
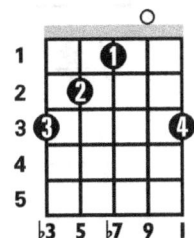
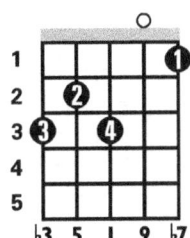
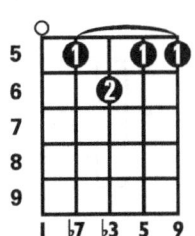

Dmaj9
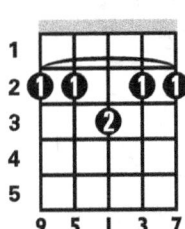
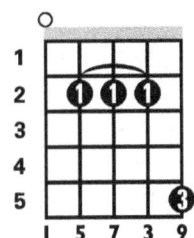
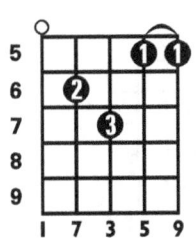

D11
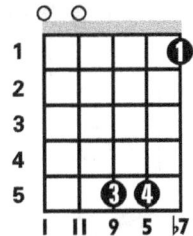
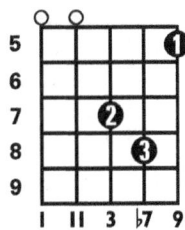
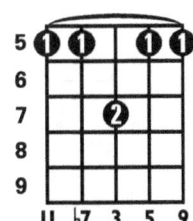

D13
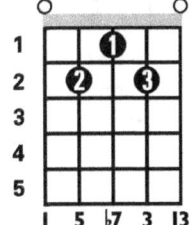
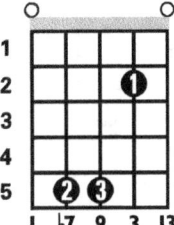
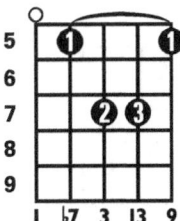

D Chords (Advanced)

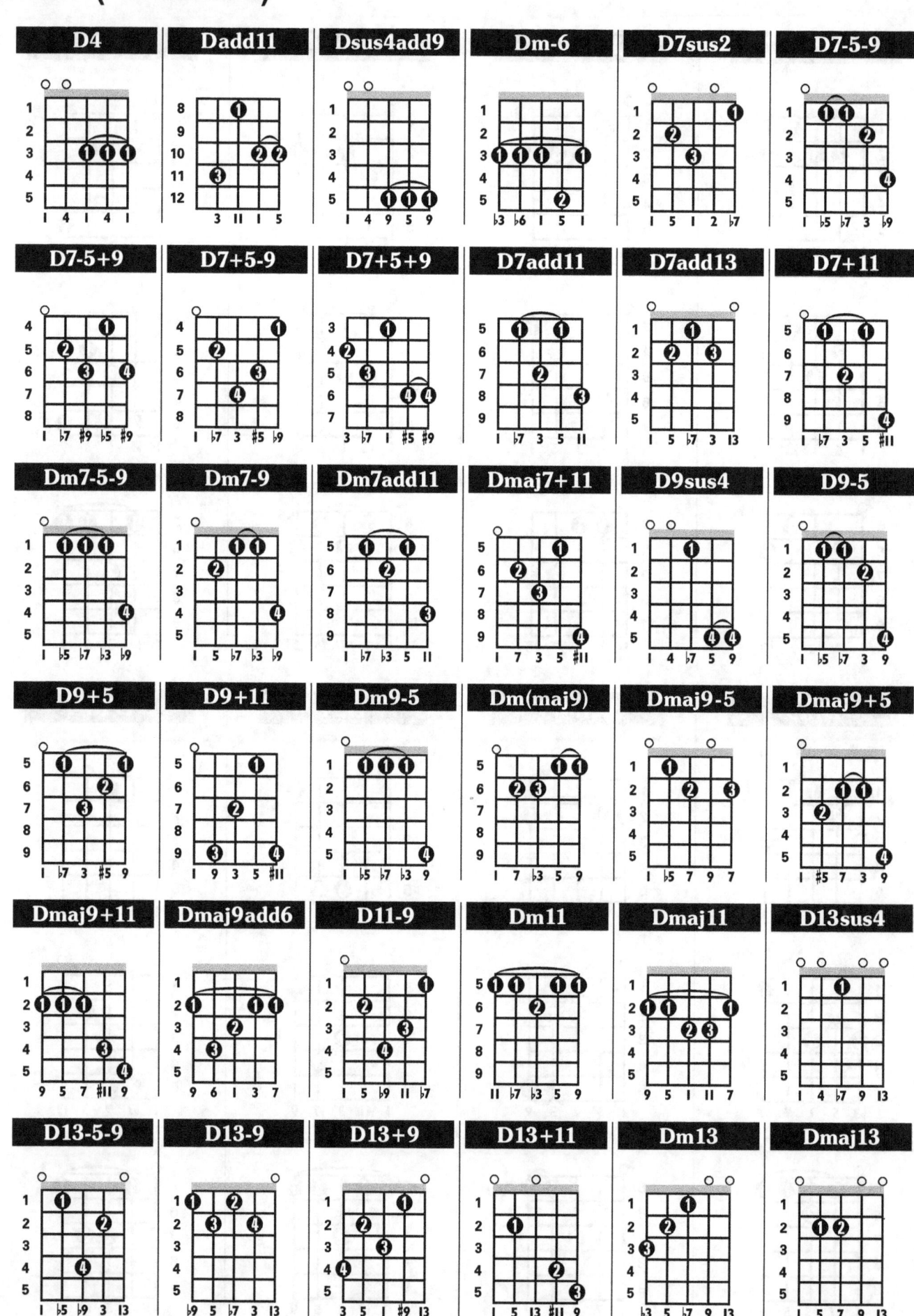

D#/ E♭ Chords

E♭
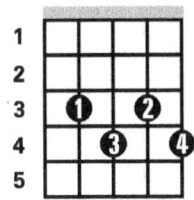
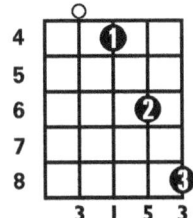
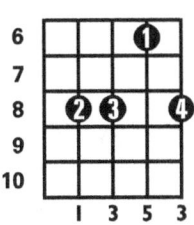

E♭m
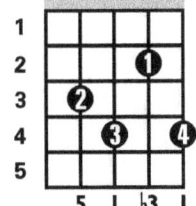
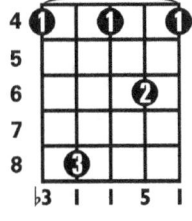
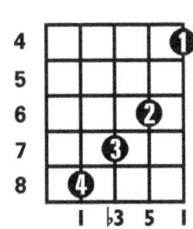

E♭7
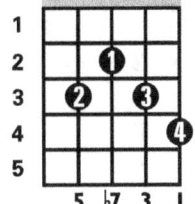
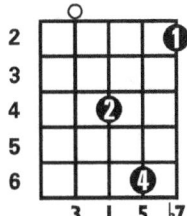
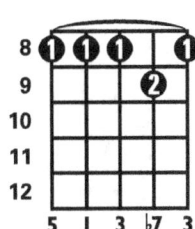

E♭m7
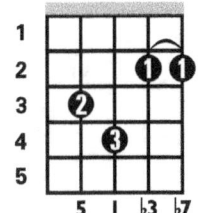
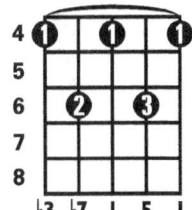
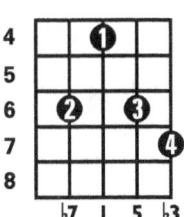

E♭5
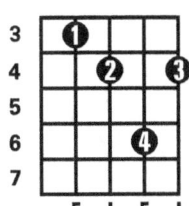
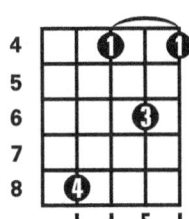
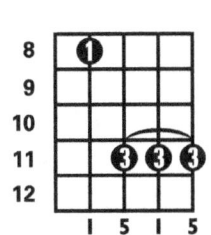

E♭6
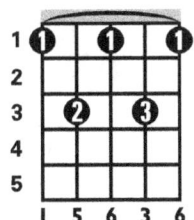
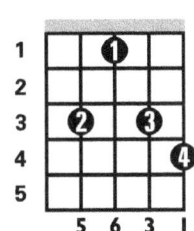
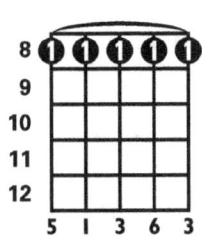

E♭m6
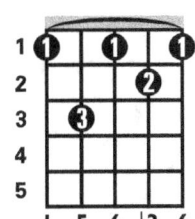
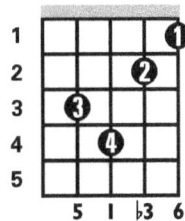
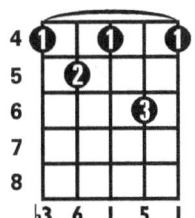

E♭maj7
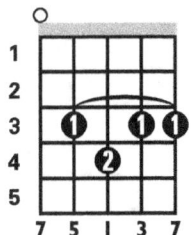
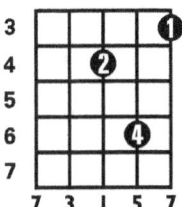
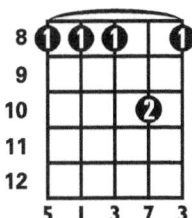

D#/ E♭ Chords

E♭°
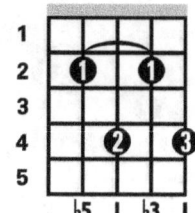
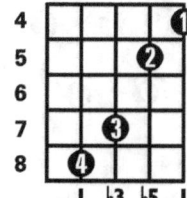
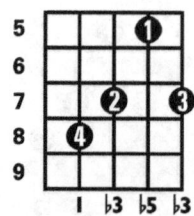

E♭°7
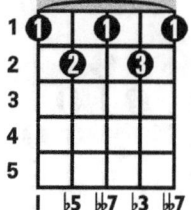
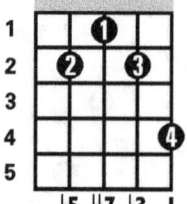
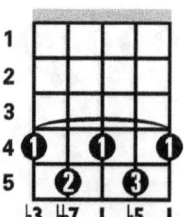

E♭-5
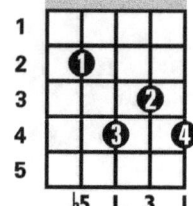
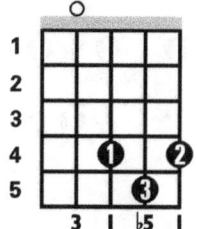
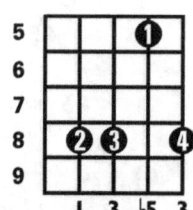

E♭+
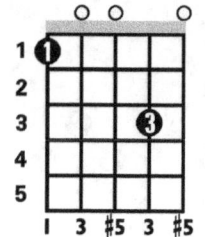
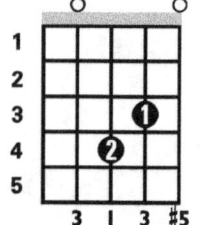
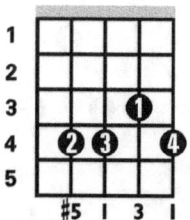

E♭sus2
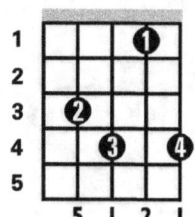
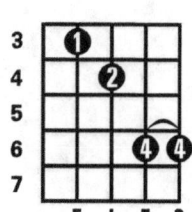
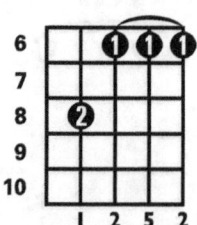

E♭sus4
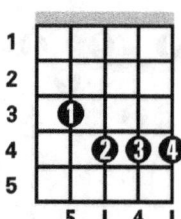
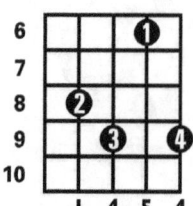
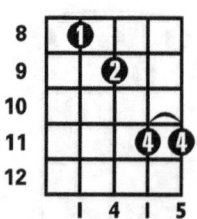

E♭7sus4
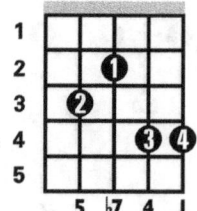
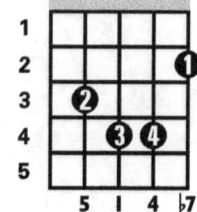
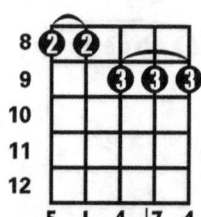

E♭m7-5
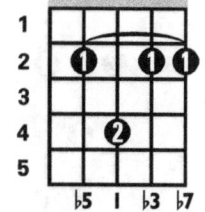
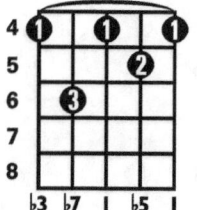
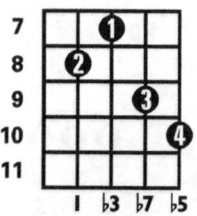

D#/ E♭ Chords

E♭add9
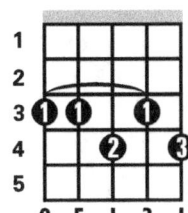
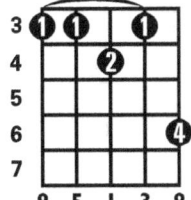
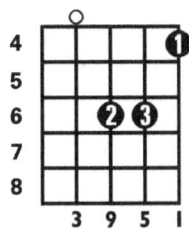

E♭madd9
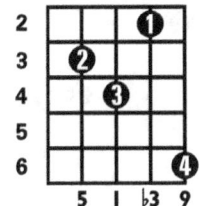
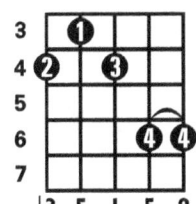
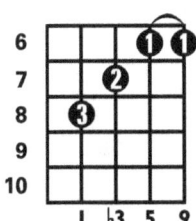

E♭6add9
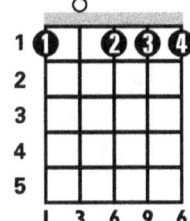
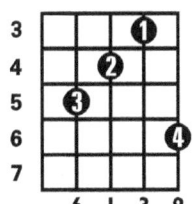
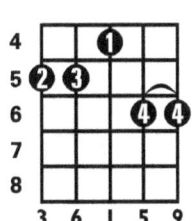

E♭m6add9
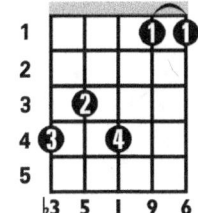
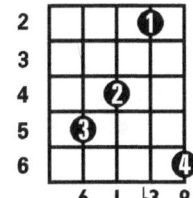
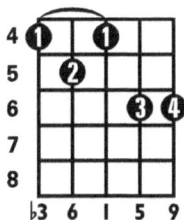

E♭7-5
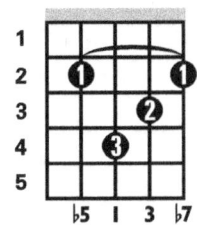
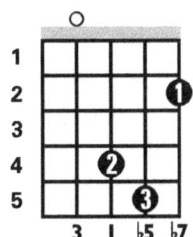
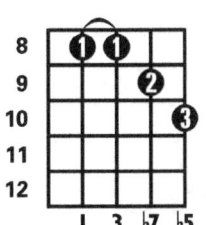

E♭7+5
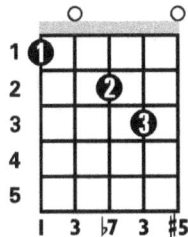
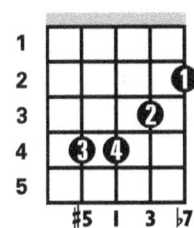
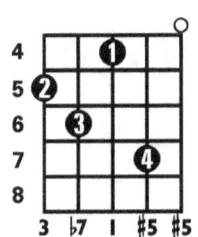

E♭7-9
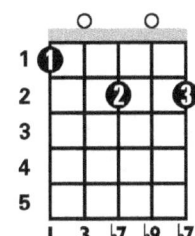
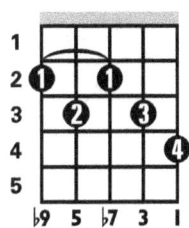
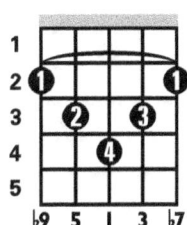

E♭7+9
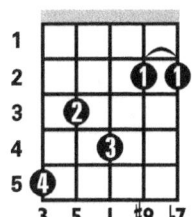
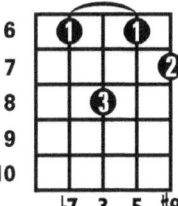
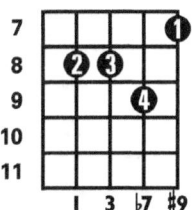

D#/ E♭ Chords

E♭m(maj7)	E♭maj7-5	E♭maj7+5	E♭9
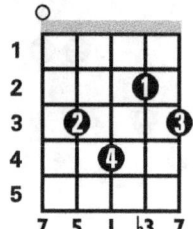	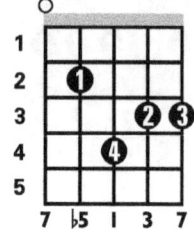	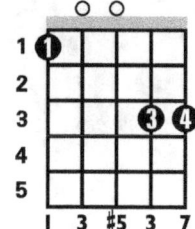	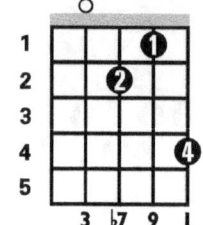
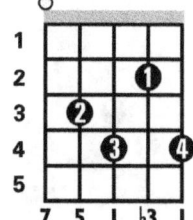	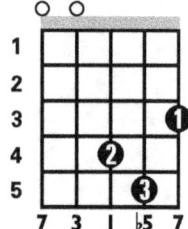	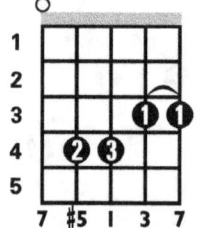	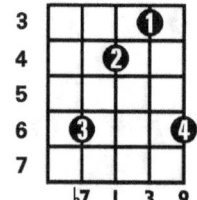
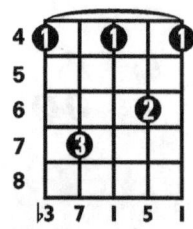	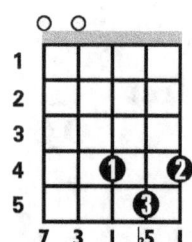	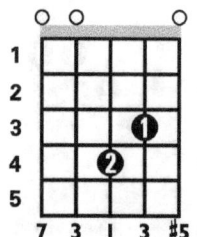	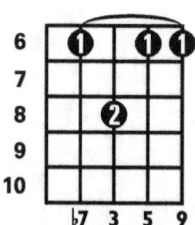

E♭m9	E♭maj9	E♭11	E♭13
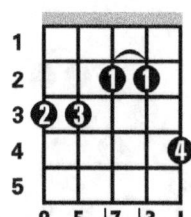	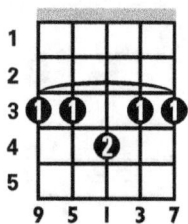	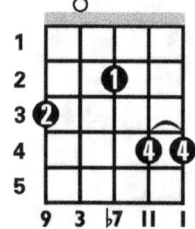	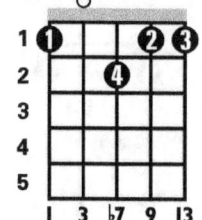
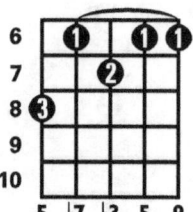	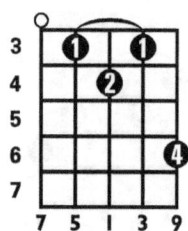	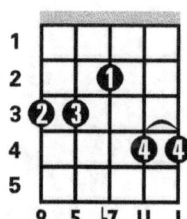	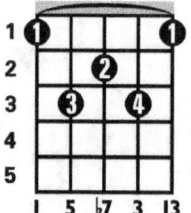
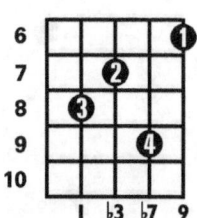	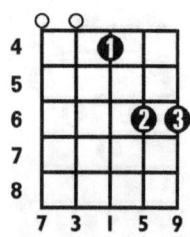	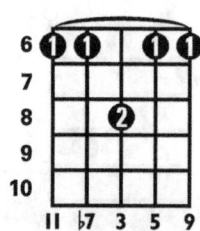	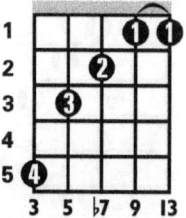

D♯/ E♭ Chords (Advanced)

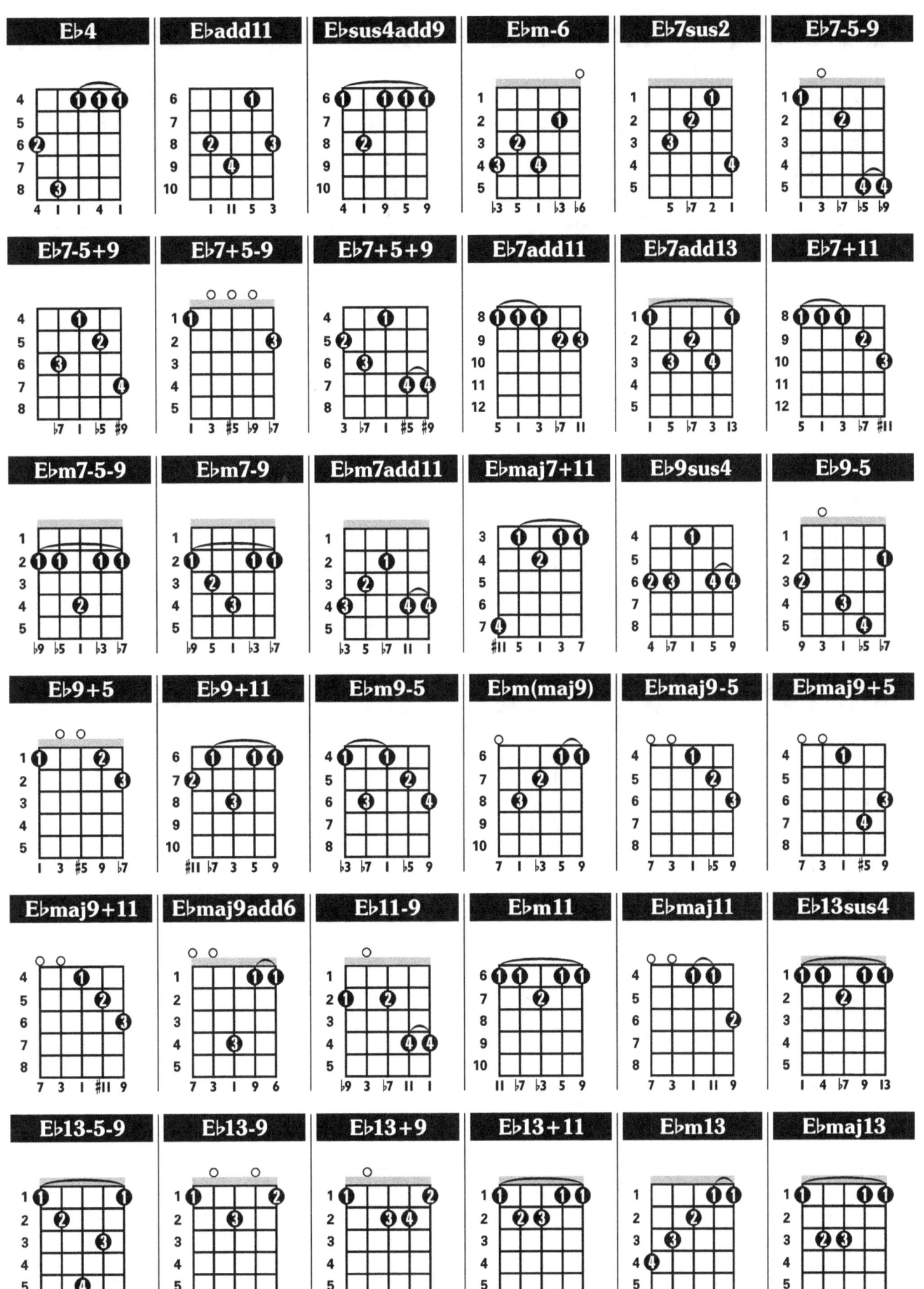

E Chords

E	Em	E7	Em7
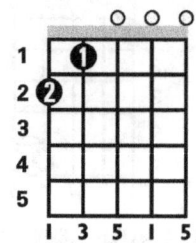	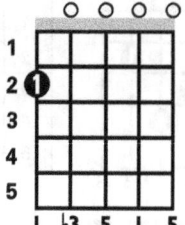	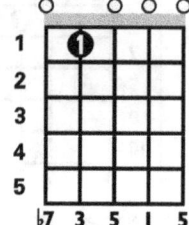	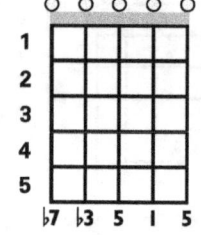
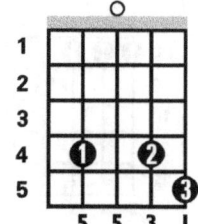	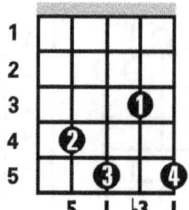	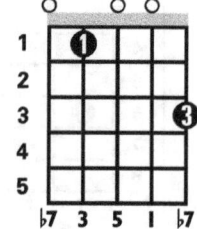	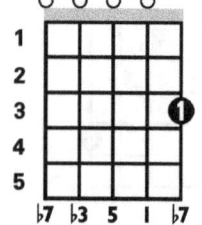
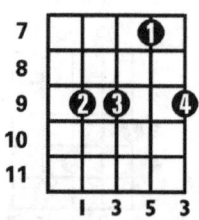	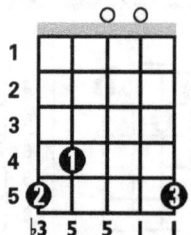	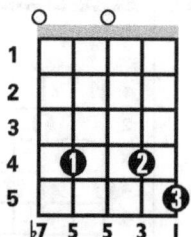	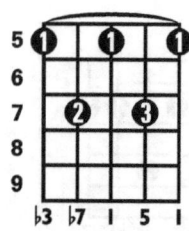

E5	E6	Em6	Emaj7
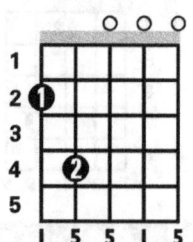	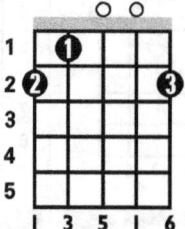	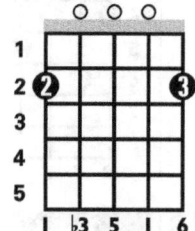	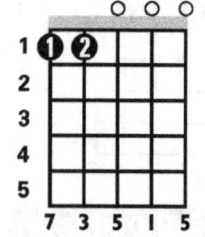
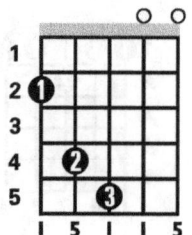	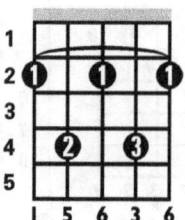	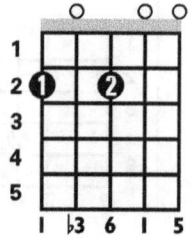	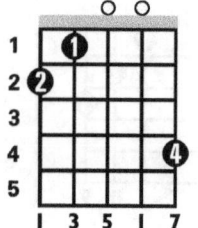
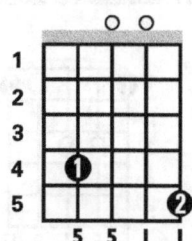	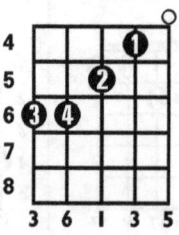	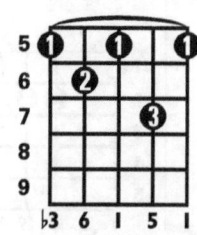	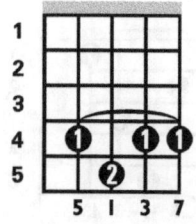

E Chords

E°
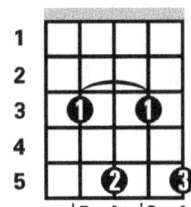
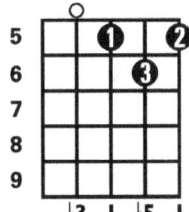
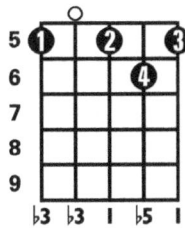

E°7
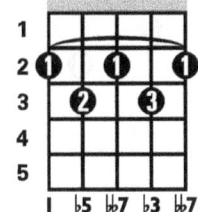
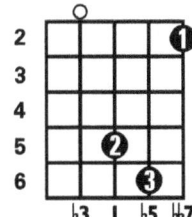
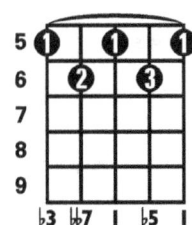

E-5
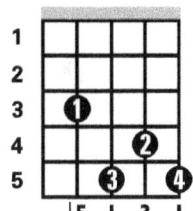
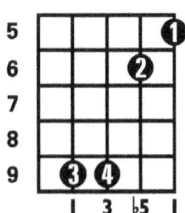
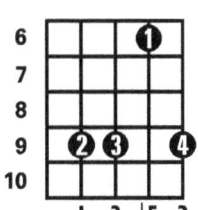

E+
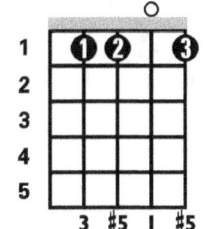
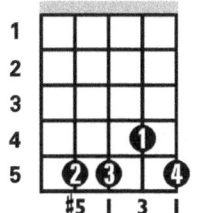
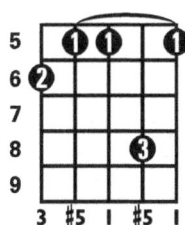

Esus2
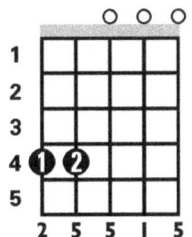
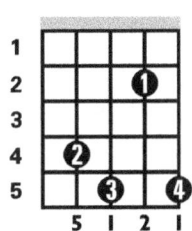
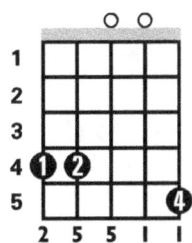

Esus4
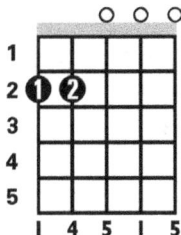
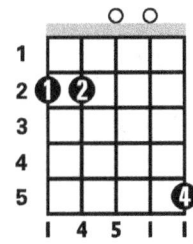
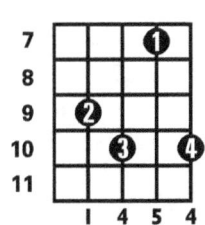

E7sus4
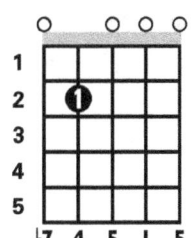
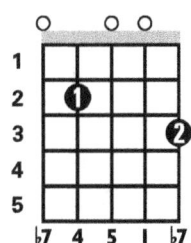
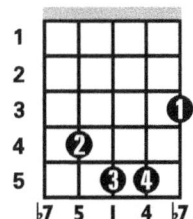

Em7-5
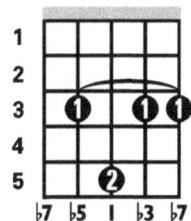
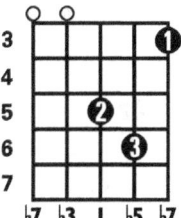
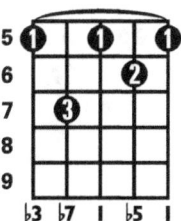

E Chords

Eadd9	Emadd9	E6add9	Em6add9
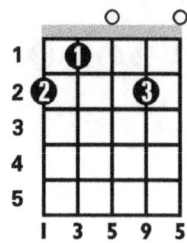	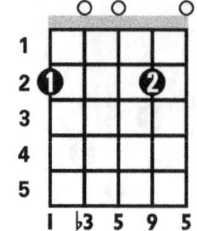	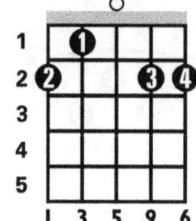	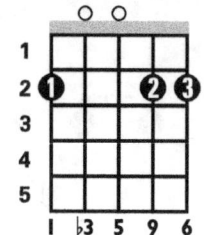
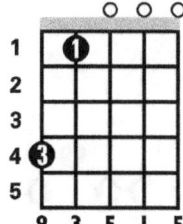	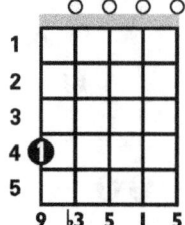	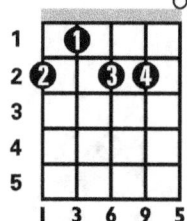	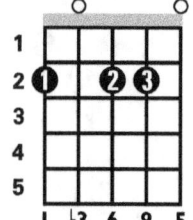
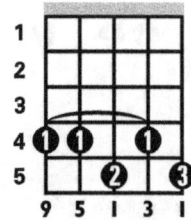	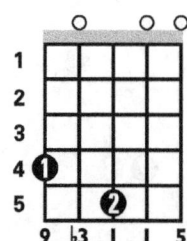	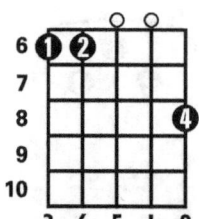	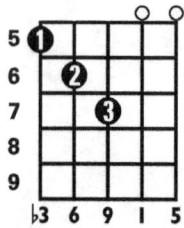

E7-5	E7+5	E7-9	E7+9
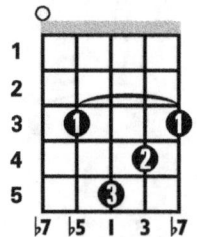	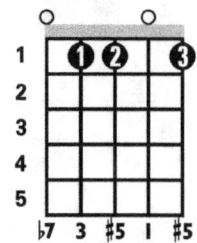	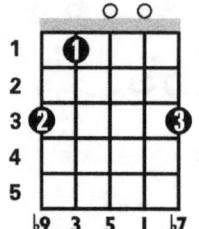	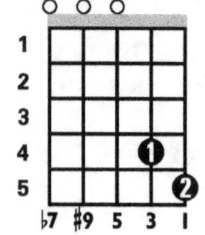
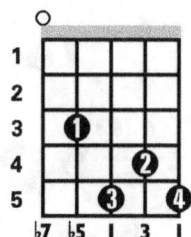	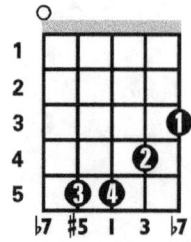	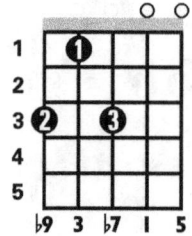	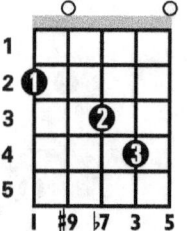
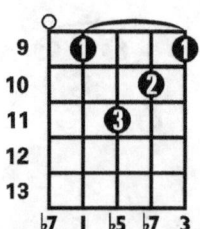	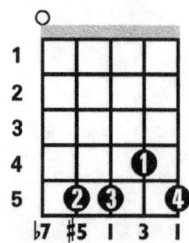	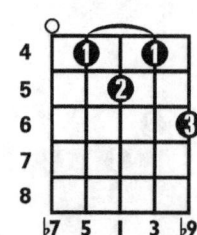	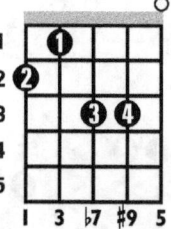

E Chords

Em(maj7)
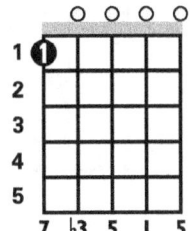
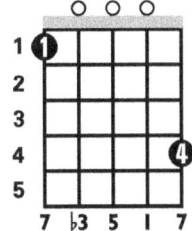
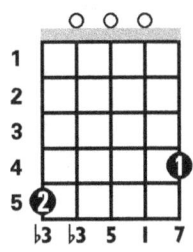

Emaj7-5
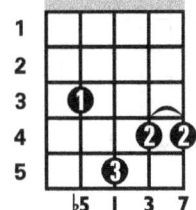
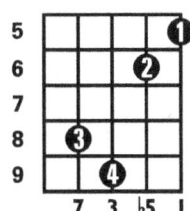
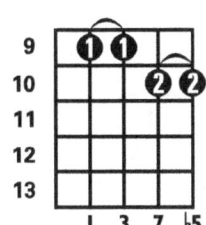

Emaj7+5
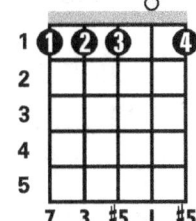
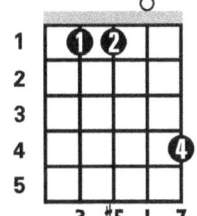
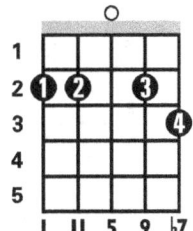

E9
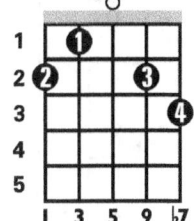
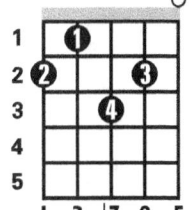
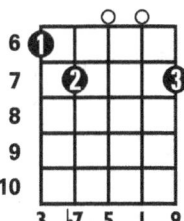

Em9
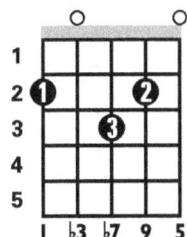
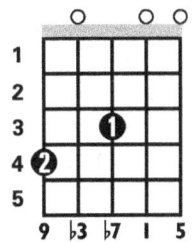
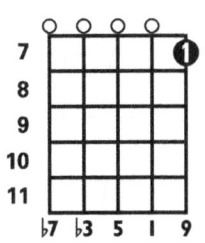

Emaj9
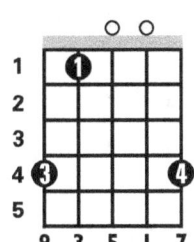
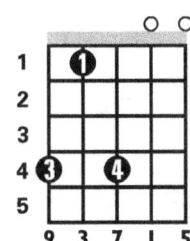
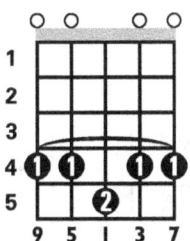

E11
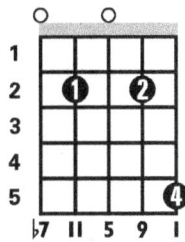
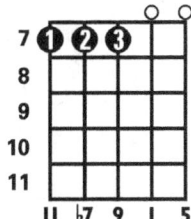

E13
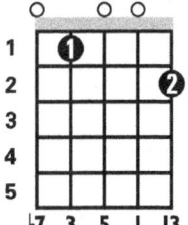
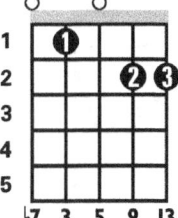
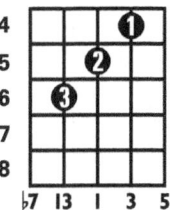

E Chords (Advanced)

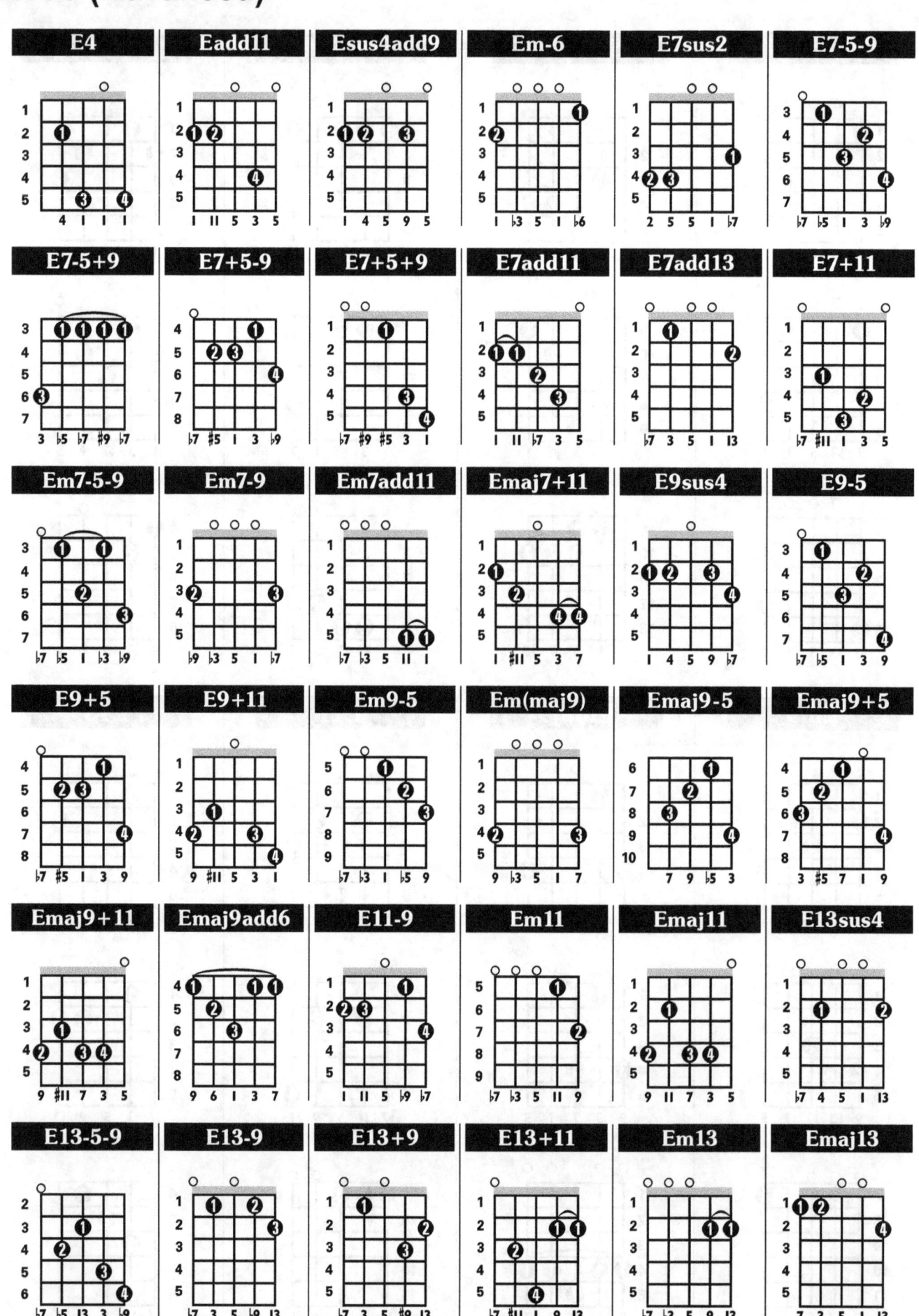

F Chords

F
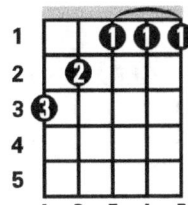
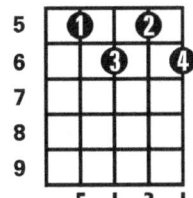
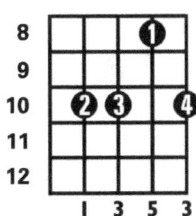

Fm
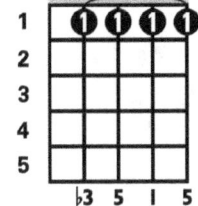
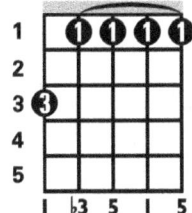
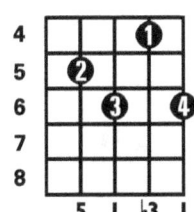

F7
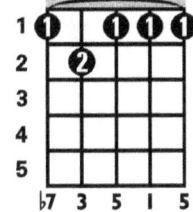
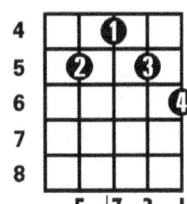
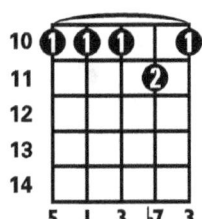

Fm7
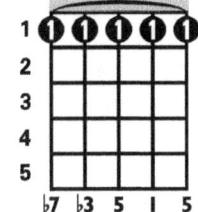
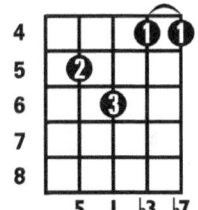
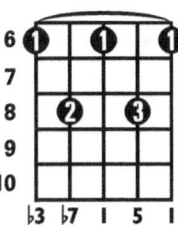

F5
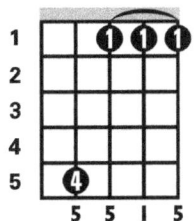
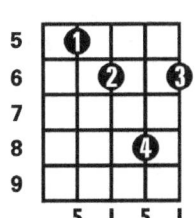
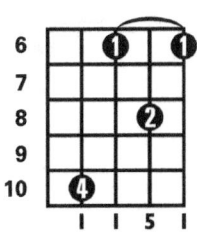

F6
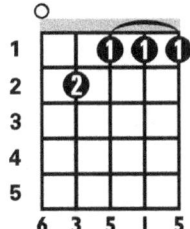
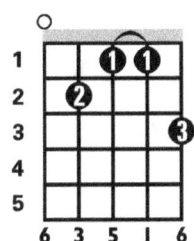
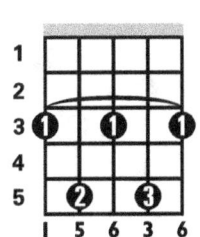

Fm6
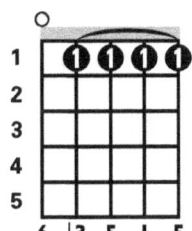
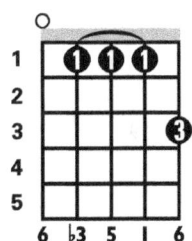
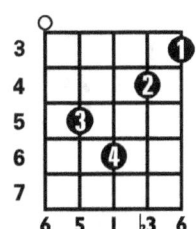

Fmaj7
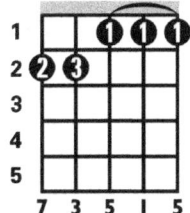
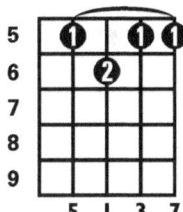
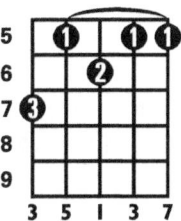

F Chords

F°	F°7	F-5	F+
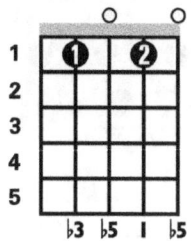	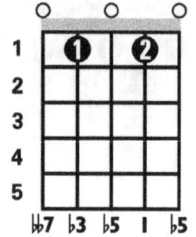	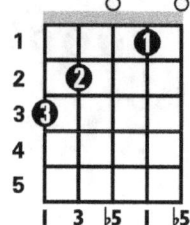	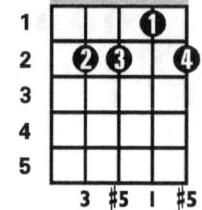
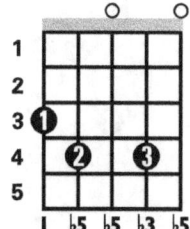	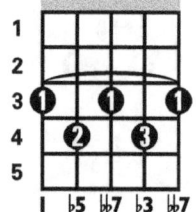	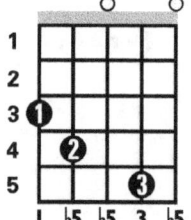	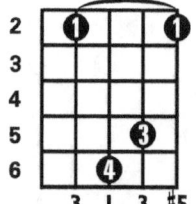
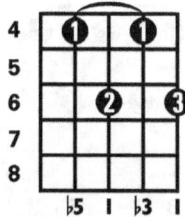	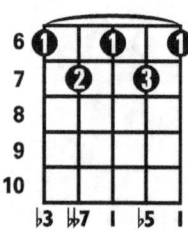	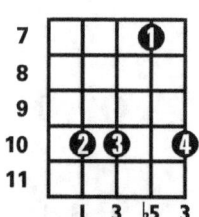	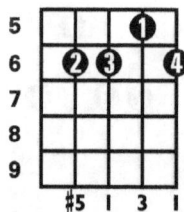

Fsus2	Fsus4	F7sus4	Fm7-5
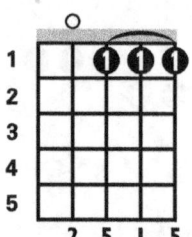	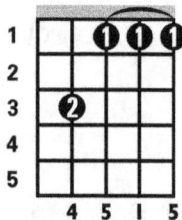	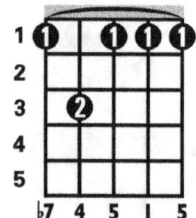	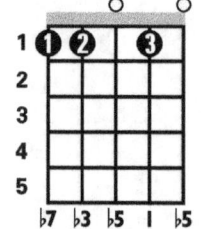
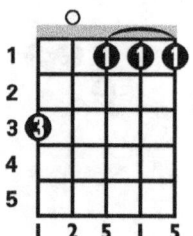	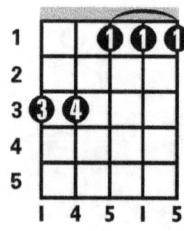	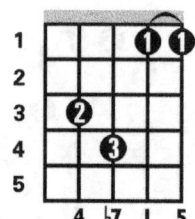	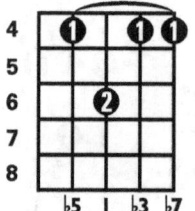
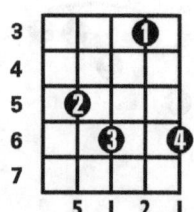	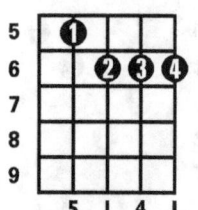	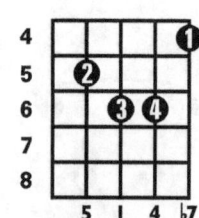	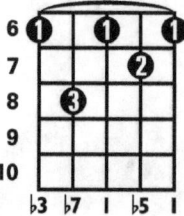

F Chords

Fadd9
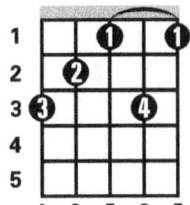
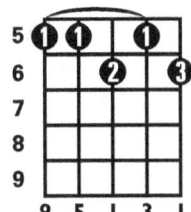
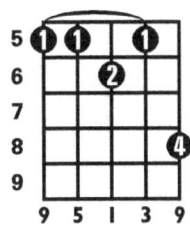

Fmadd9
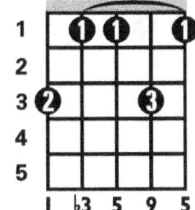
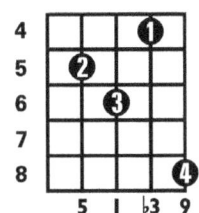
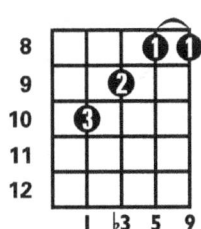

F6add9
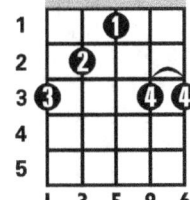
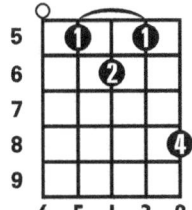
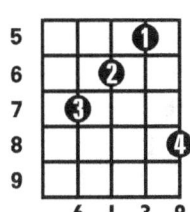

Fm6add9
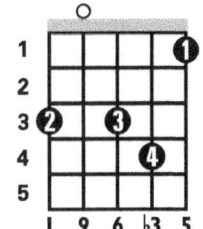
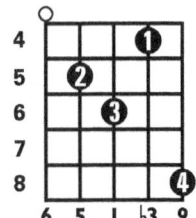
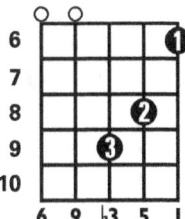

F7-5
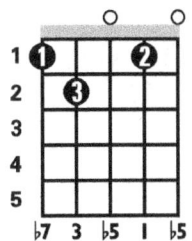
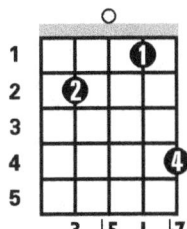
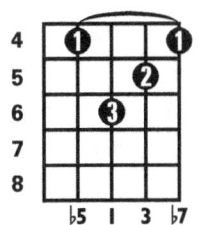

F7+5
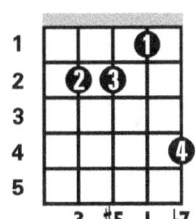
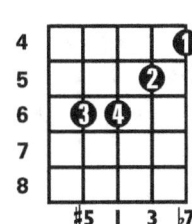
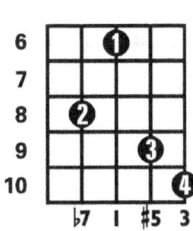

F7-9
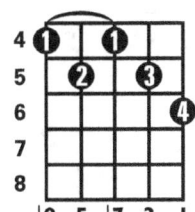
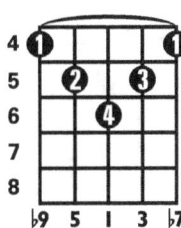
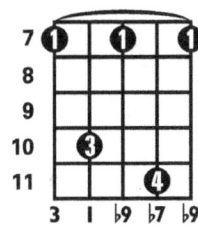

F7+9
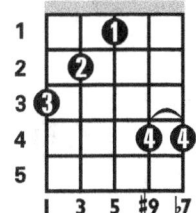
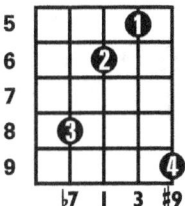
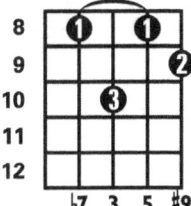

F Chords

Fm(maj7)	Fmaj7-5	Fmaj7+5	F9
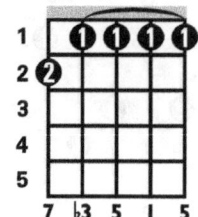	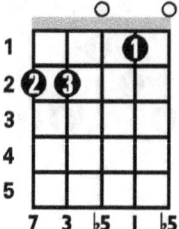	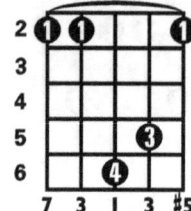	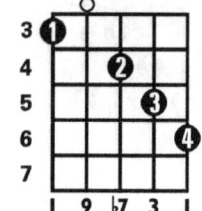
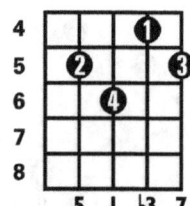	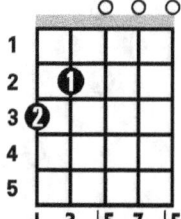	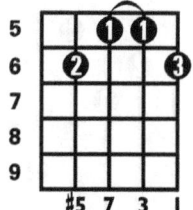	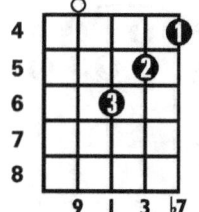
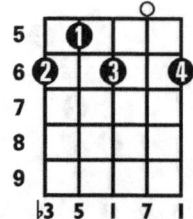	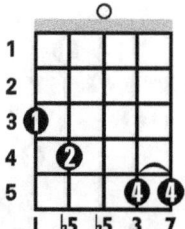	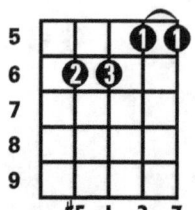	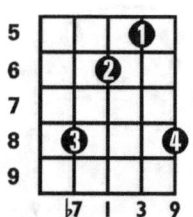

Fm9	Fmaj9	F11	F13
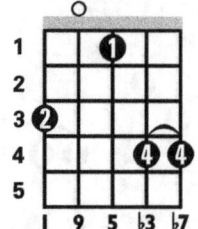	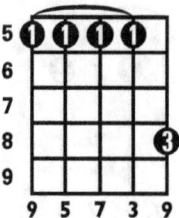	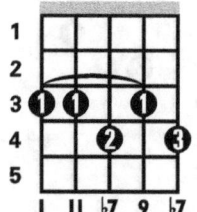	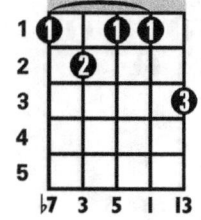
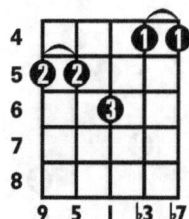	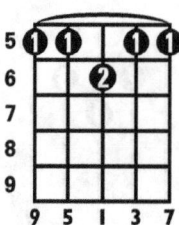	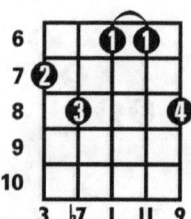	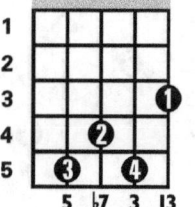
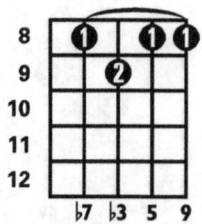	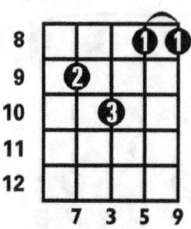	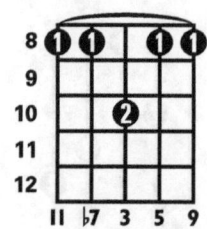	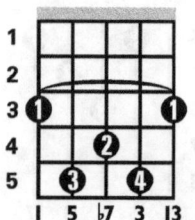

F Chords (Advanced)

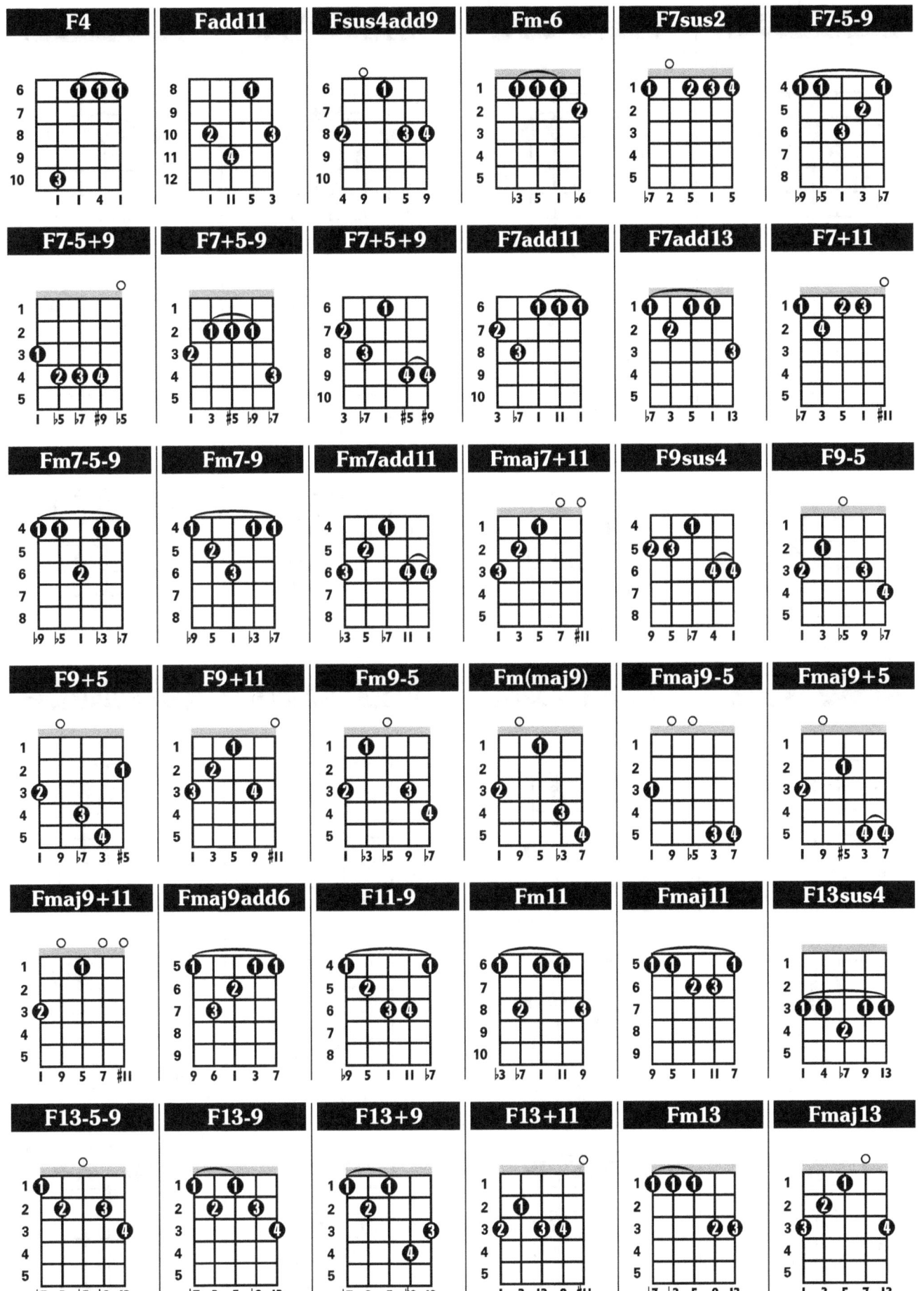

F#/Gb Chords

F#	F#m	F#7	F#m7
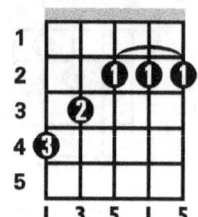	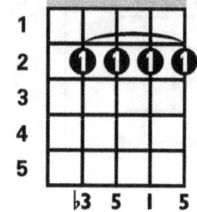	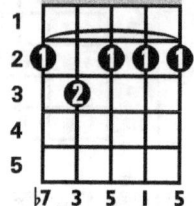	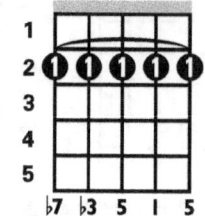
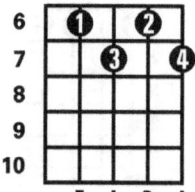	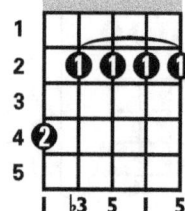	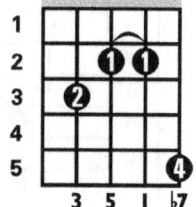	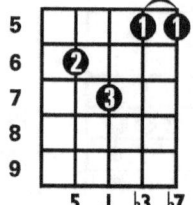
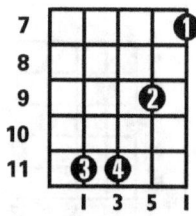	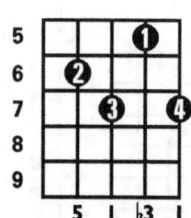	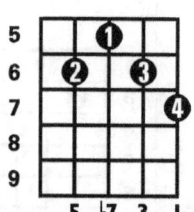	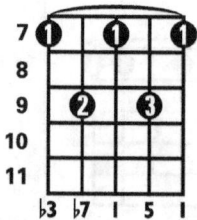

F#5	F#6	F#m6	F#maj7
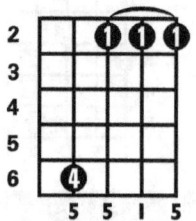	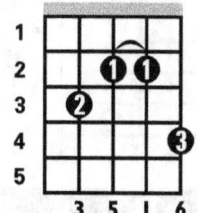	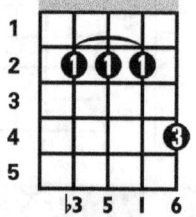	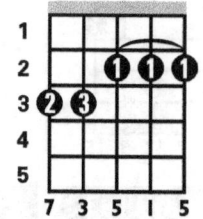
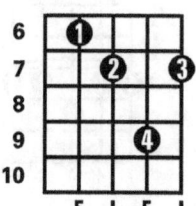	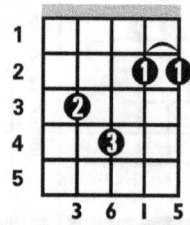	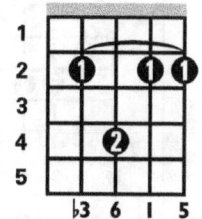	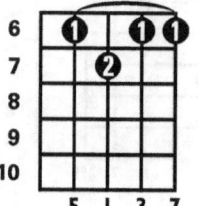
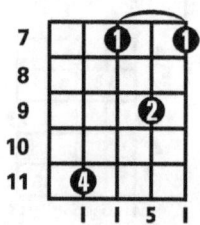	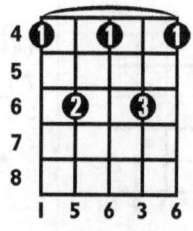	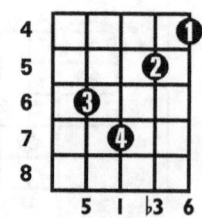	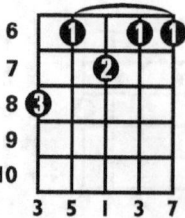

F#/G♭ Chords

F#°
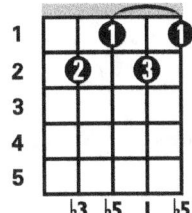
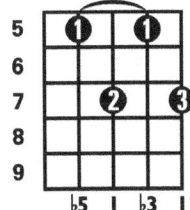
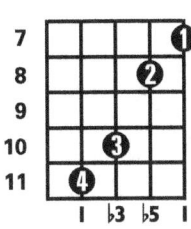

F#°7
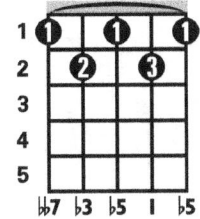
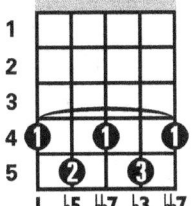
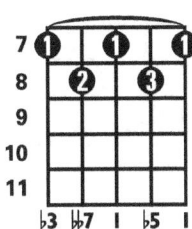

F#-5
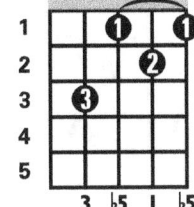
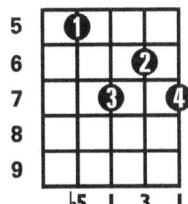
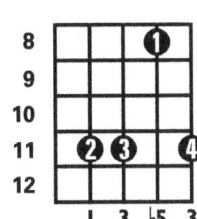

F#+
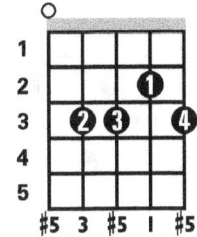
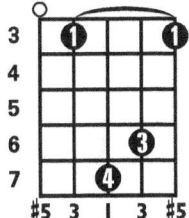
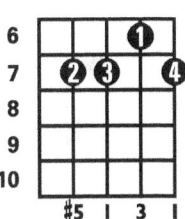

F#sus2
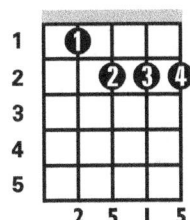
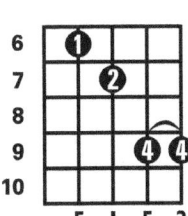
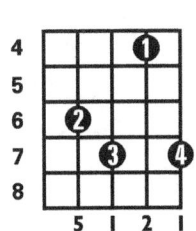

F#sus4
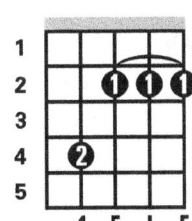
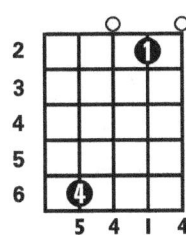
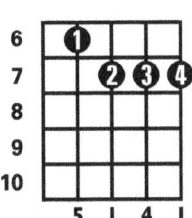

F#7sus4
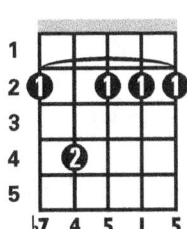
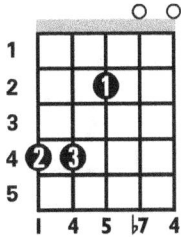
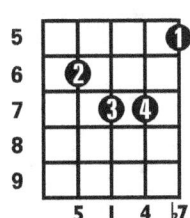

F#m7-5
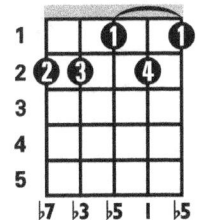
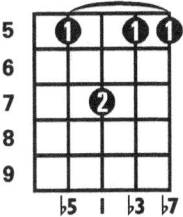
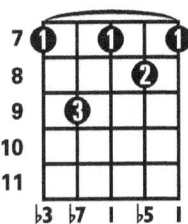

F#/G♭ Chords

F#add9	F#madd9	F#6add9	F#m6add9
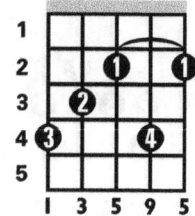	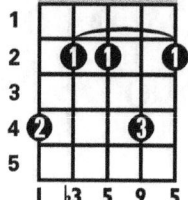	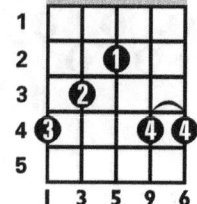	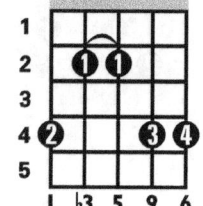
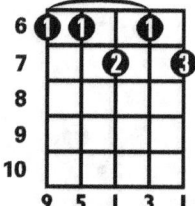	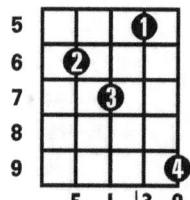	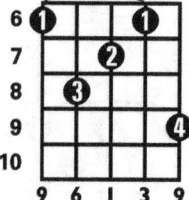	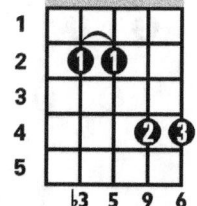
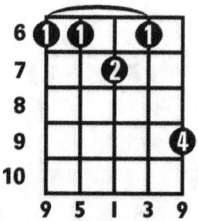	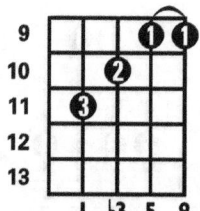	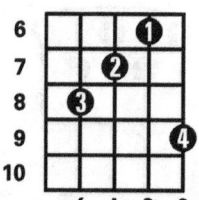	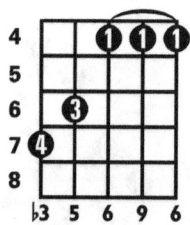

F#7-5	F#7+5	F#7-9	F#7+9
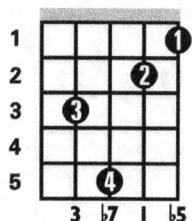	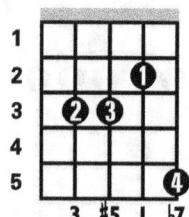	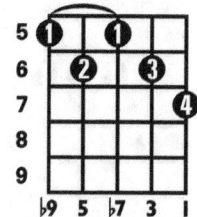	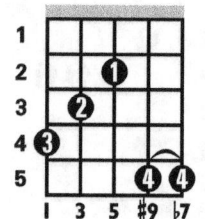
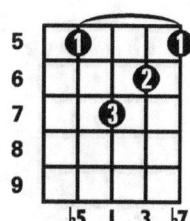	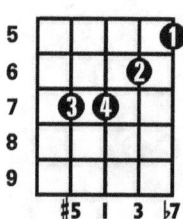	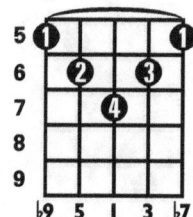	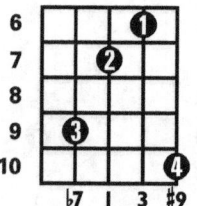
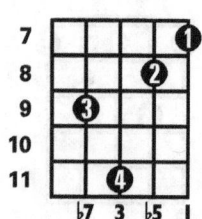	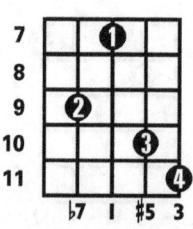	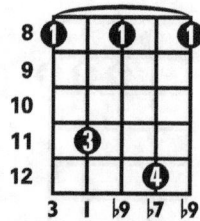	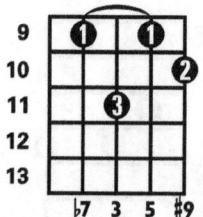

F#/G♭ Chords

F#m(maj7)
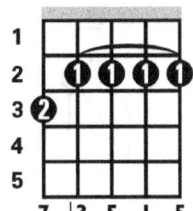
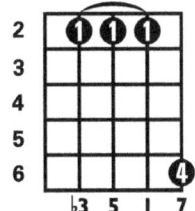
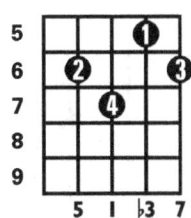

F#maj7-5
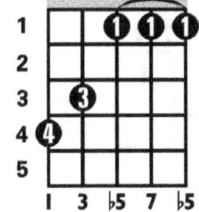
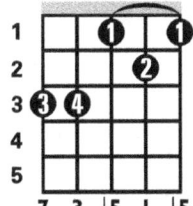
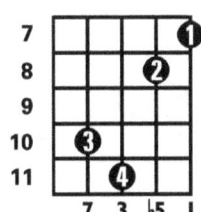

F#maj7+5
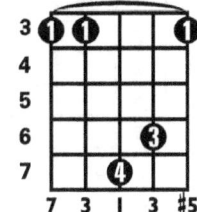
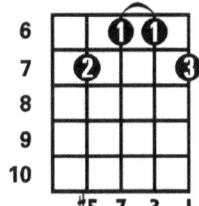
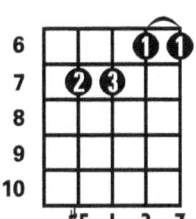

F#9
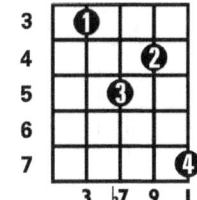
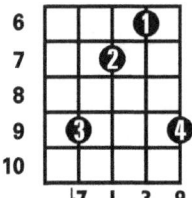
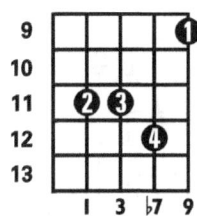

F#m9
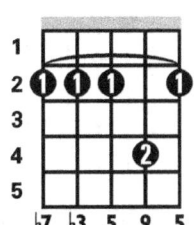
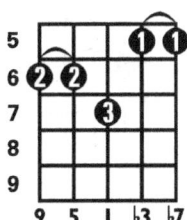
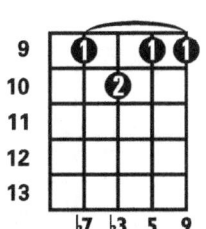

F#maj9
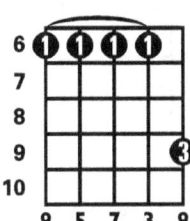
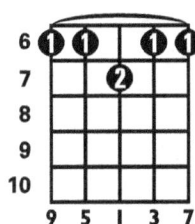
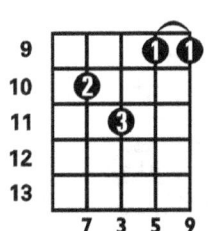

F#11
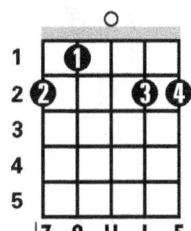
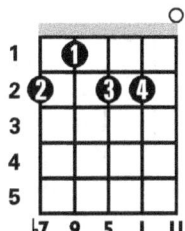
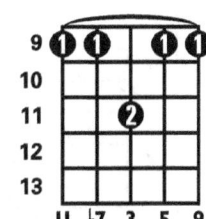

F#13
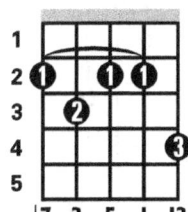
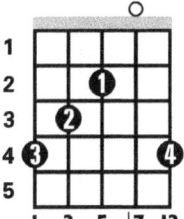
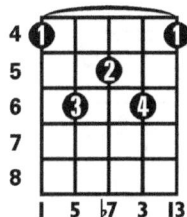

F#/G♭ Chords (Advanced)

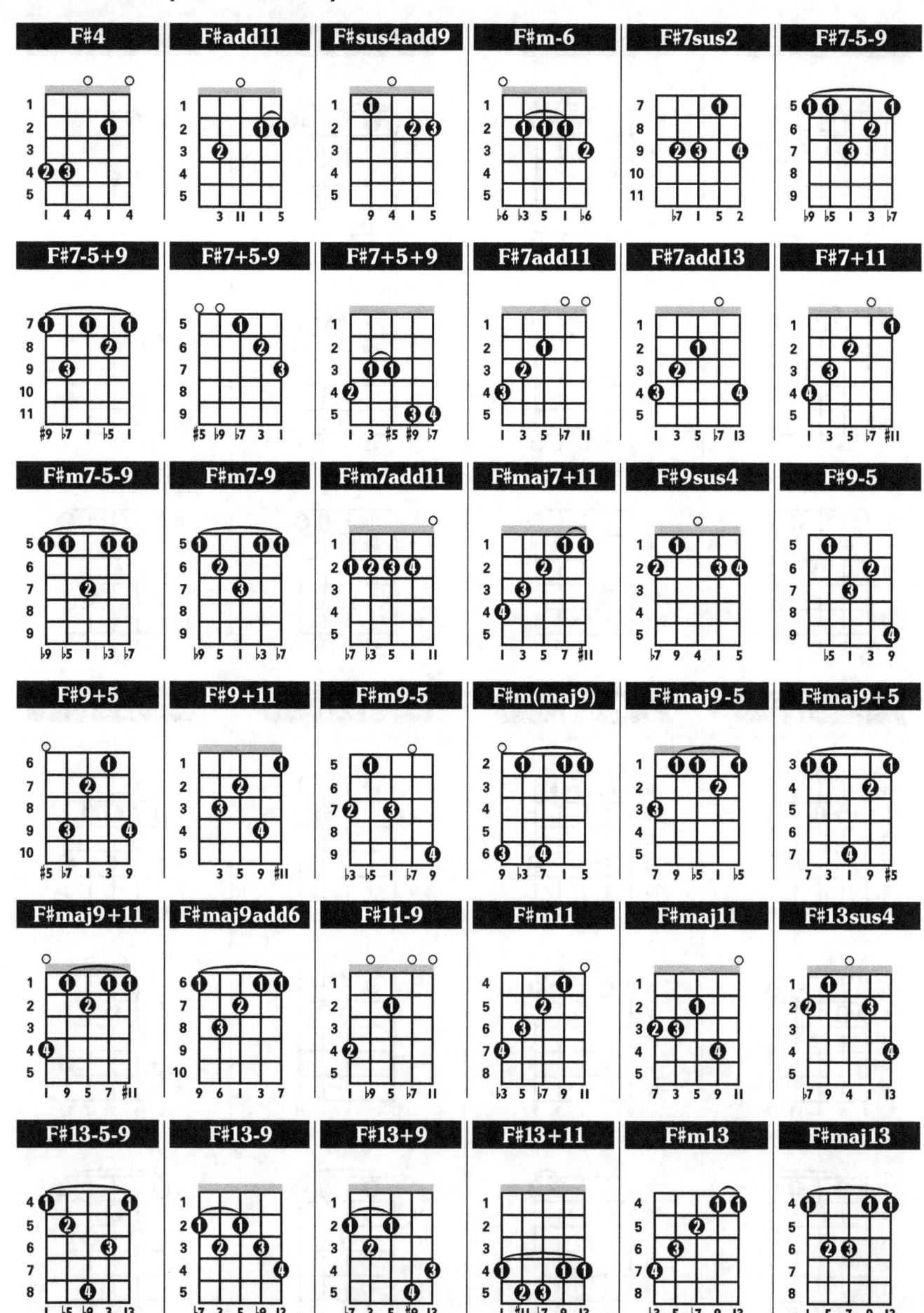

G Chords

G
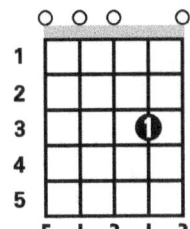
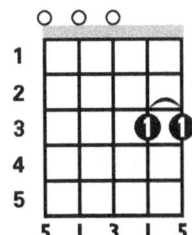
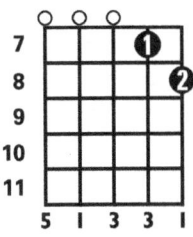

Gm
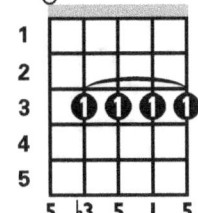
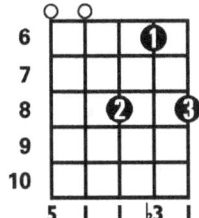
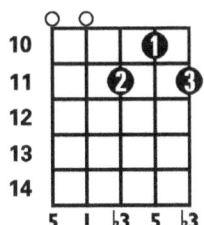

G7
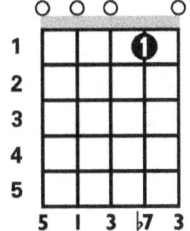
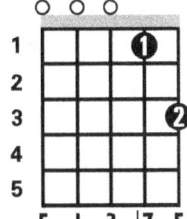
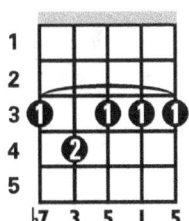

Gm7
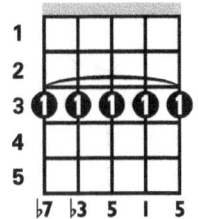
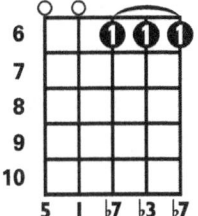
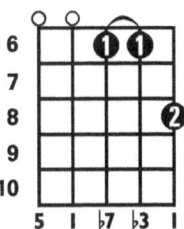

G5
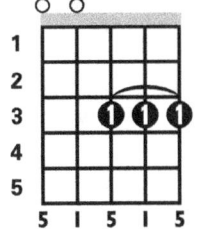
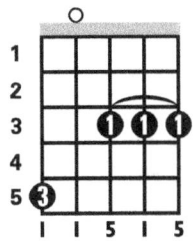
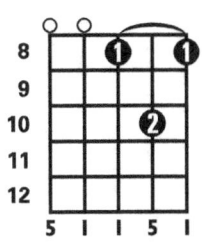

G6
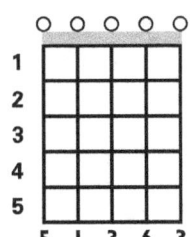
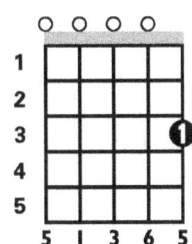
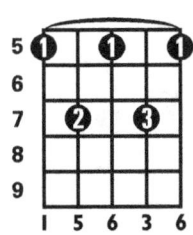

Gm6
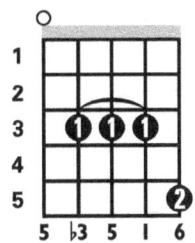
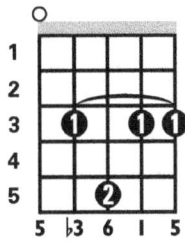
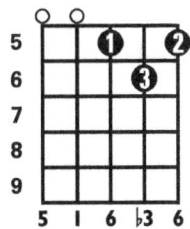

Gmaj7
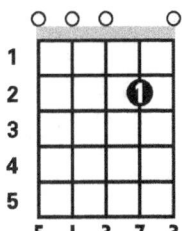
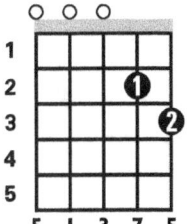
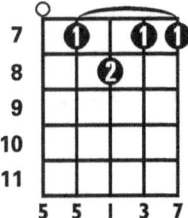

G Chords

G°	G°7	G-5	G+
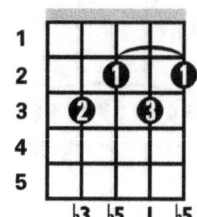	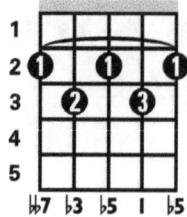	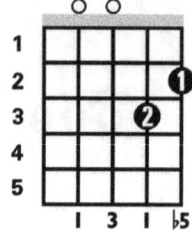	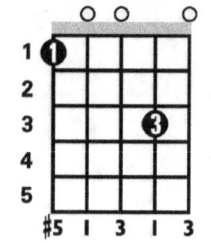
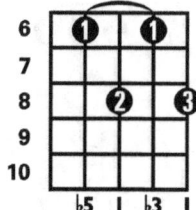	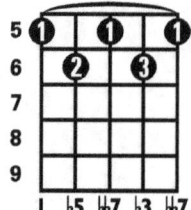	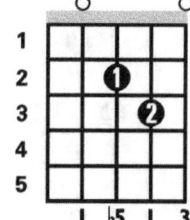	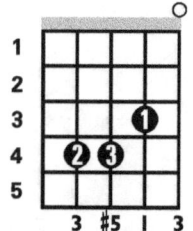
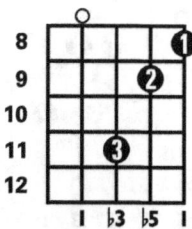	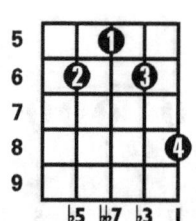	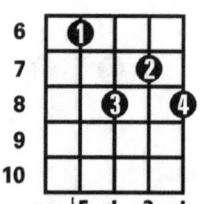	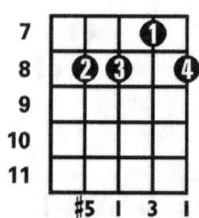

Gsus2	Gsus4	G7sus4	Gm7-5
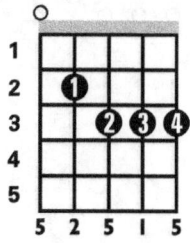	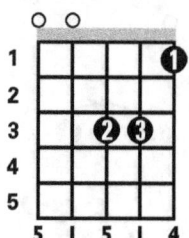	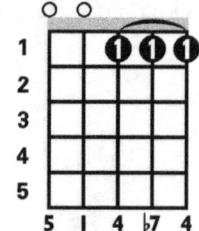	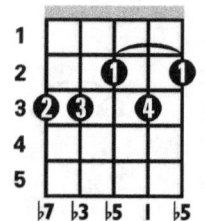
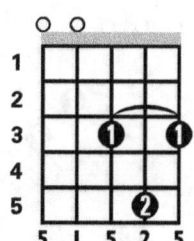	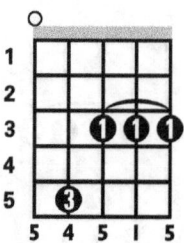	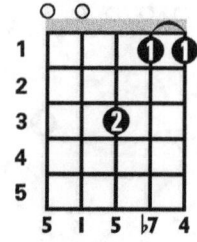	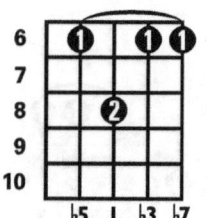
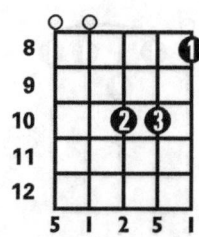	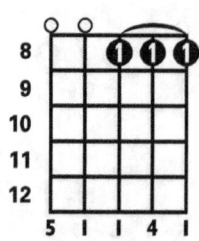	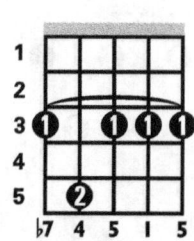	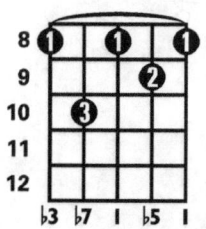

G Chords

Gadd9
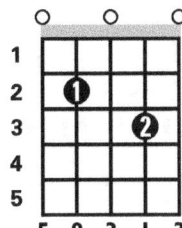
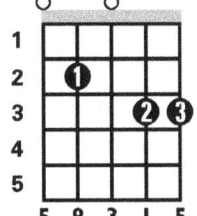
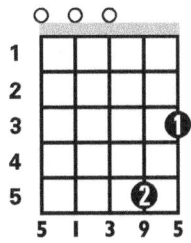

Gmadd9
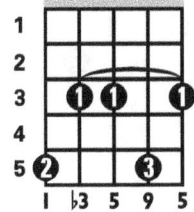
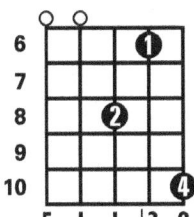
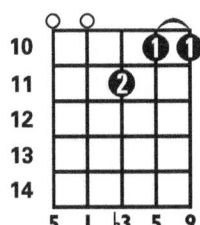

G6add9
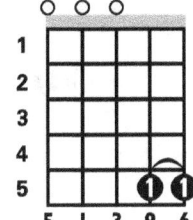
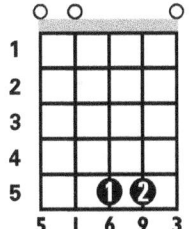
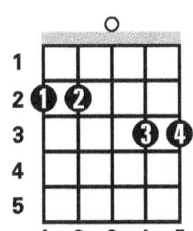

Gm6add9
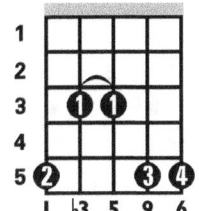
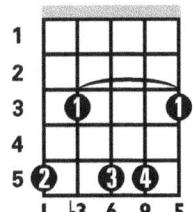
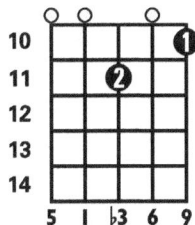

G7-5
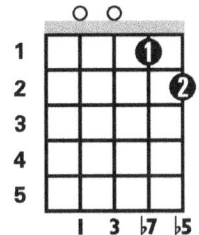
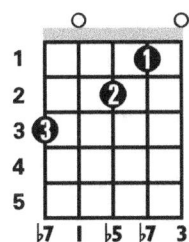
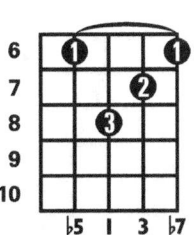

G7+5
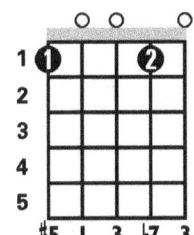
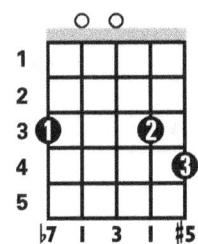
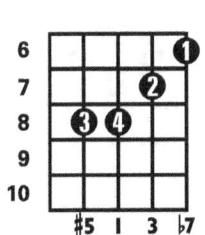

G7-9
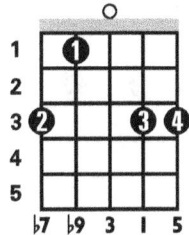
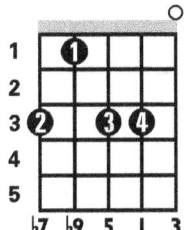
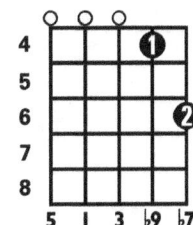

G7+9
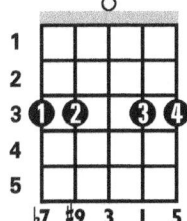
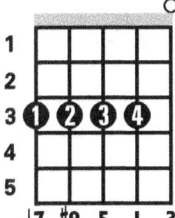
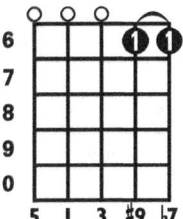

G Chords

Gm(maj7)	Gmaj7-5	Gmaj7+5	G9
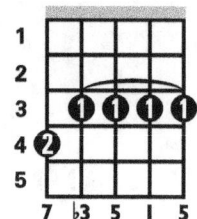	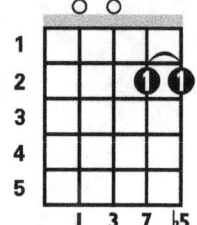	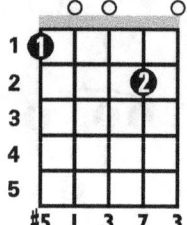	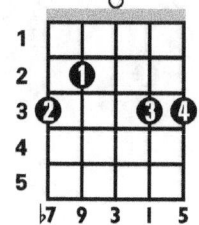
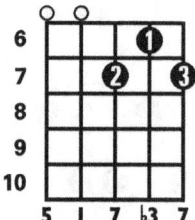	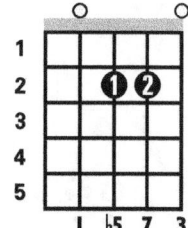	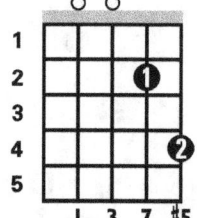	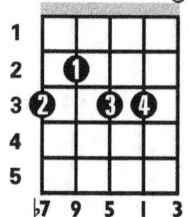
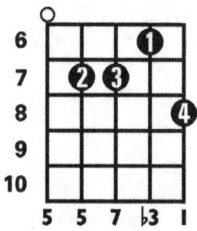	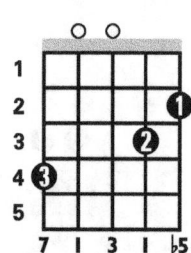	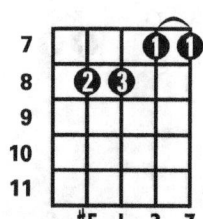	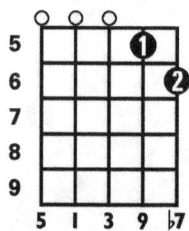

Gm9	Gmaj9	G11	G13
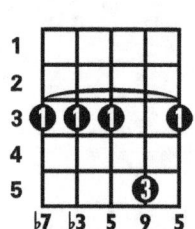	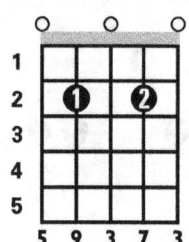	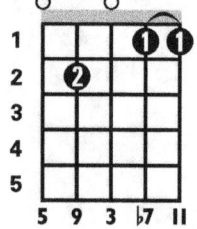	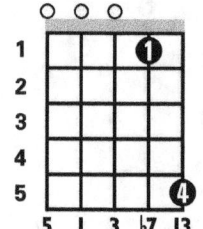
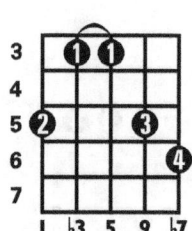	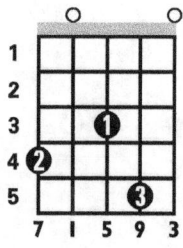	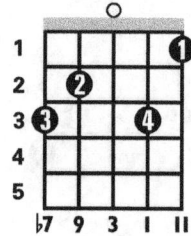	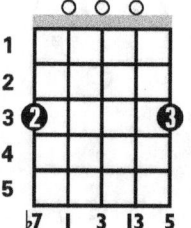
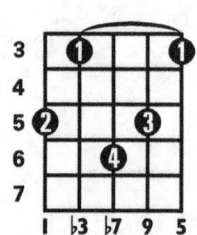	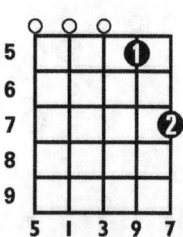	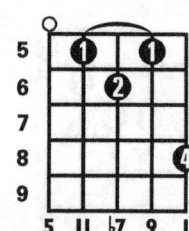	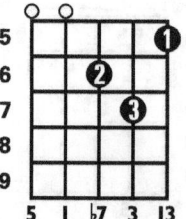

G Chords (Advanced)

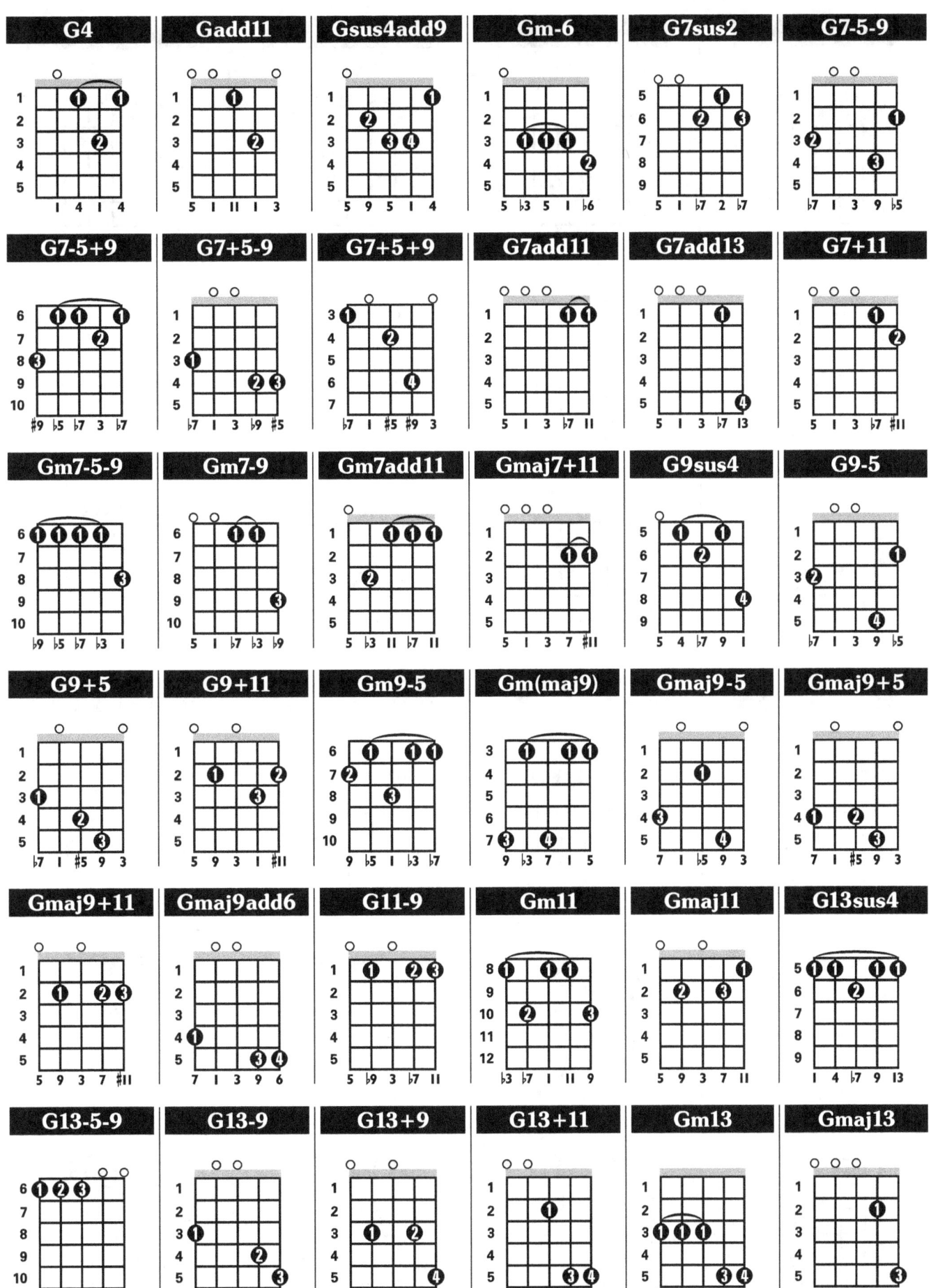

G# / A♭ Chords

A♭	A♭m	A♭7	A♭m7
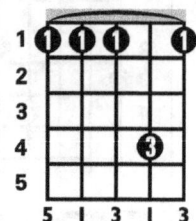	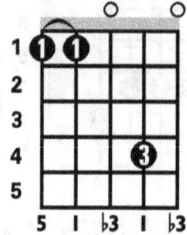	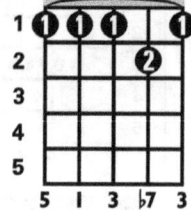	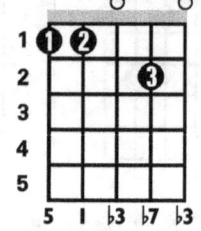
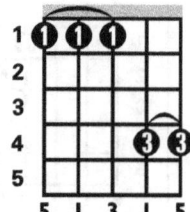	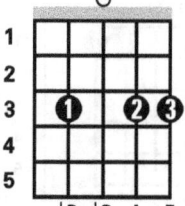	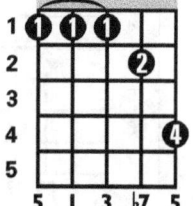	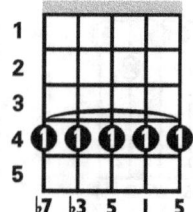
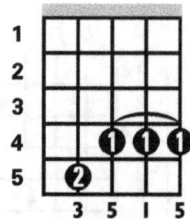	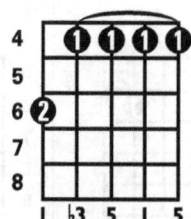	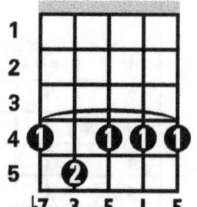	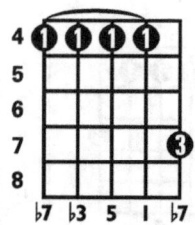

A♭5	A♭6	A♭m6	A♭maj7
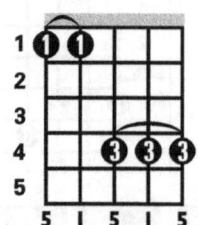	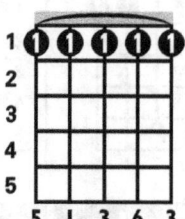	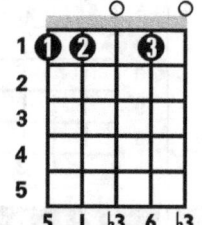	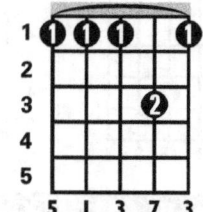
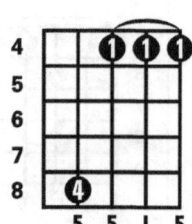	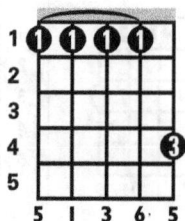	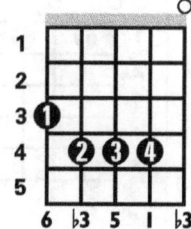	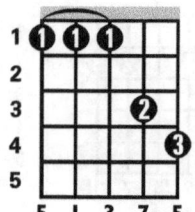
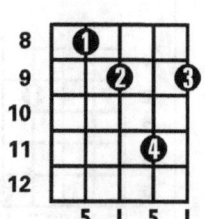	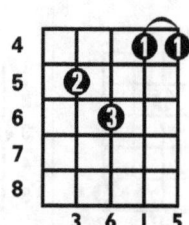	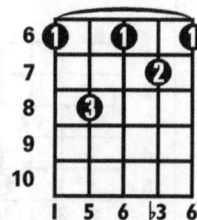	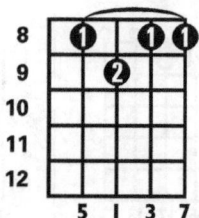

G#/A♭ Chords

A♭°
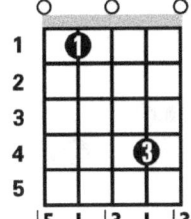
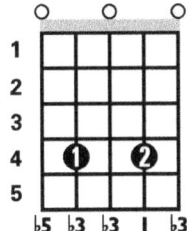
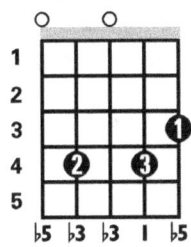

A♭°7
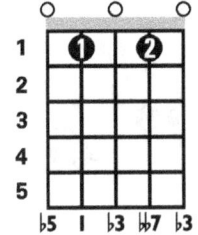
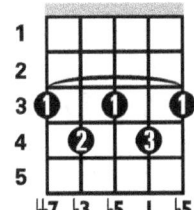
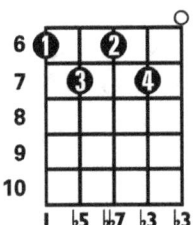

A♭-5
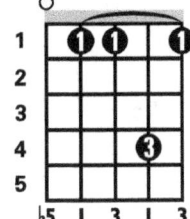
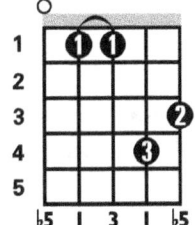
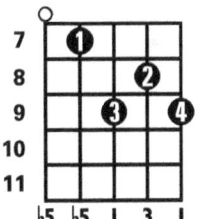

A♭+
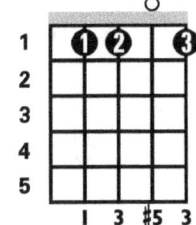
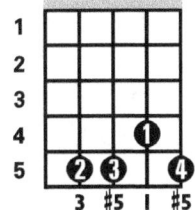
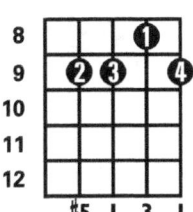

A♭sus2
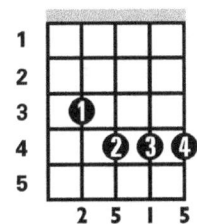
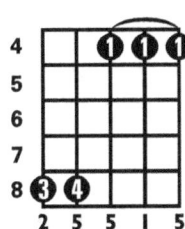
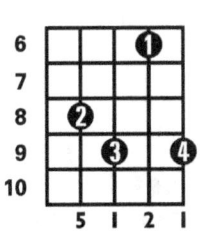

A♭sus4
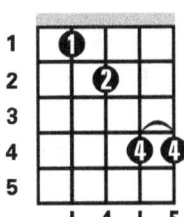
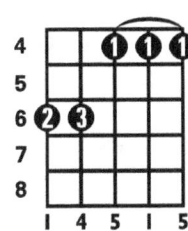
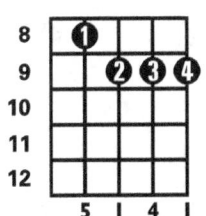

A♭7sus4
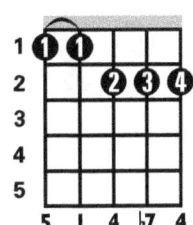
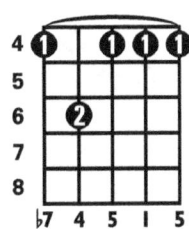
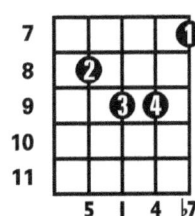

A♭m7-5
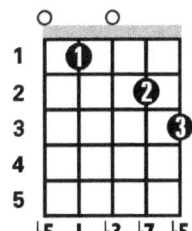
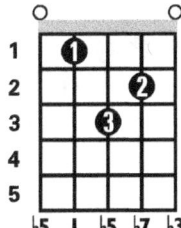
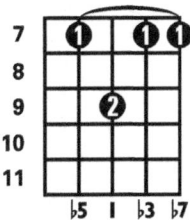

G# / A♭ Chords

A♭add9	A♭madd9	A♭6add9	A♭m6add9
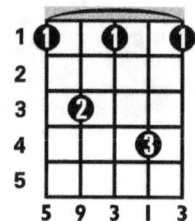	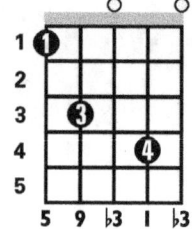	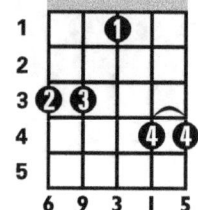	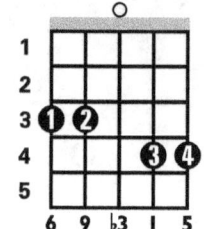
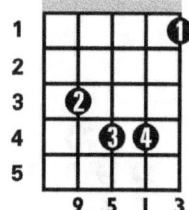	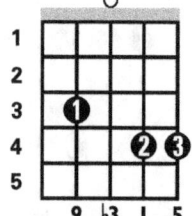	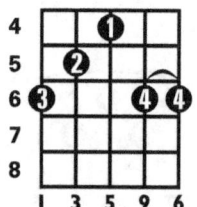	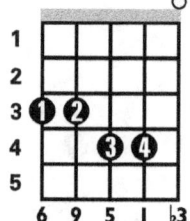
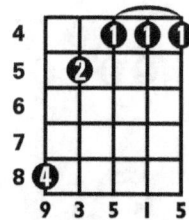	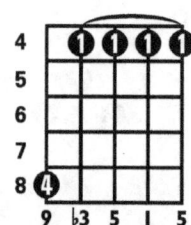	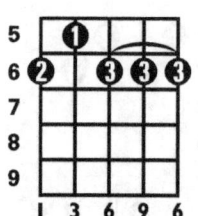	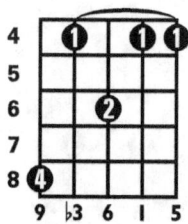

A♭7-5	A♭7+5	A♭7-9	A♭7+9
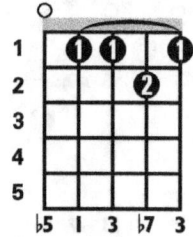	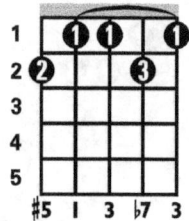	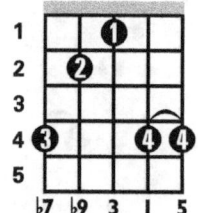	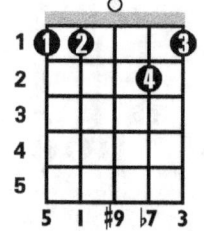
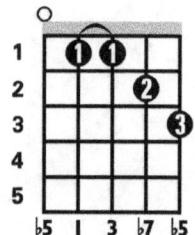	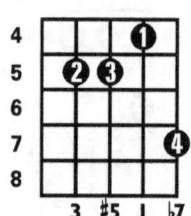	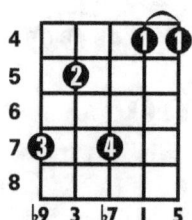	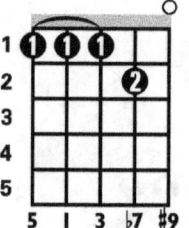
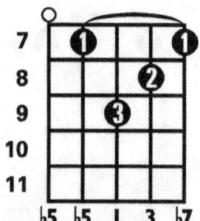	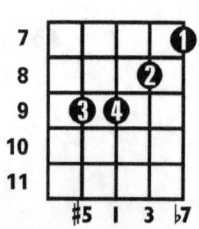	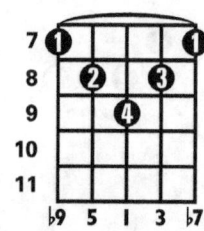	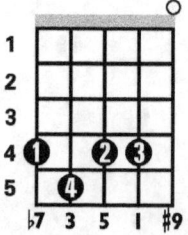

G#/A♭ Chords

A♭m(maj7)
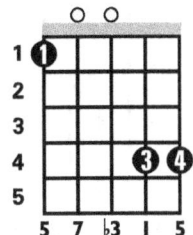
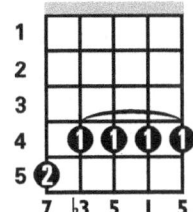
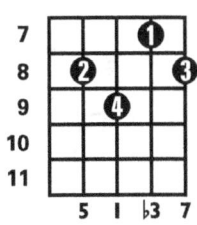

A♭maj7-5
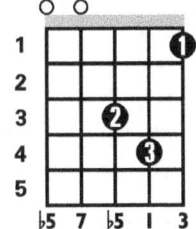
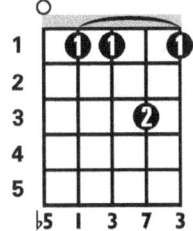
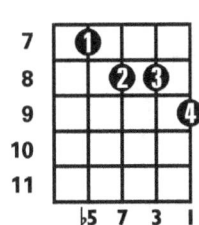

A♭maj7+5
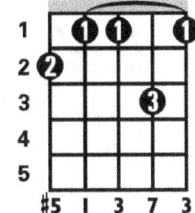
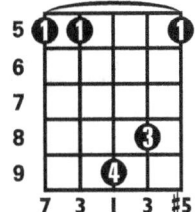
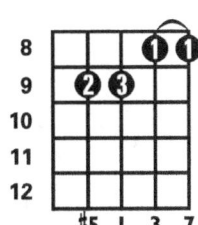

A♭9
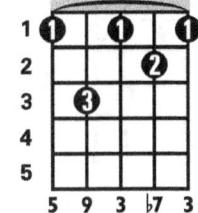
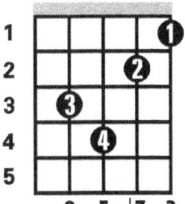
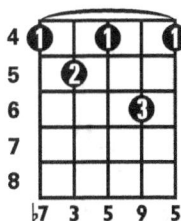

A♭m9
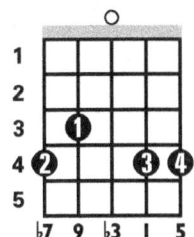
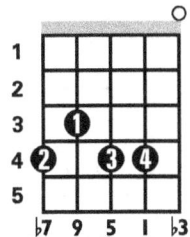
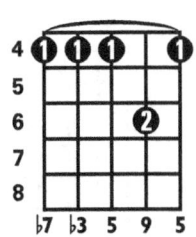

A♭maj9
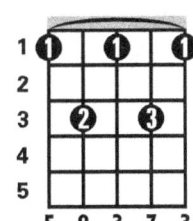
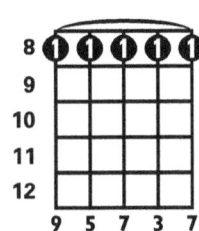
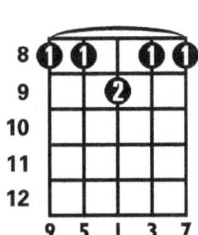

A♭11
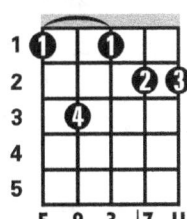
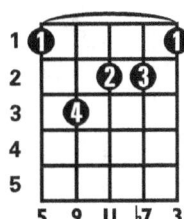
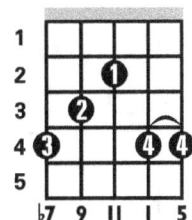

A♭13
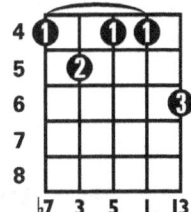
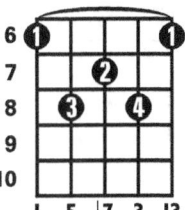
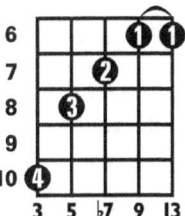

G# / A♭ Chords (Advanced)

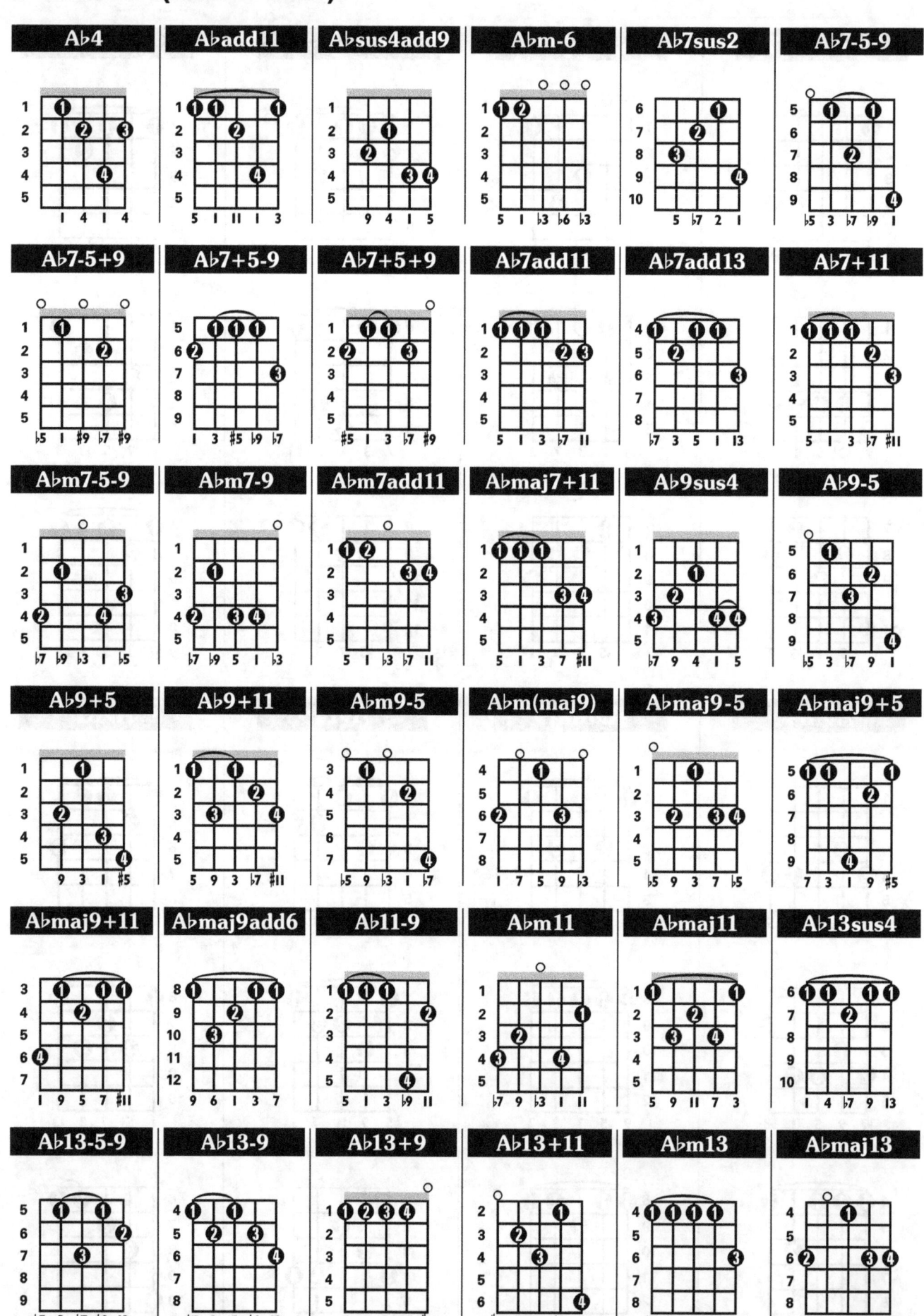

A Chords

A	Am	A7	Am7
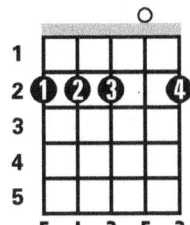	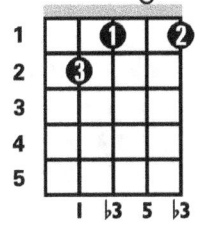	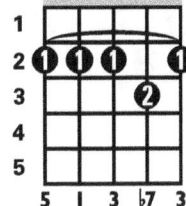	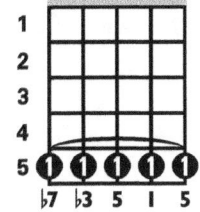
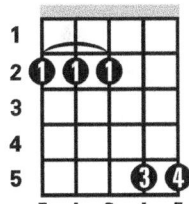	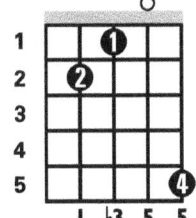	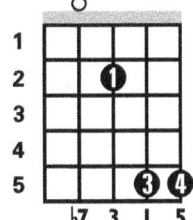	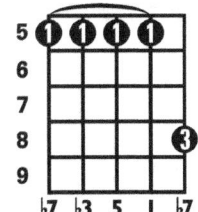
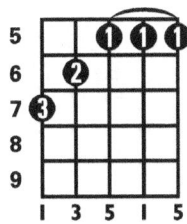	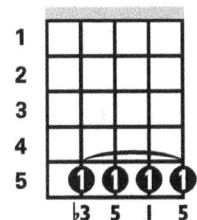	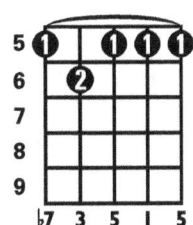	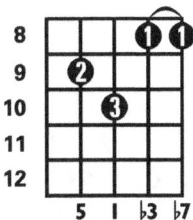

A5	A6	Am6	Amaj7
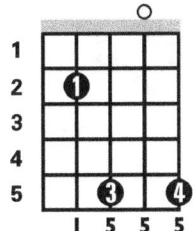	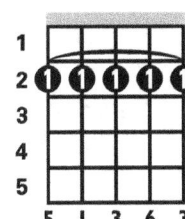	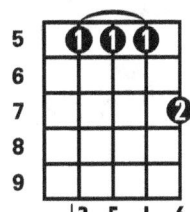	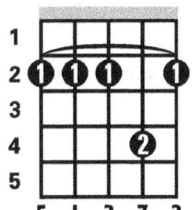
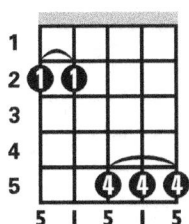	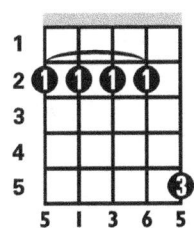	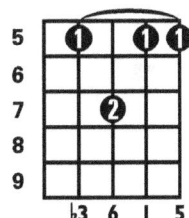	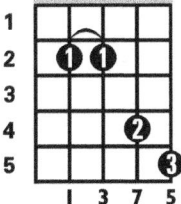
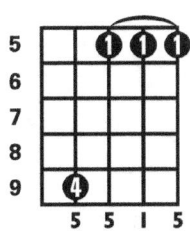	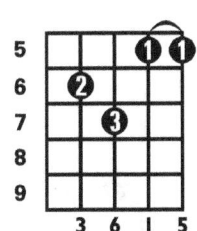	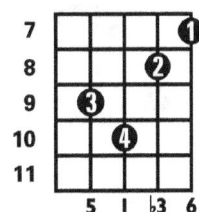	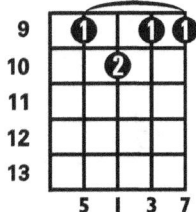

A Chords

A°	A°7	A-5	A+
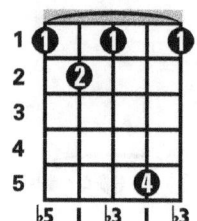	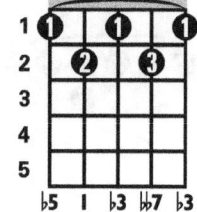	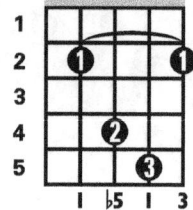	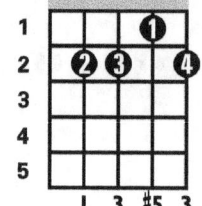
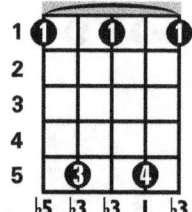	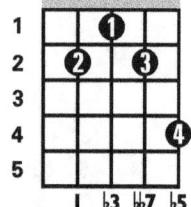	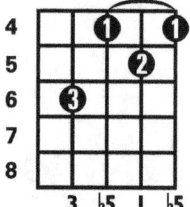	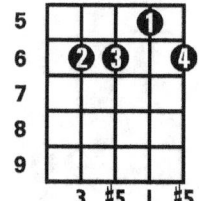
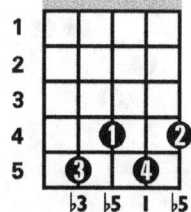	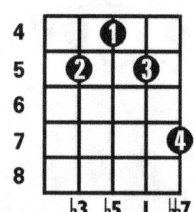	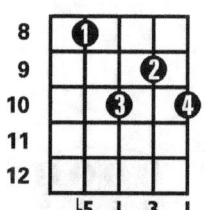	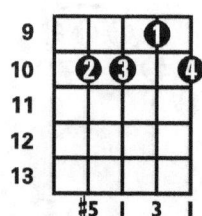

Asus2	Asus4	A7sus4	Am7-5
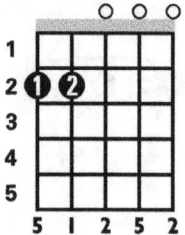	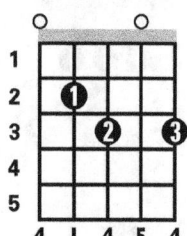	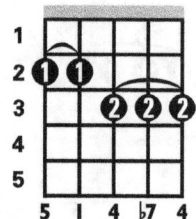	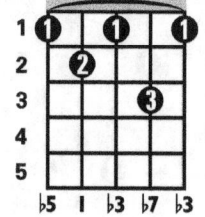
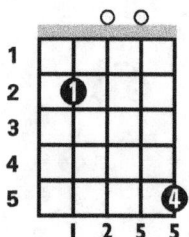	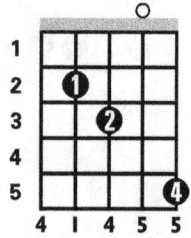	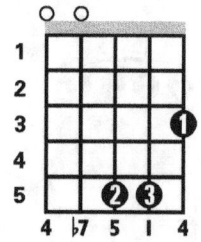	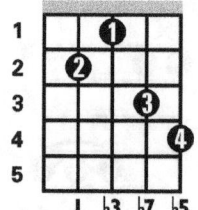
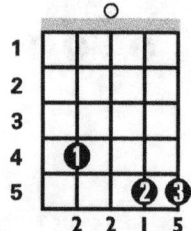	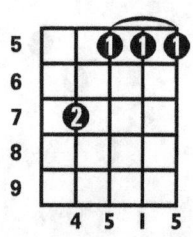	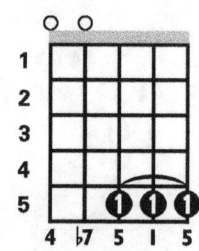	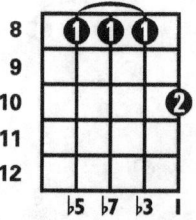

A Chords

Aadd9
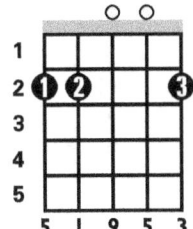
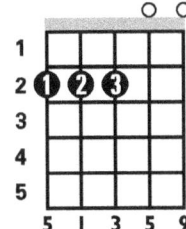
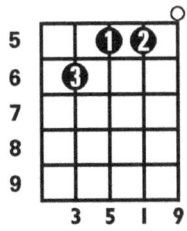

Amadd9
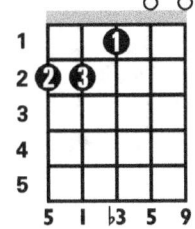
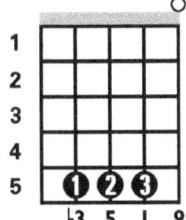
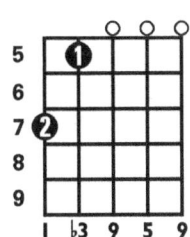

A6add9
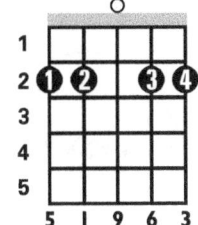
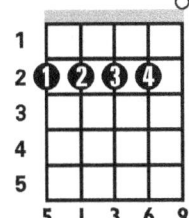
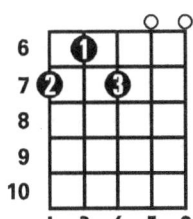

Am6add9
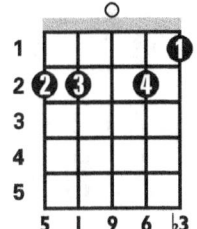
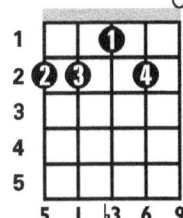
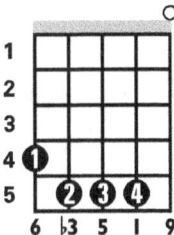

A7-5
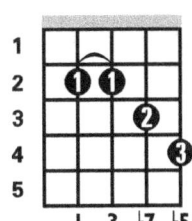
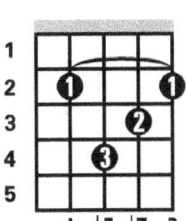
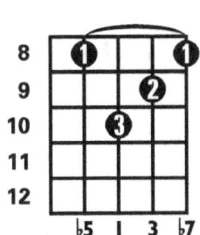

A7+5
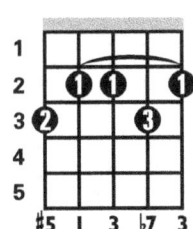
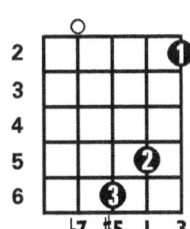
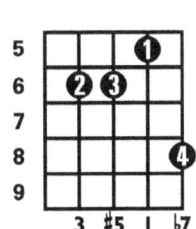

A7-9
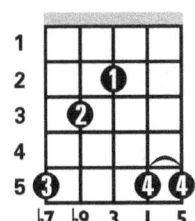
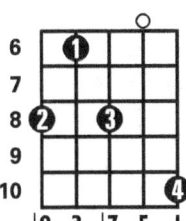
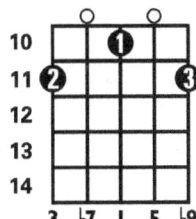

A7+9
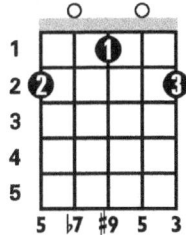
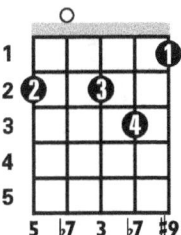
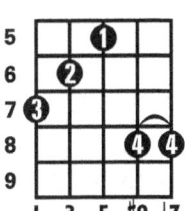

A Chords

Am(maj7)
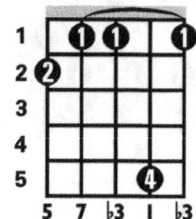
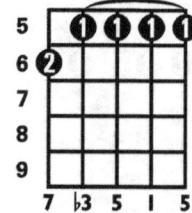
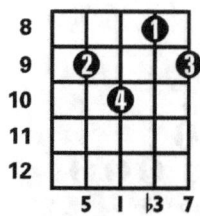

Amaj7-5
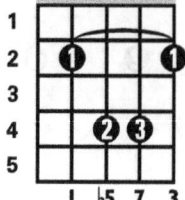
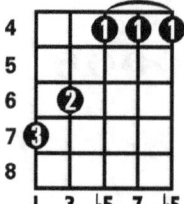
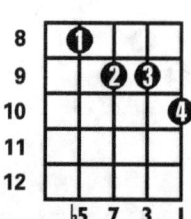

Amaj7+5
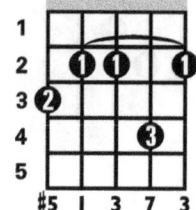
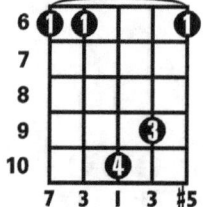
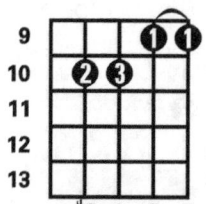

A9
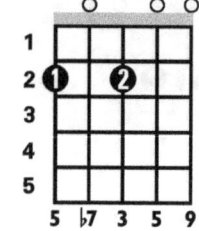
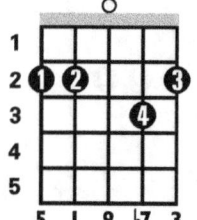
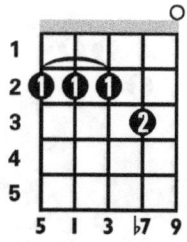

Am9
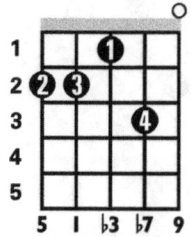
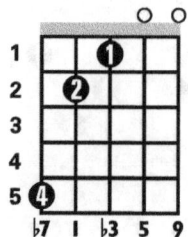
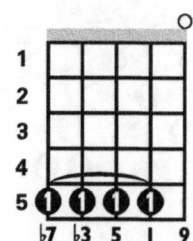

Amaj9
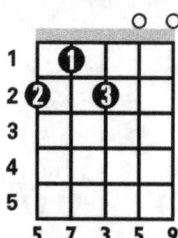
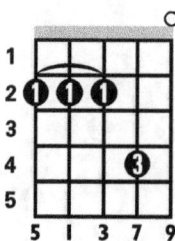
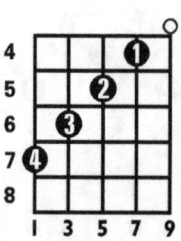

A11
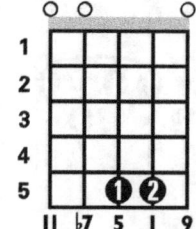
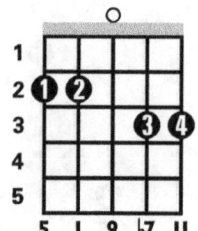
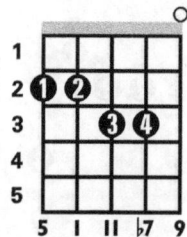

A13
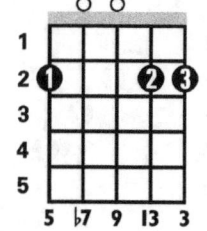
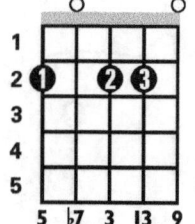
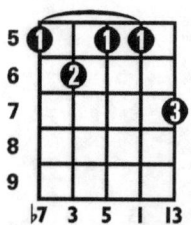

A Chords (Advanced)

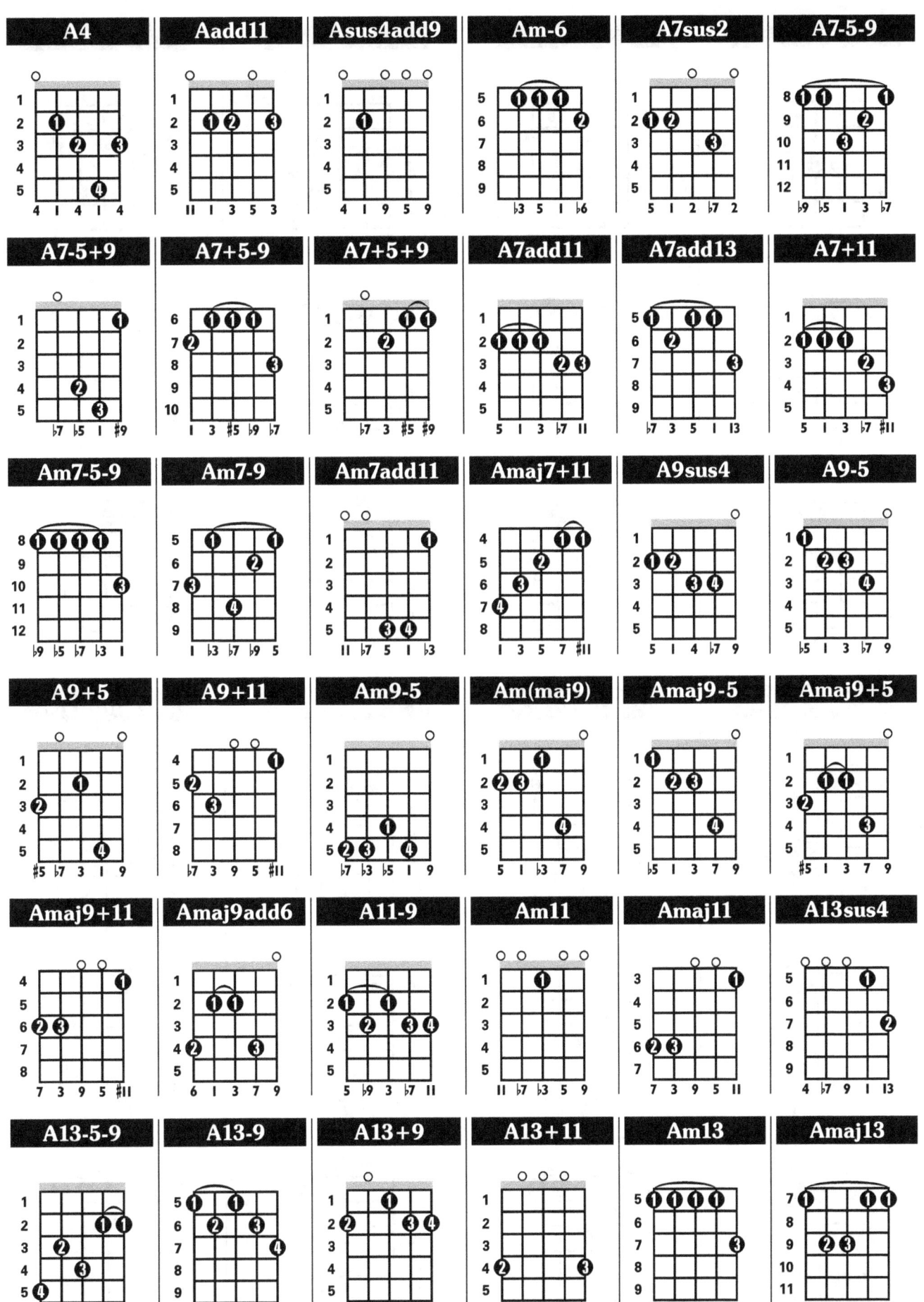

A# / B♭ Chords

B♭
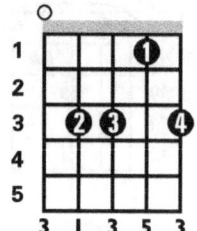
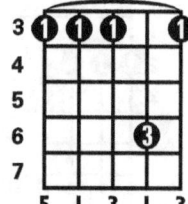
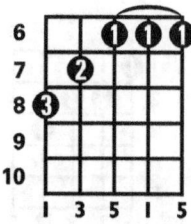

B♭m
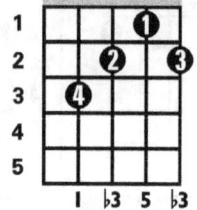
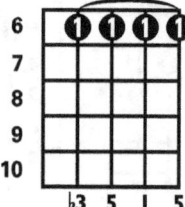
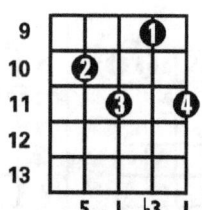

B♭7
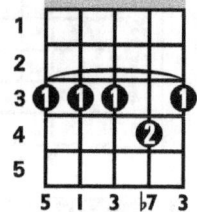
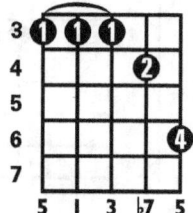
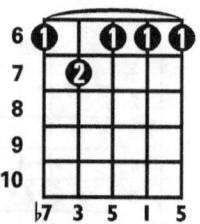

B♭m7
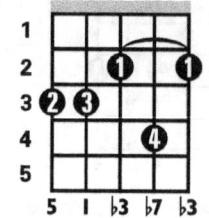
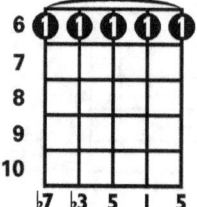
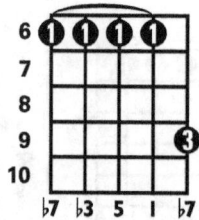

B♭5
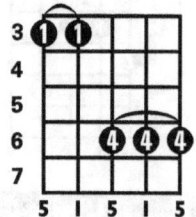
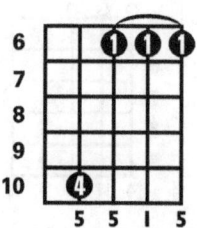
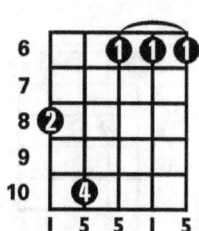

B♭6
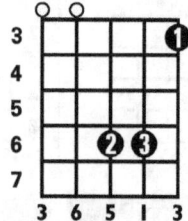
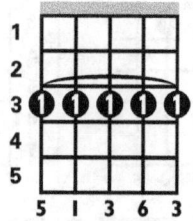
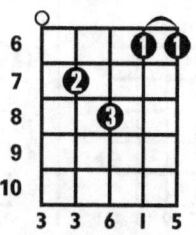

B♭m6
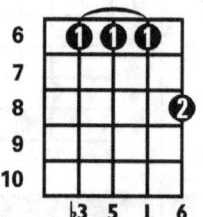
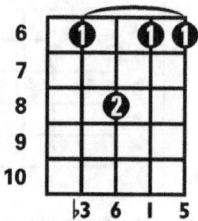
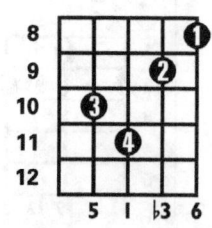

B♭maj7
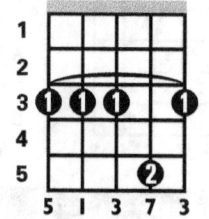
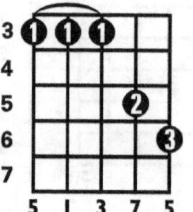
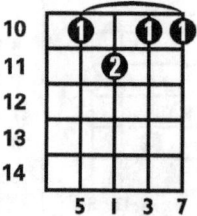

A#/B♭ Chords

B♭°
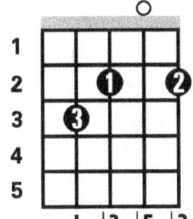
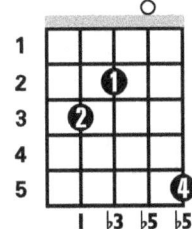
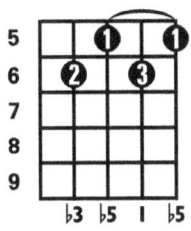

B♭°7
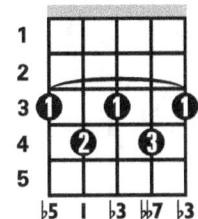
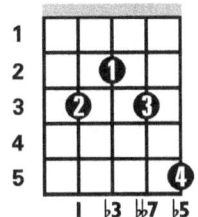
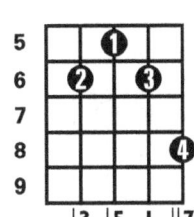

B♭-5
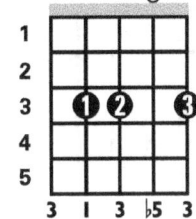
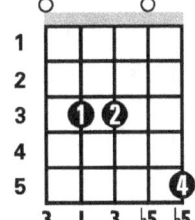
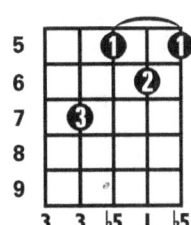

B♭+
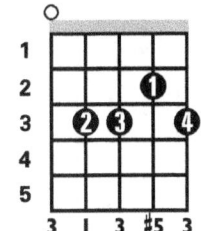
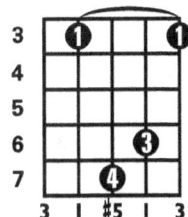
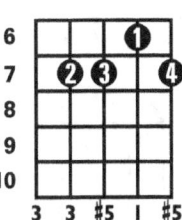

B♭sus2
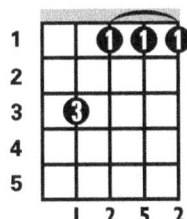
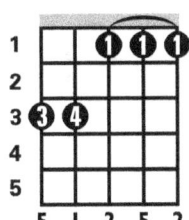
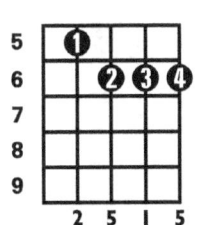

B♭sus4
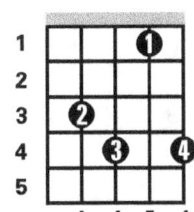
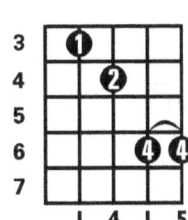
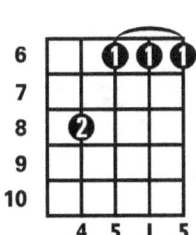

B♭7sus4
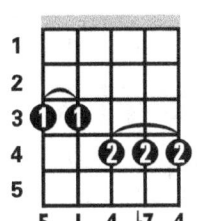
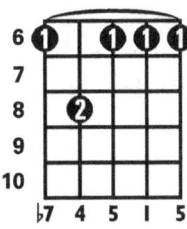
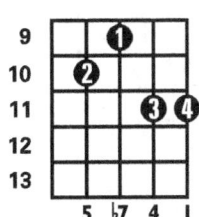

B♭m7-5
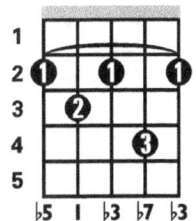
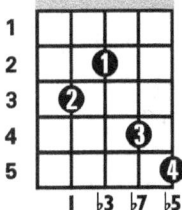
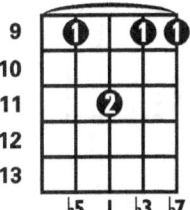

A♯ / B♭ Chords

B♭add9	B♭madd9	B♭6add9	B♭m6add9
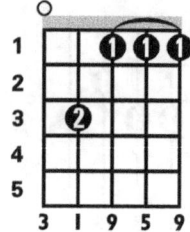	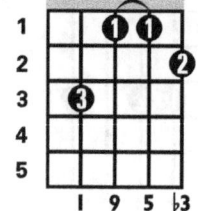	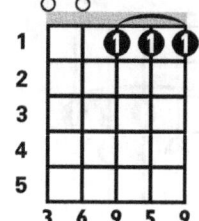	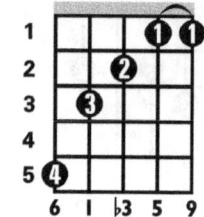
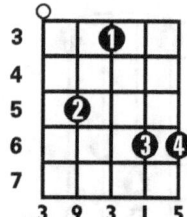	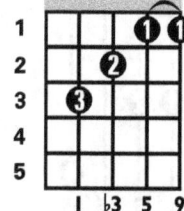	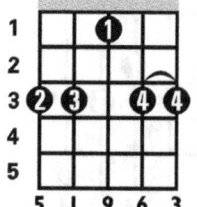	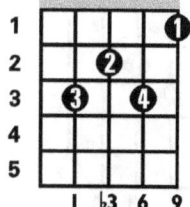
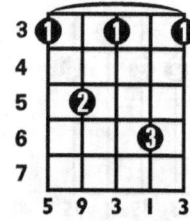	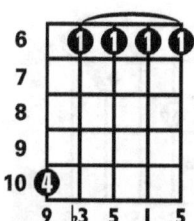	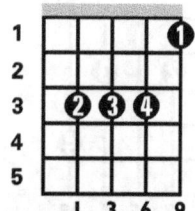	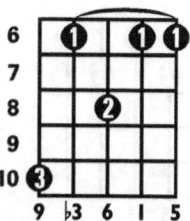

B♭7-5	B♭7+5	B♭7-9	B♭7+9
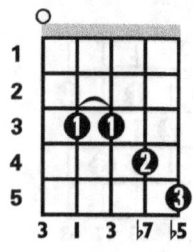	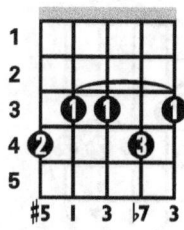	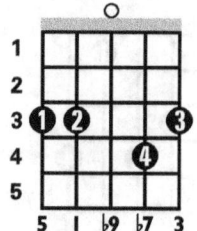	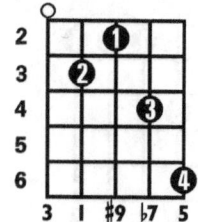
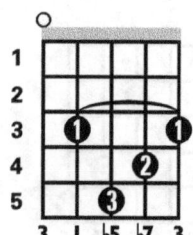		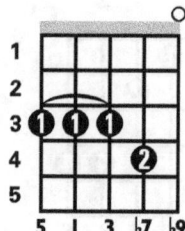	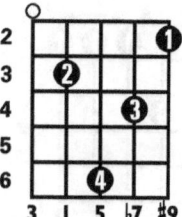
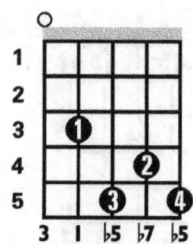	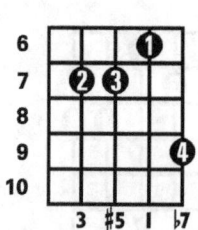	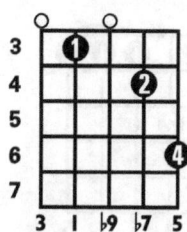	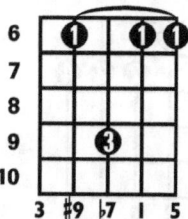

A#/B♭ Chords

B♭m(maj7)
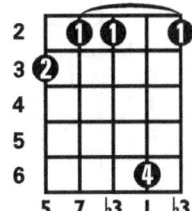
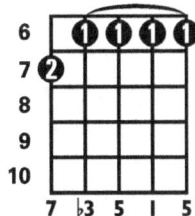
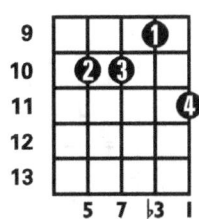

B♭maj7-5
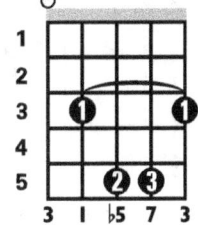
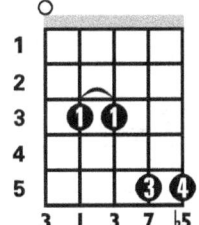
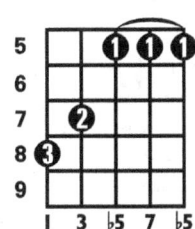

B♭maj7+5
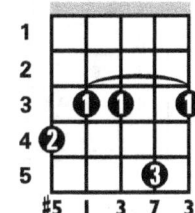
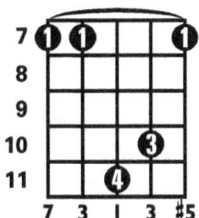
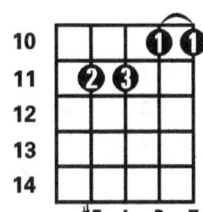

B♭9
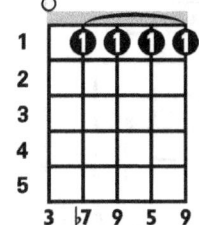
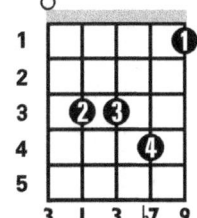
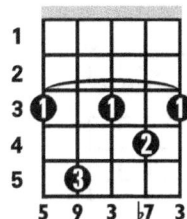

B♭m9
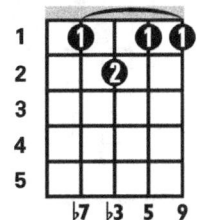
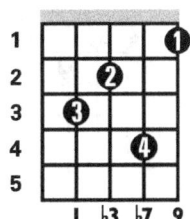
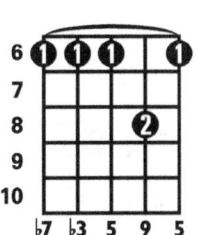

B♭maj9
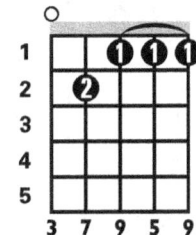
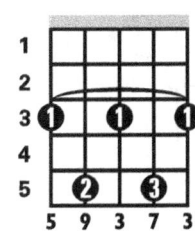
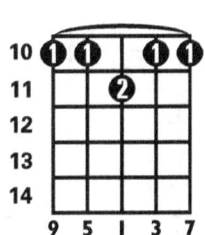

B♭11
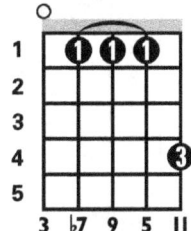
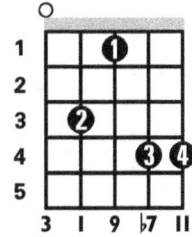
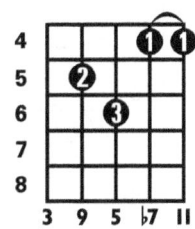

B♭13
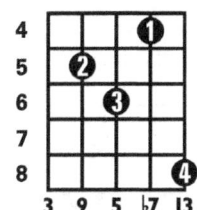
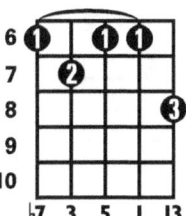
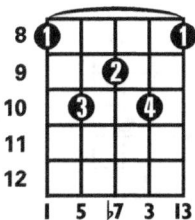

A# / B♭ Chords (Advanced)

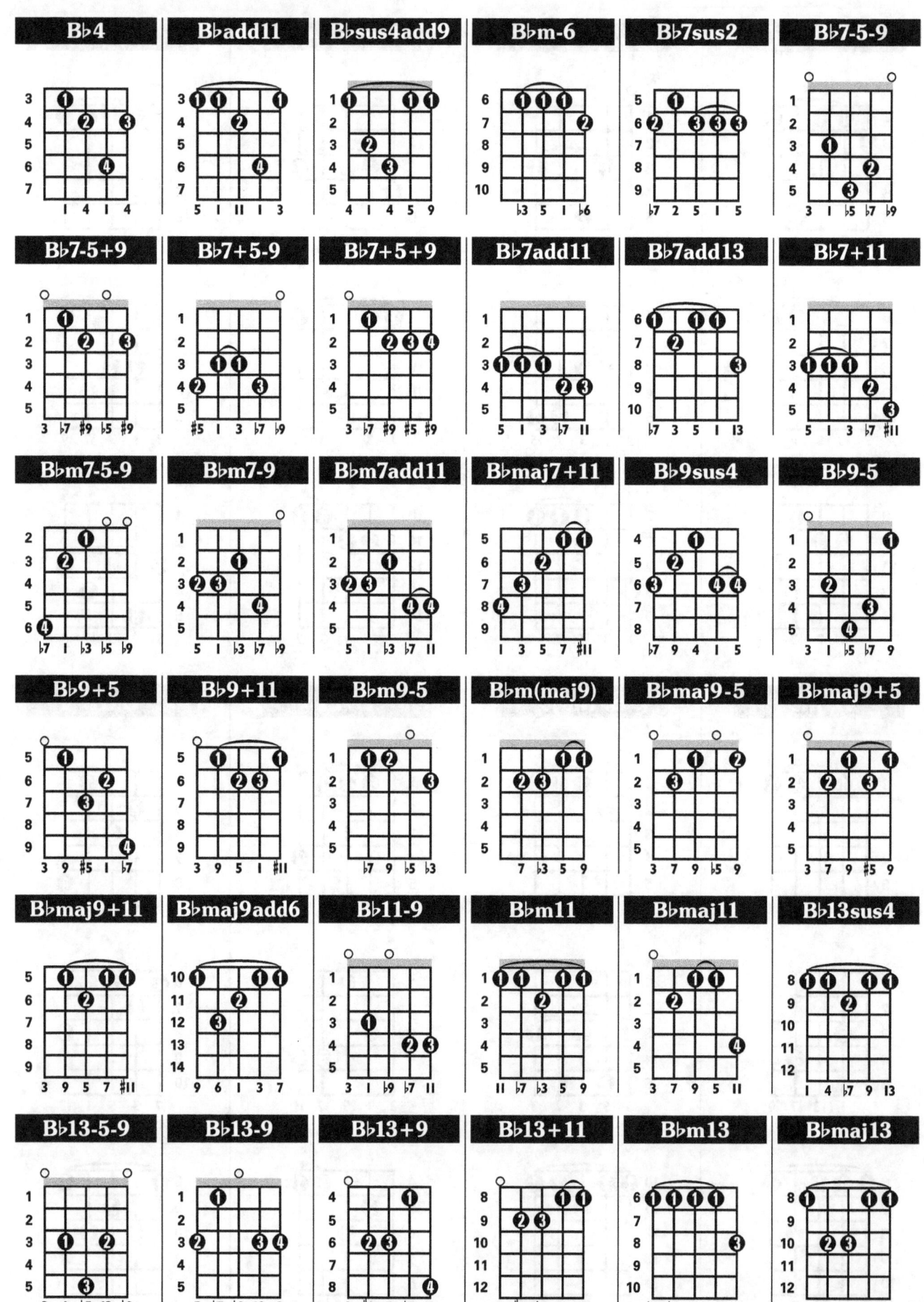

B Chords

B
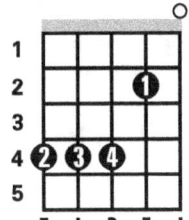
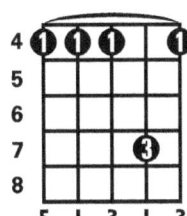
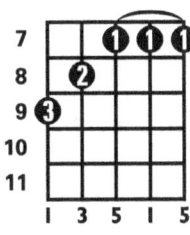

Bm
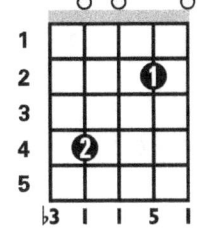
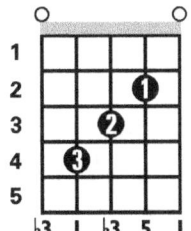
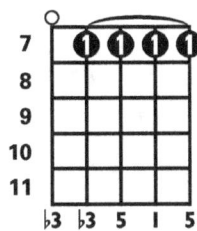

B7
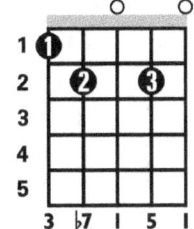
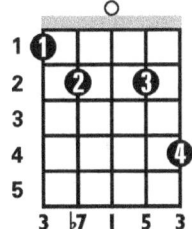
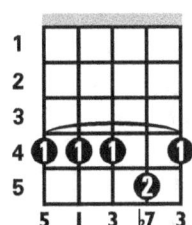

Bm7
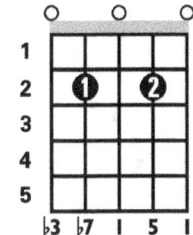
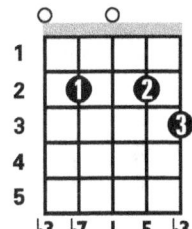
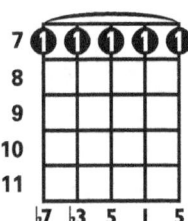

B5
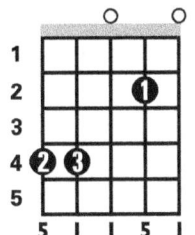
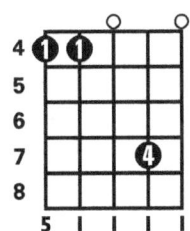
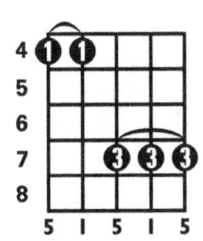

B6
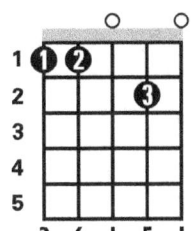
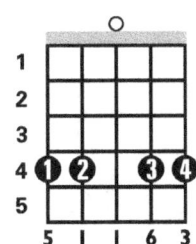
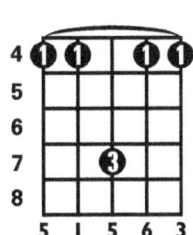

Bm6
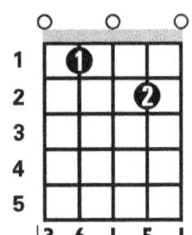
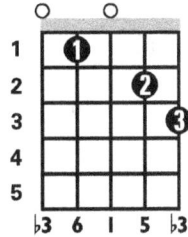
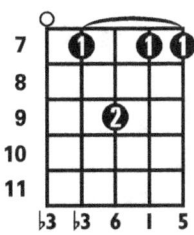

Bmaj7
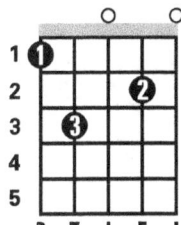
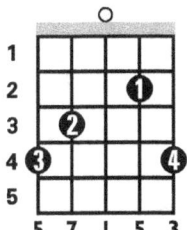
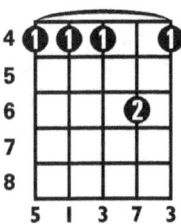

B Chords

Bº	Bº7	B-5	B+
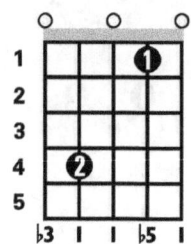	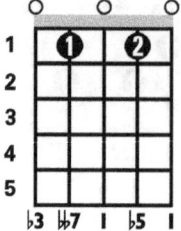	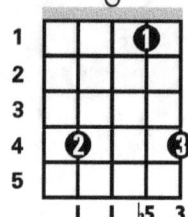	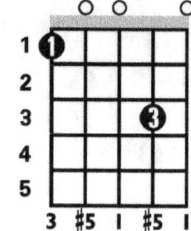
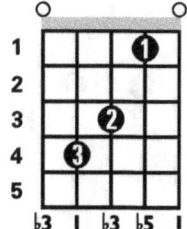	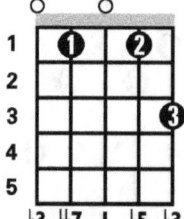	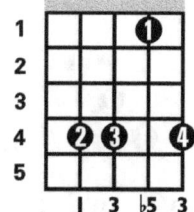	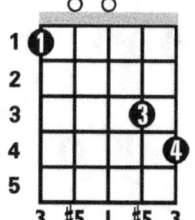
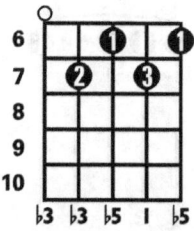	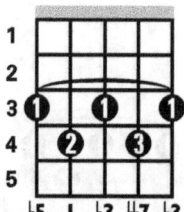	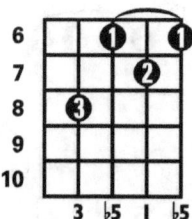	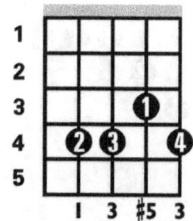

Bsus2	Bsus4	B7sus4	Bm7-5
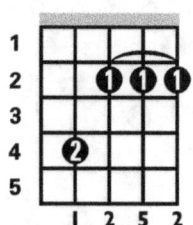	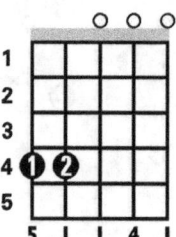	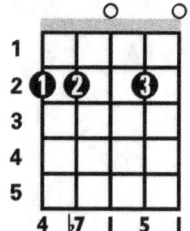	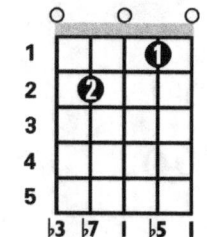
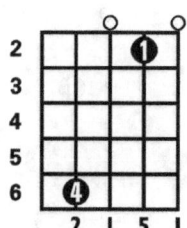	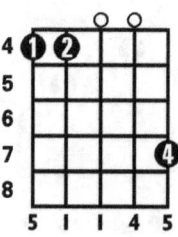	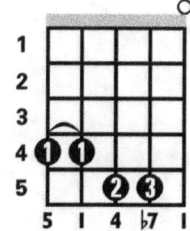	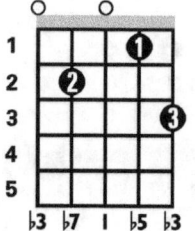
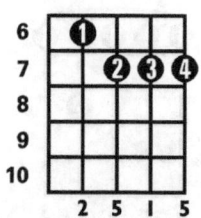	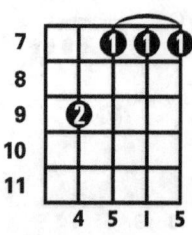	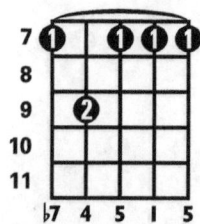	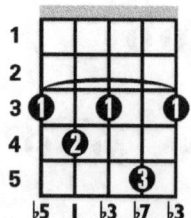

B Chords

Badd9
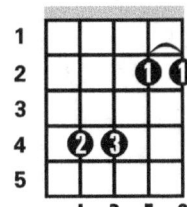
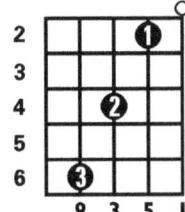
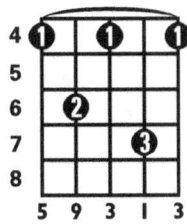

Bmadd9
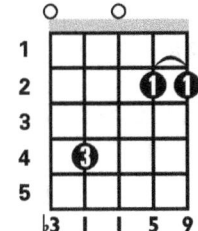
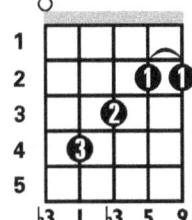
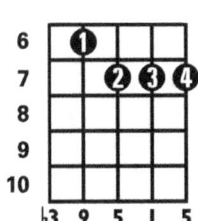

B6add9
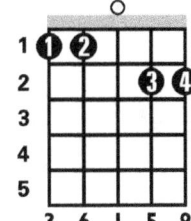
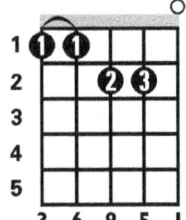
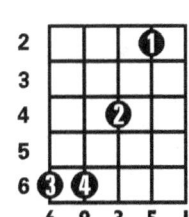

Bm6add9
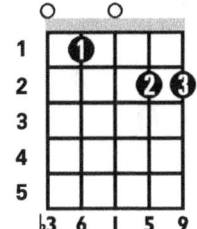
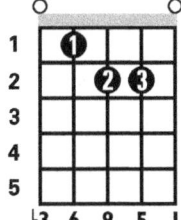
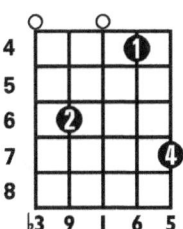

B7-5
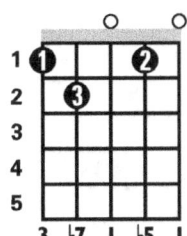
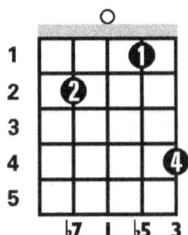
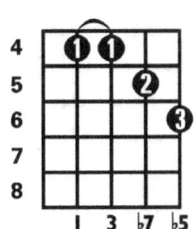

B7+5
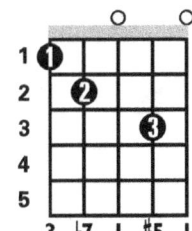
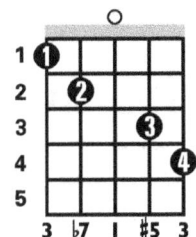
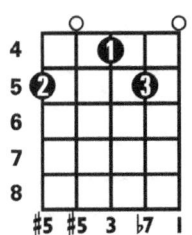

B7-9
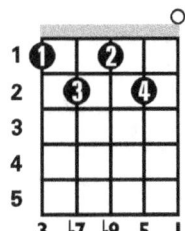
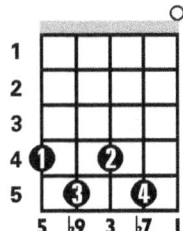
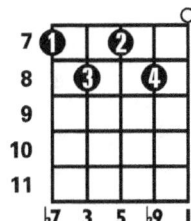

B7+9
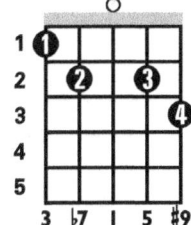
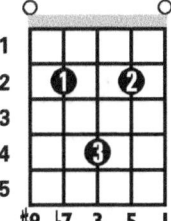
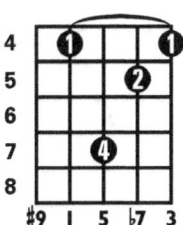

B Chords

Bm(maj7)	Bmaj7-5	Bmaj7+5	B9
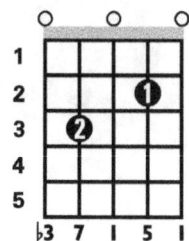	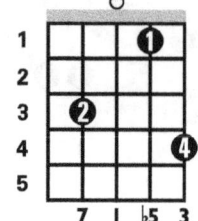	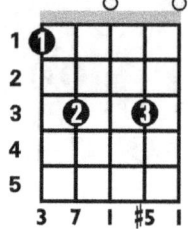	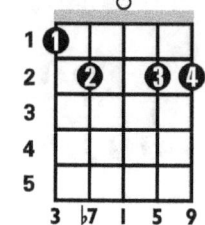
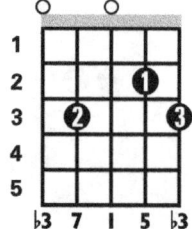	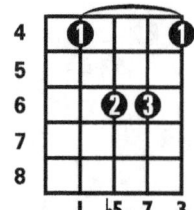	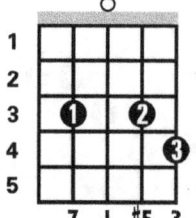	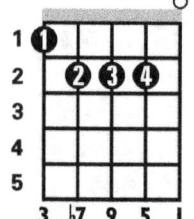
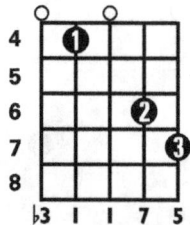	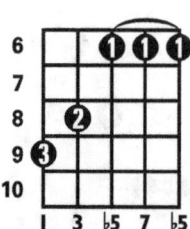	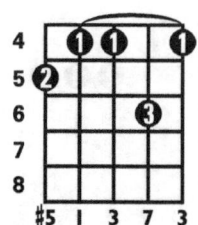	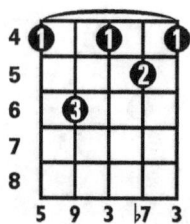

Bm9	Bmaj9	B11	B13
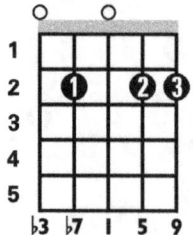	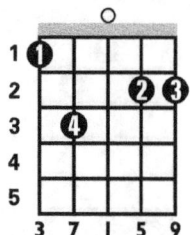	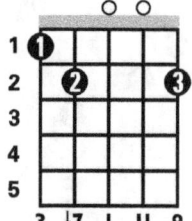	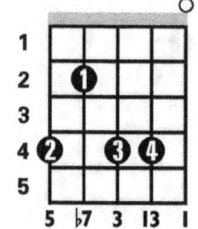
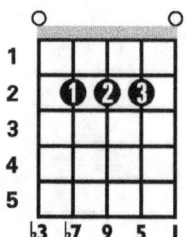	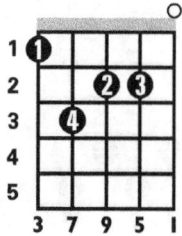	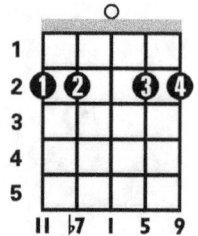	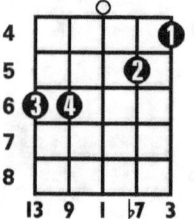
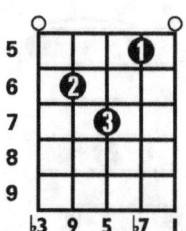	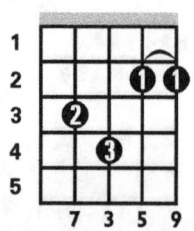	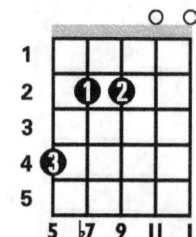	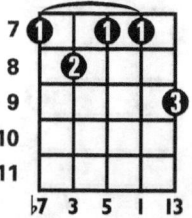

B Chords (Advanced)

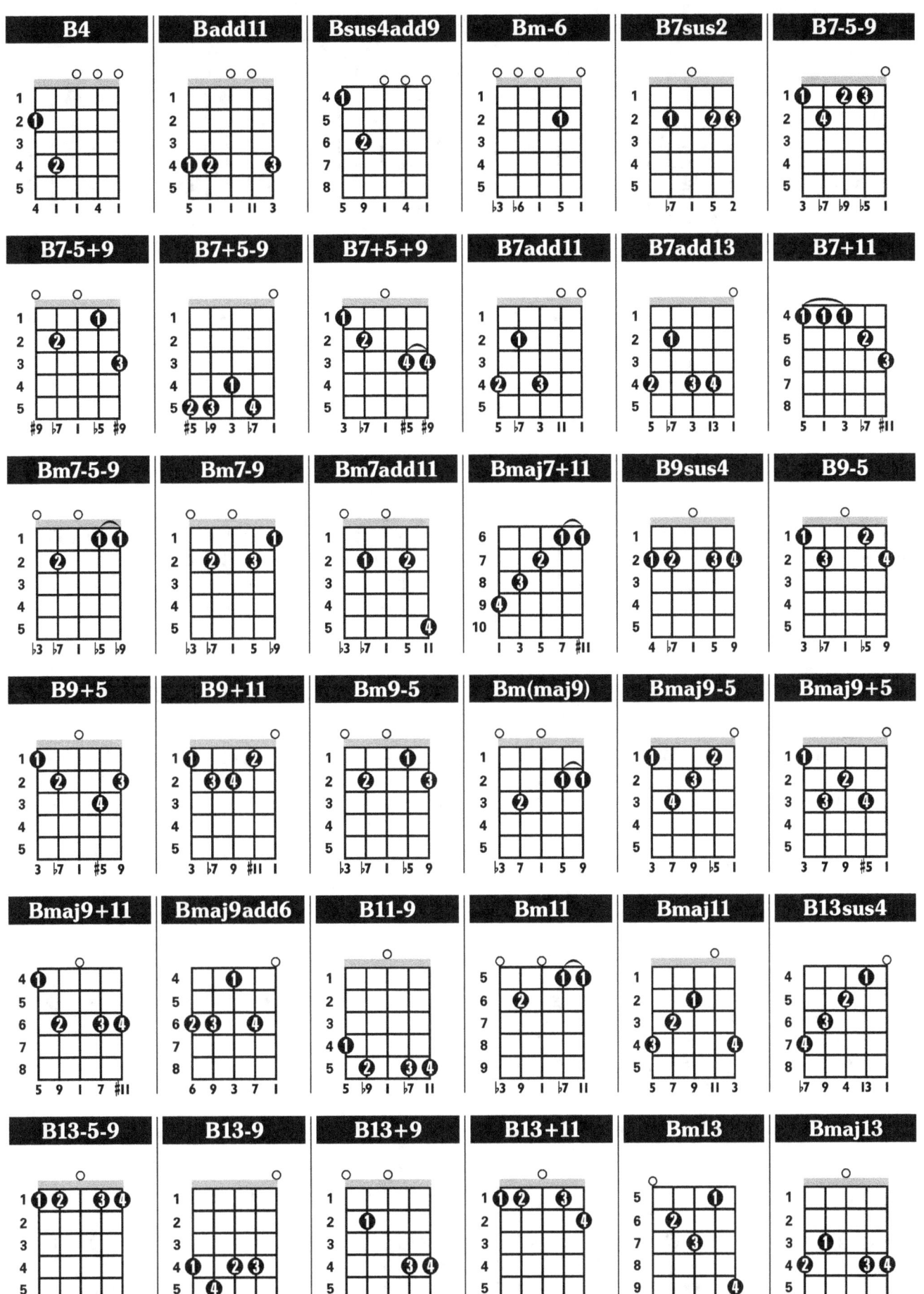

Major Slash Chords

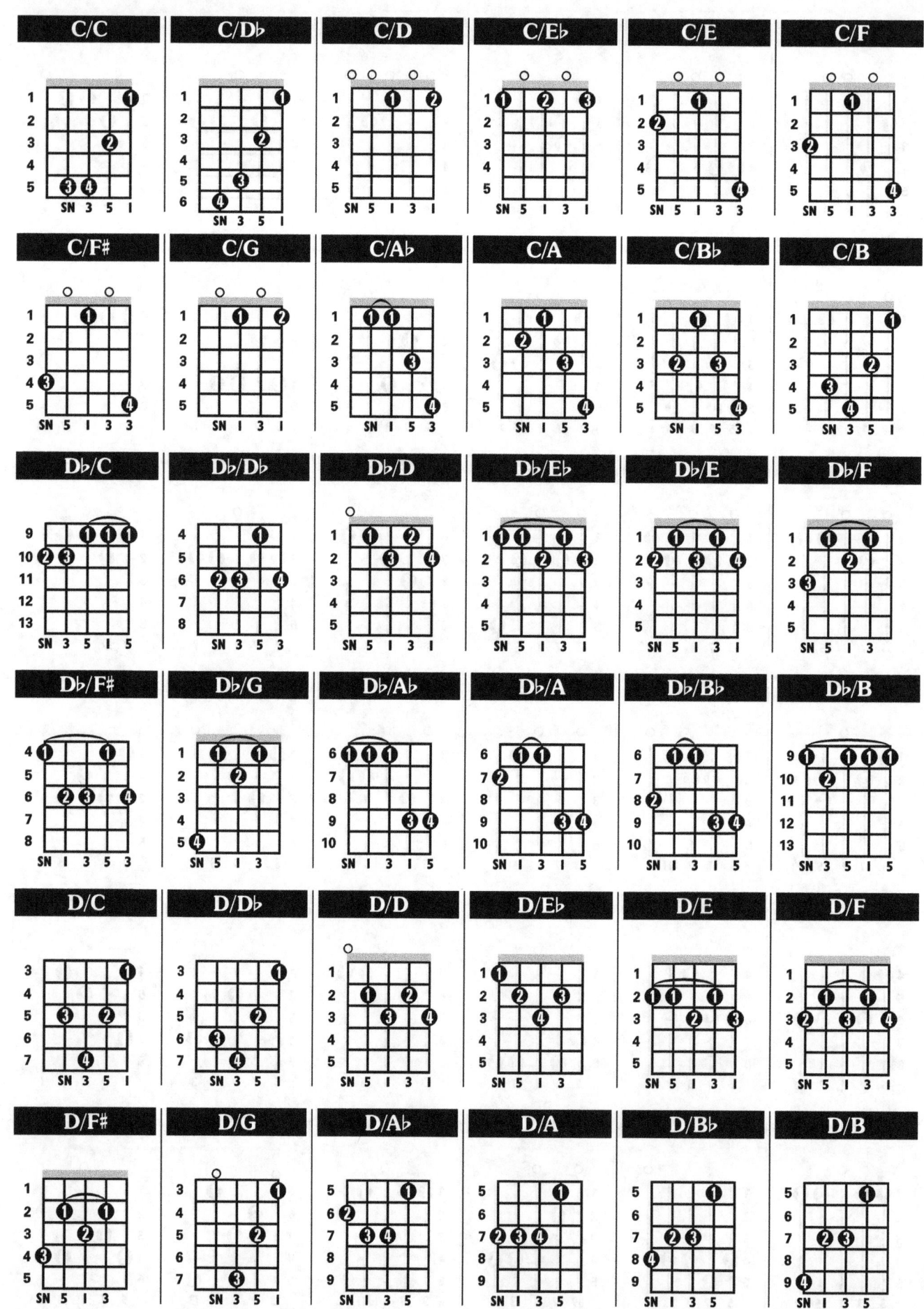

Major Slash Chords

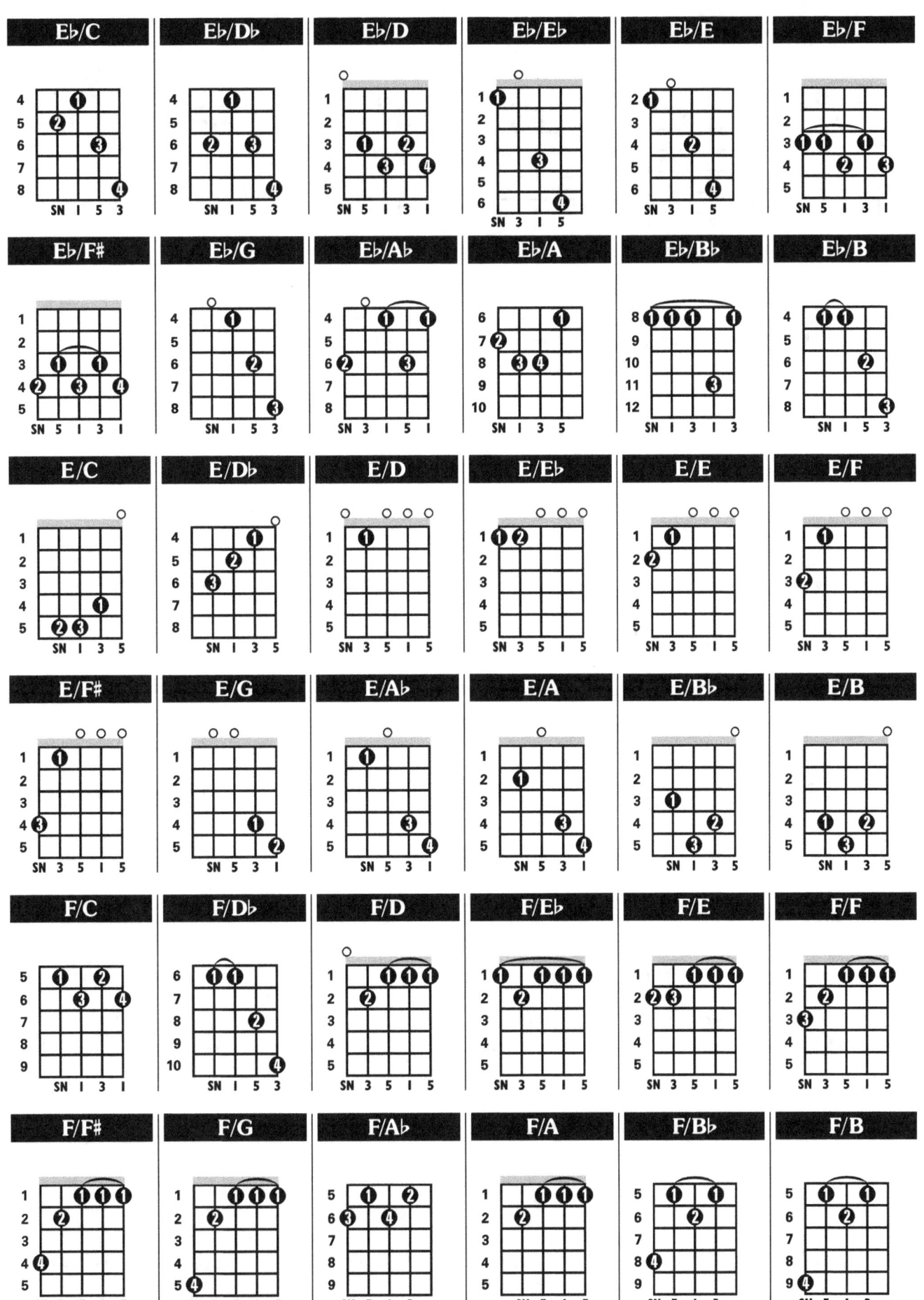

Major Slash Chords

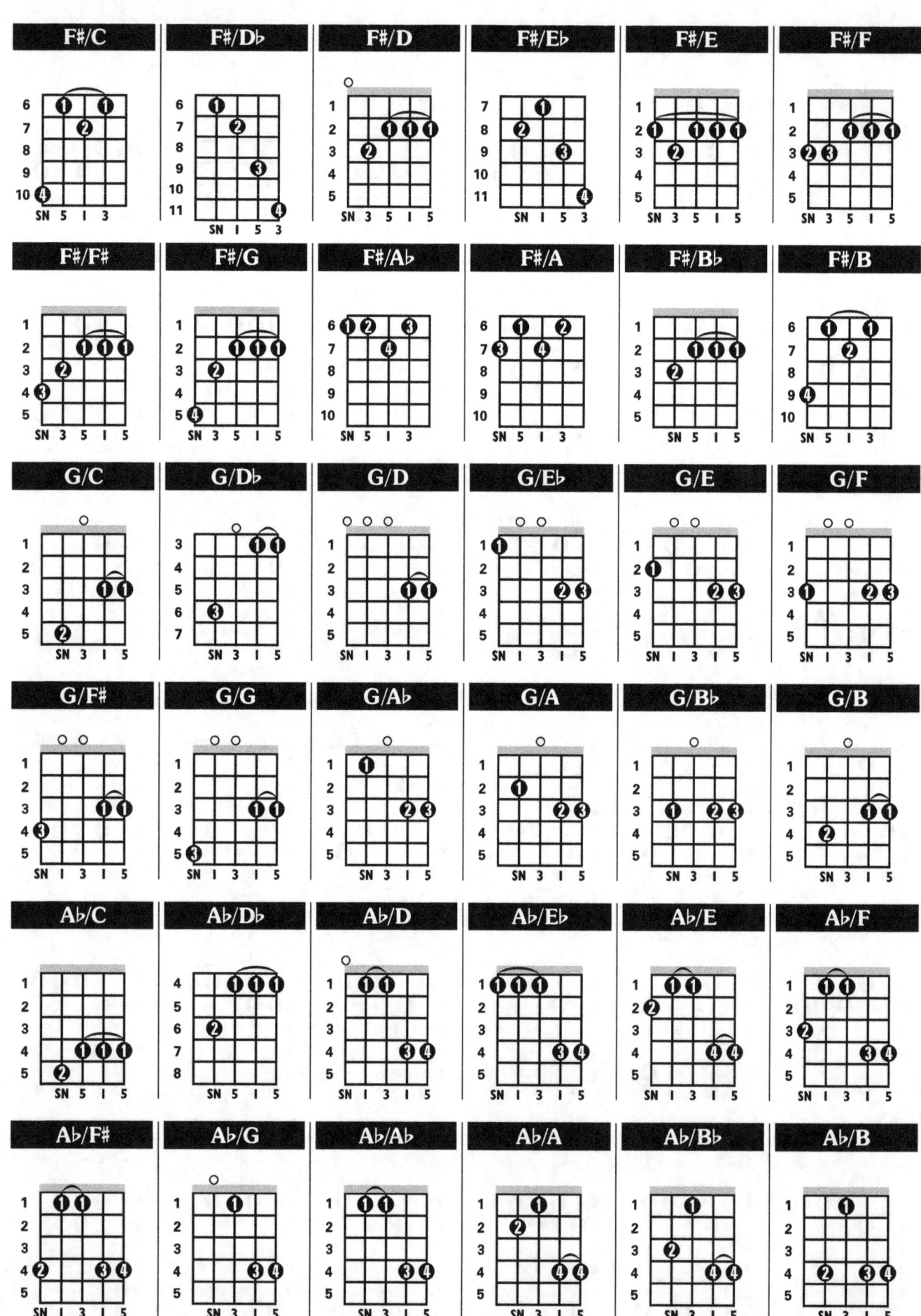

Major Slash Chords

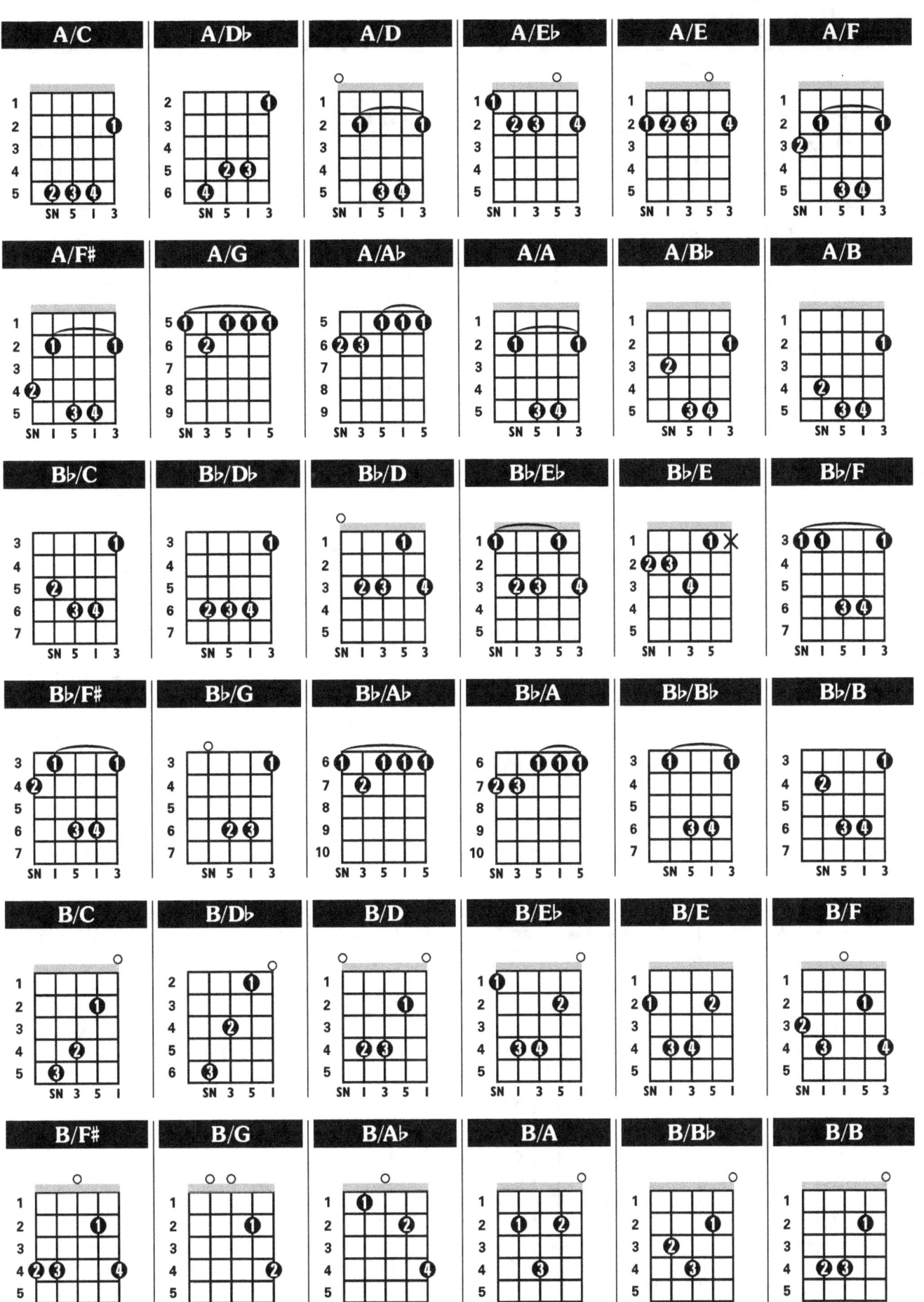

A Selection of Moveable Chord Shapes

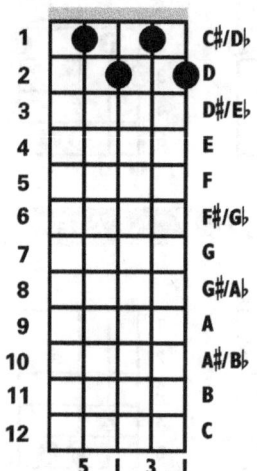
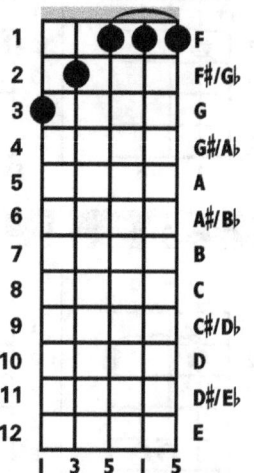
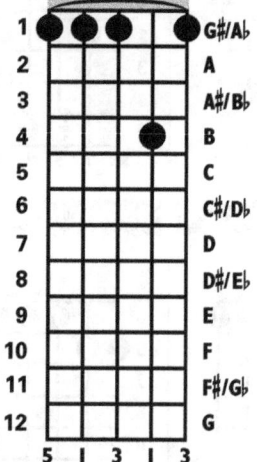
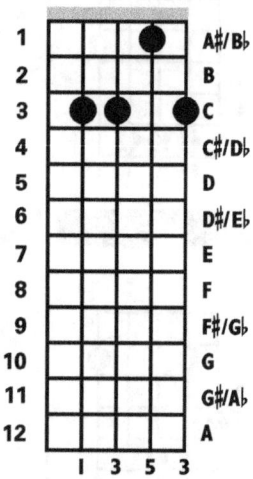

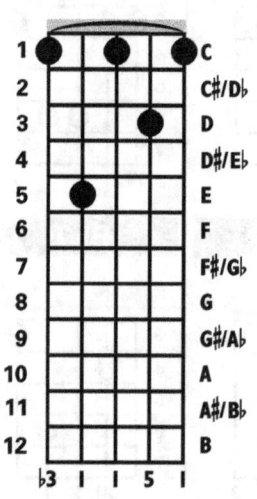
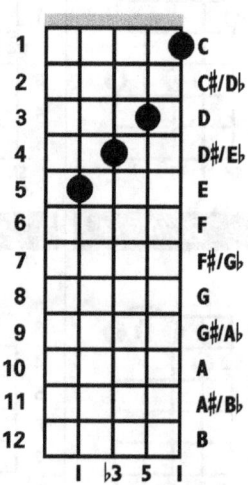
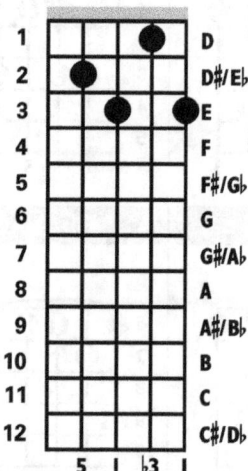
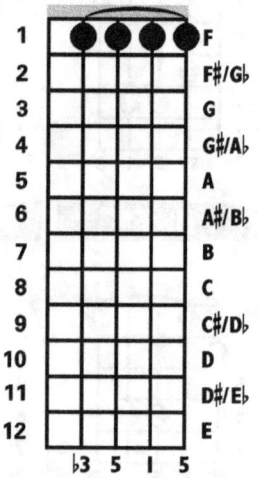

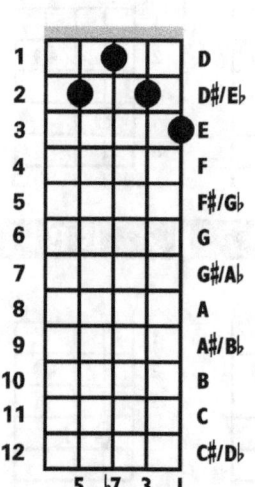
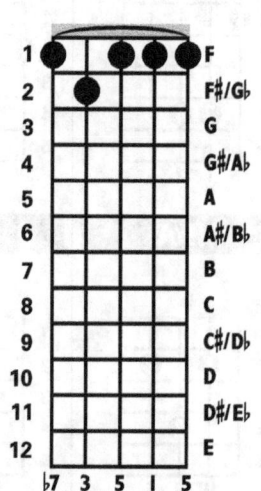
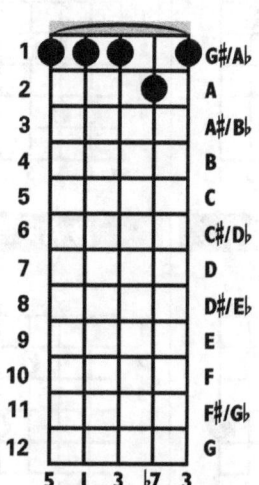
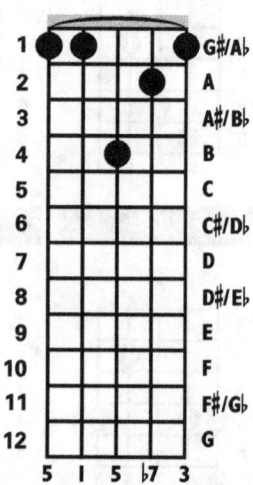

A Selection of Moveable Chord Shapes

Minor Seventh

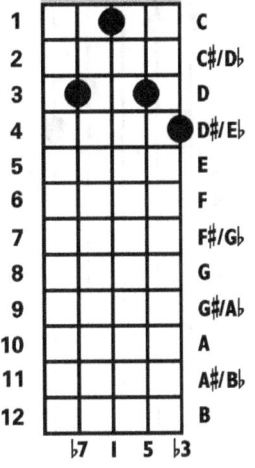
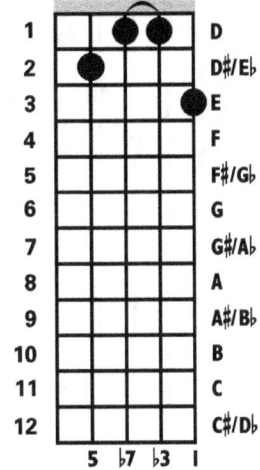
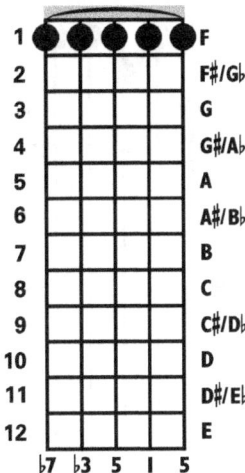

Sixth

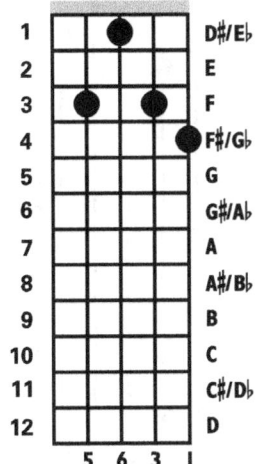
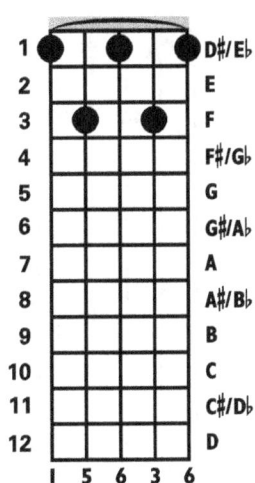
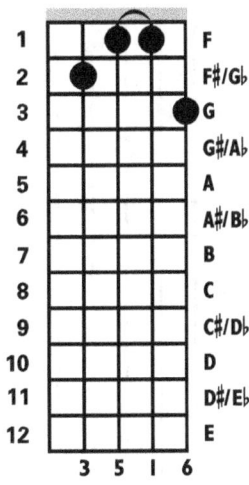
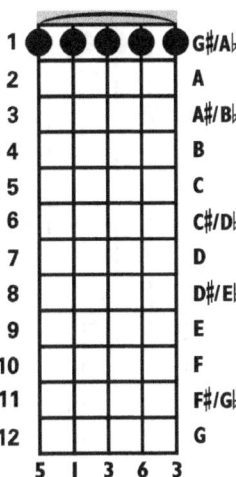

Minor Sixth

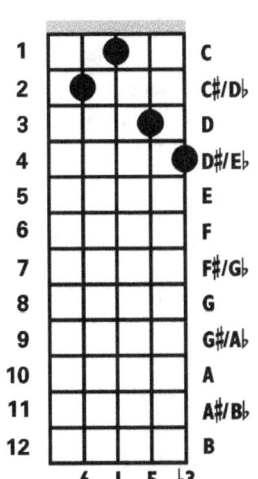
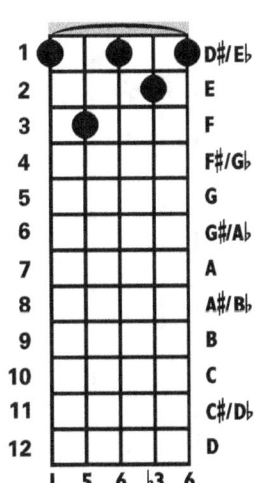
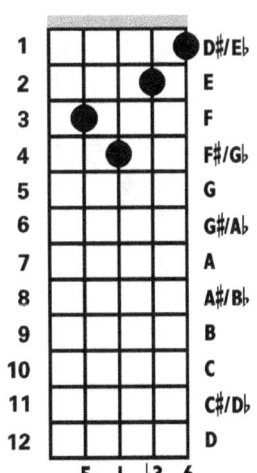
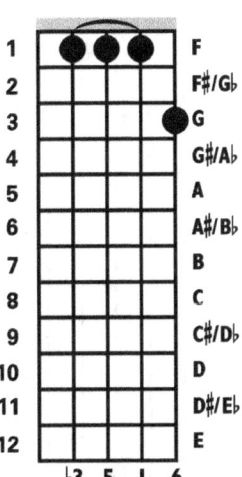

A Selection of Moveable Chord Shapes

Major Seventh
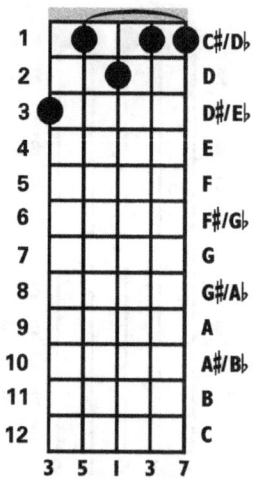

Major Seventh
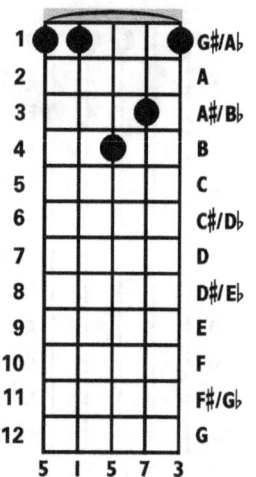

Major Seventh
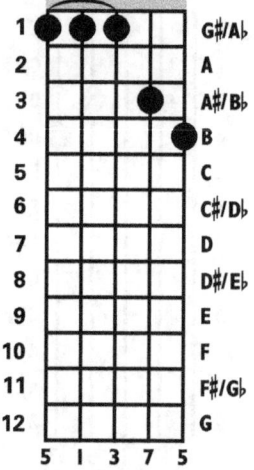

Suspended Fourth
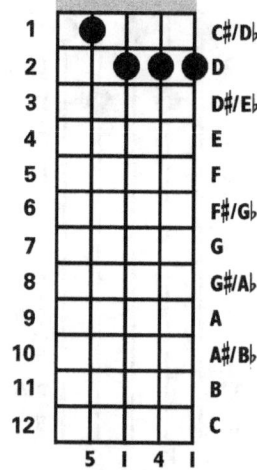

Suspended Fourth
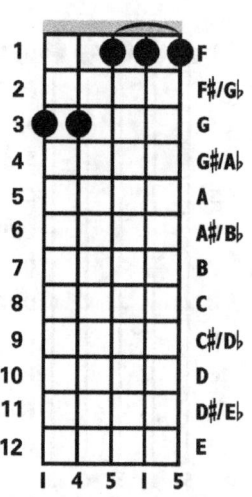

Suspended Fourth
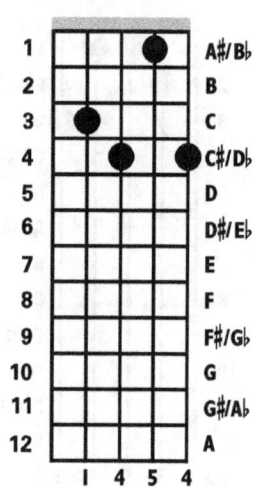

Diminished
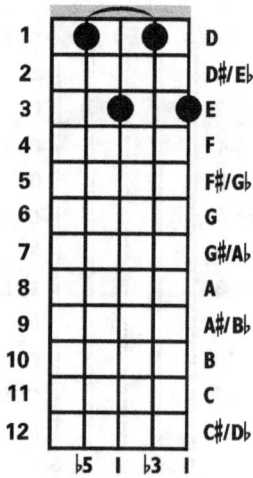

Diminished
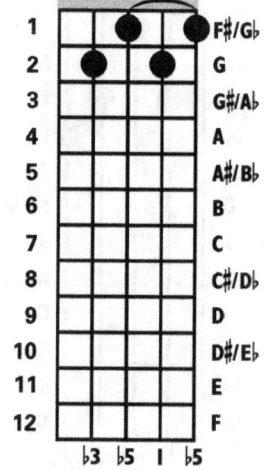

Diminished
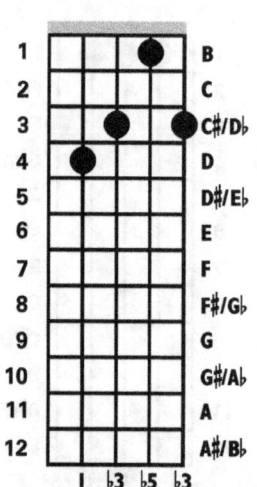

Augmented
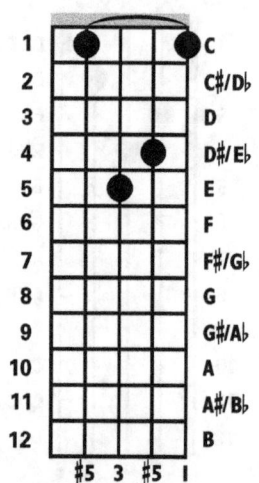

Augmented
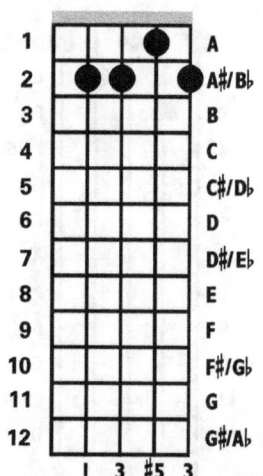

Augmented
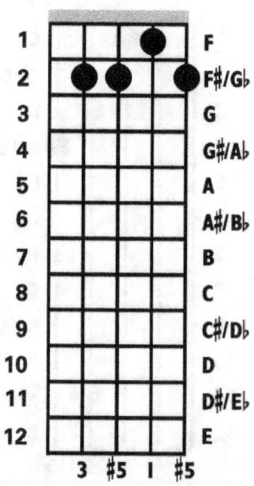

A Selection of Moveable Chord Shapes

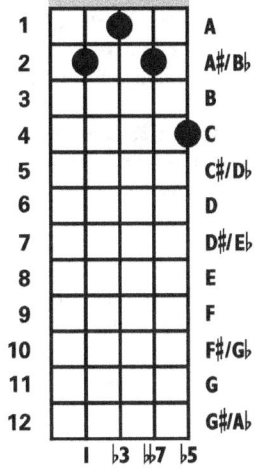
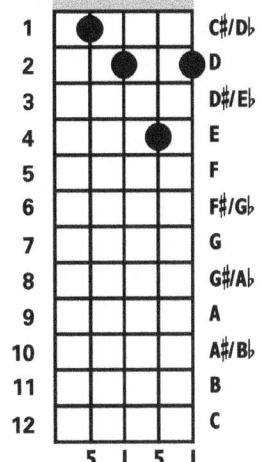
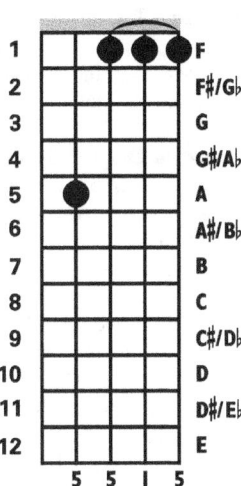
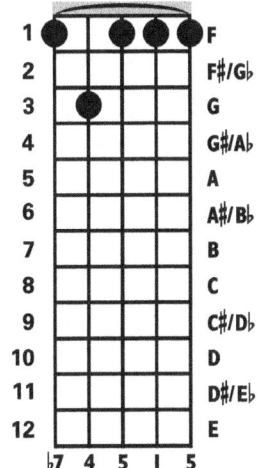
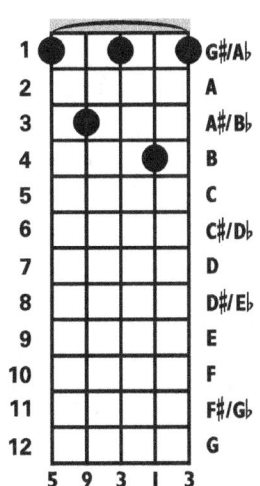
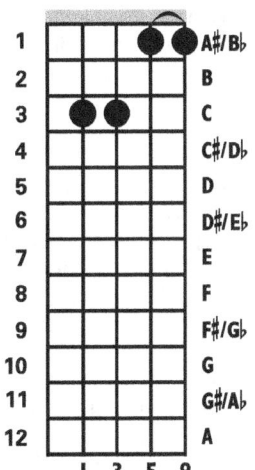
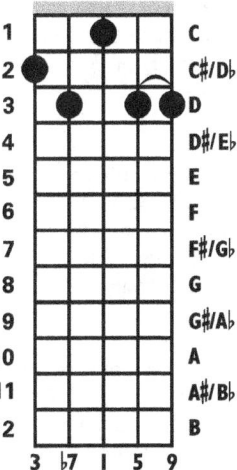
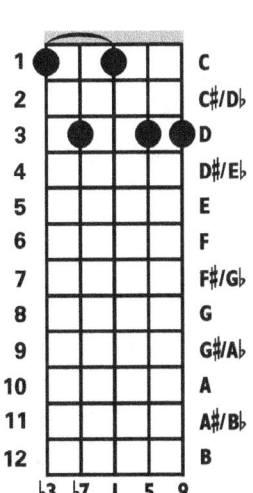
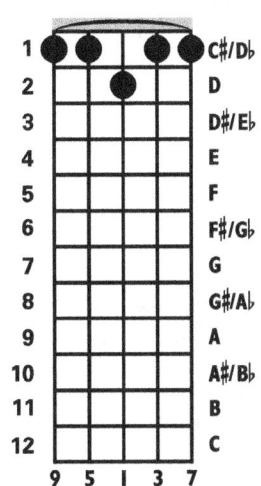
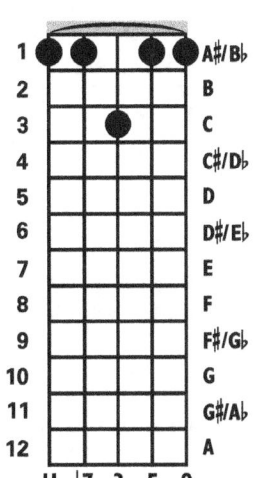
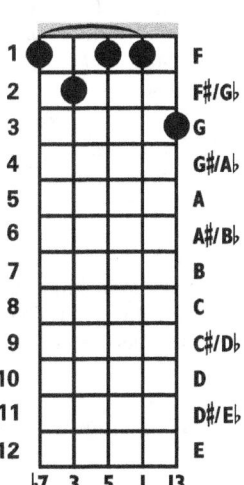

CHARANGO & UKULELE FAMILY FACTFILE

Braguinha
A Madeiran instrument said to have been the main ancestor of today's ukulele. The Braguinha features the same scale length as a standard soprano uke, but is tuned roughly a fourth lower to an open G major chord (D-G-B-D). The name of the instrument itself is taken from the Madeiran city of Braga.

Charango - Its Origins and Future
Although the charango is considered to be a cultural symbol of several South American countries encompassing the Andean region (Bolivia, Peru, Argentina, Chile and Ecuador), the original instrument took its musical inspiration from the *vihuela da mano*, an early relative of the guitar brought over by the Spanish conquistadors. Because the indigenous Inca peoples had very limited technological know-how and trees were in short supply, they had to use the materials at hand. Sadly for the little Andean armadillo (or *quirquincho*), their hardened shells became a ready source of pre-formed charango bodies. Today, quirquincho charangos are still available, but have been largely superceded by the much more ecologically sensitive solid wood designs based on the armadillo carapace. Arguably, these have much better acoustic qualities and tend to be the popular choice of most musicians.

In its traditional setting, the charango can be found entertaining at weddings and fiestas, as well as at funerals and other official occasions. With the growth of global internet commerce, the charango has become far more readily available, making the future popularity of this versatile little instrument virtually assured. For trivia lovers, it's even found its way into a Hollywood movie in the final wedding scene of the comedy, *Meet the Fockers*.

Charangon
Mainly tuned a fifth or a fourth down from the standard charango (CFADA or DGBEB) and virtually the same physical size as a ronroco. The body shape is more akin to the guitar-shaped charango and not the more angular rustic looking ronroco. It's sometimes referred to as the baritone charango.

Charanguero
A charango maker or luthier, with charanguera being the female equivalent. Well known makers include: Pablo Richter and Jorge Espinosa (Argentina), Rene Gamboa, El Chasqui, Juan Acha, Waldo Panoso, Jorge Martinez, Ruben Garcia, Clarken Orosco, Tylor Orosco, Inti Marka, Jesuz Aruquipa, Alberto Torrico, Cerudo Torrico/Maxima Colque, Roberto Licona and Mario Morales (Bolivia), Justo Baca (Peru), Yelkon Montero (Chile) and Paco Jimenez (Spain).

Charanguista
A charango player. Famous charanguistas include: Ernesto Cavour, Rolando Goldman, Mauro Nuñez, Jaime Guardia, Hector Soto, Jaime Torres, Eddy Navía, William Centallas, Celestino Campos, Alejandro Cámara, Klarken Orozco, Jorge Milchberg, Horacio Duran, Donato Espinoza, Gastón Ávila, Florencio Oros, Fernando Torrico, Alberto Arteaga and others. Western musicians and groups who've experimented with the charango include: Bob Brozman, Bruce Cockburn, Incantation and Mocheeba.

Charanguita
A hybrid design combining both charango and classical guitar into a double-necked instrument. The charango, being the smaller instrument is nearest to the player's chin.

Charanquena
Another hybrid instrument featuring a standard charango with a quena flute built into the headstock and neck.

Chillador
Constructed like a little guitar with a flat back and steel strings. The string layout can vary from 5 or 6, up to 10 or 12. Found in the Puno, Cuzco, Apurimac and Arequipa regions.

Construction & Design
Designs vary according to both region and luthier, but most instruments are constructed from one piece of timber which forms the body, neck and headstock, unlike the majority of fretted instruments where the neck and body are constructed separately. The choice of local woods for the one piece design include naranjillo, jarka, quina quina, tarco, sotomora, orange tree and nacna. The top or soundboard is generally built from one of the several varieties of pine, while the fingerboard is usually ebony or rosewood. The tuners, although not exclusively so, tend to be geared machines in the style of the classical guitar, apart from a few designs featuring traditional vertical pegs. Soundhole configurations vary quite a bit from luthier to luthier, but the majority favour a circle or oval. Butterfly designs are also popular. The body shape again is much like a little classical guitar, apart from the *Kjarkas* models with their angular, slightly rustic looking appearance. Electric or electro-acoustic charangos have also made an appearance in the last few years, making them ideal for recording and live performance. The scale length of an average charango is around 370mm or 14½ inches.

Guitarlele
Arguably, the guitarlele can be viewed as a scaled down guitar, rather than a true member of the ukulele family. The physical size is around that of the baritone uke, but with a wider fretboard to accommodate the two additional lower strings. The tuning is identical to a regular guitar (E-A-D-G-B-E).

Maulincho
An alternative name for the walaycho.

Music
Mainstream popular music has yet to fully exploit the unique qualities of the charango, but it has made notable appearances on the combined and solo recordings of Simon & Garfunkel. Firstly, in *El Condor Pasa*, a traditional tune with lyrics adapted by Simon, featuring the Andean group, Los Incas. Then again on two of the duo's solo albums, notably on the tracks *Duncan* (Simon) and *Woyaya* (Garfunkel) - the latter featuring Jorge Milchberg of Los Incas. In the UK, the charango made its chart debut on the Andean tune, *Cachapaya* by the British group Incantation, reaching number twelve in late 1982.

Quirquincho
A charango made from the shell of an armadillo. The origin of the word comes from the Quechua name of the animal itself.

Rajão
The 5-string rajão, like it's sister instrument, the braguinha, originates in the Portuguese island of Madeira where it's used mainly for rhythm accompaniment. The D-G-C-E-A tuning is re-entrant like the soprano ukulele, except it employs this configuration on both the 4th and 5th strings.

Ronroco (*or* Ronrroco)
The big brother of the charango, generally tuned an octave lower than its little sibling (GCEAE). The Argentine version is tuned down a fourth. The length of the instrument is around 750mm, with a scale length of approximately 450mm.

Strings
Traditionally early charangos were strung with gut or animal tendons, but today the majority use nylon or other synthetic materials. The use of steel strings is also popular with instruments like the flat backed chillador and some types of walaycho. Popular string manufacturers include: *Medina Artigas*, *Hispana* and *Gauchita* (Argentina), *Aquilacorde* (Italy), *La Bella* and *Daniel Mari* (USA) and *Pyramid* (Germany).

Timple
A close relative of the ukulele originating in the Canary Islands and Murcia, the timple (pronounced *teem-play*) has an additional fifth string and a distinctive rounded back. The tuning is generally A-D-F#-B-E (from low to high). Basically, a traditional ukulele D6 tuning with an additional high E string. 4-string versions also exist. The timple is thought to have Berber origins.

Tiple
Unlike its Hawaiian relative, the tiple in its many incarnations, is generally strung with steel strings which are arranged in triple and double courses. The version familiar to American and Western musicians was designed by *C.F. Martin & Company*, better known for their prowess in acoustic guitar design. The *Martin* tiple is usually tuned A-D-F#-B with the middle two courses tripled and the two outer courses doubled.

Other types of tiple include:
Banjo Tiple (Peru): *A little banjo with 4 double courses of strings.*
Colombian Tiple: *12-string guitar-like instrument divided up into 4 triple stringed courses*
Marxochime Hawaiian Tiple: *A zither-lap steel guitar hybrid tiple.*
Spanish Tiple (Spain): *A little guitar style tiple from Menorca.*
Tiple Argentino (Argentina): *Little guitar-style instrument with 6 strings.*
Tiple Cubano (Cuba): *Cuban instrument with either 5 single string or 5 double courses (like the taropatch or charango).*
Tiple Doliente (Puerto Rico): *A popular five stringed instrument.*
Tiple Dominicano (Dominican Republic): *5 double coursed bandurria-like instrument*
Tiple Grande de Ponce (Puerto Rico): *A narrow waisted, larger member of the tiple group.*
Tiple Peruano (Peru): *Peruvian tiple with 4 single or double strings.*
Tiple Requinto Costanero (Puerto Rico): *Small version of the tiplón.*
Tiple Requinto de la Montaña (Puerto Rico): *Small 3-stringed version of the doliente.*
Tiple Uruguayo (Uruguay): *A little guitar-style of tiple with 6 strings.*
Tiple Venezolano (Venezuela): *Smaller version of the Colombian tiple, featuring 4 triple string courses.*
Tiplón or Tiple con Macho (Puerto Rico): *The largest family member with a 5th tuning peg much like the 5-string banjo.*

Tuning and Octave Designation Systems
From the 10th to the 1st string. *Acoustical Society of America* system: G4 pair, C5 pair, E5 & E4 octave pair, A4 pair and E5 pair. *Heimholtz* system: g1 pair, c2 pair, e2 and e1 octave pair, a1 pair and e2 pair. *Alternative Heimholtz* system: g' pair, c'' pair, e'' and e' octave pair, a' pair and e'' pair. These systems provide an alternative way of describing the tuning of an instrument without using standard notation. The charango employs re-entrant tuning much like the ukulele, meaning that the strings don't follow a normal high to low progression like the guitar or mandolin.

Ukulele
Musically, the charango shares many of the attributes of the ukulele including the size, the use of nylon strings and a very similar tuning configuration. The main difference being the addition of an extra course of strings at the high end. A standard uke is tuned GCEA.

Venezuelan Cuatro
The South American cuatro's history can be traced back to its long defunct ancestor, the 4-string Spanish guitar. Again, like several of the instruments in this family group, the cuatro is tuned to the same fundamental intervals as the first four strings of a classical guitar - in this case A-D-F#-B, like the soprano uke's D6 tuning. Where it differs is in the positioning of the re-entrant strings. With the ukulele and rajão, the higher strings can be found on the 4th and 5th strings. With the cuatro, the 2nd and 3rd strings are re-entrant (namely the D and F#). Although most musicians use this tuning, an alternative was created by reknowned cuatro player, Fredy Reyna in 1948. Rebelling against the re-entrant standard, Reyna re-strung the cuatro to a more recognizable low to high tuning (E-A-C#-F#), but still retained the relationship, based on guitar tuning (transposed into the key of A6).

Very much akin to the English language aide-mémoire "*my dog has fleas*", the cuatro's tuning can be remembered by singing the following two words, "*Cam-bur pin-tón*", or ripe banana!

The 4-string or Venezuelan cuatro is not to be confused with the Puerto Rican cuatro which illogically has 10 steel strings in 5 double courses. The design bares little or no resemblance to the more guitar-like mainland instrument (the tuning is B-E-A-D-G). The shape is very reminiscent of a member of the violin family with it's instantly recognizable sculpted waist and upper/lower bouts.

Walaycho (*Hualaycho or Waylacho*)
Smallest member of the charango family and tuned a fourth or a fifth higher (CFADA or DGBEB). According to region and tradition, it can be strung with either nylon or steel strings.

Ukulele Family Instrument Tunings

Baritone Ukulele Standard Tuning	DGBE (G6)
Braguinha Standard Tuning	DGBD (G Major)
Cavaquinho Standard Tuning	DGBD (G Major)
Cavaquinho Alternative tuning	GGBD (G Major)
Cavaquinho Alternative Tuning	AAC#E (A Major)
Cavaquinho Guitar Tuning	DGBE (G6)
Charango Standard Tuning	GCEAE (C6)
Charangon Standard Tuning 1	CFADA (F6)
Charangon Standard Tuning 2	DGBEB (G6)
Concert Ukulele Standard Tuning	GCEA (C6)
Concert Ukulele Alternative Tuning	ADF#B (D6)
Guitarlele Standard Tuning	EADGBE (G6/9)
Martin Tiple Standard Tuning	ADF#B (D6)
Rajão Standard Tuning	DGCEA (C6/9)
Ronroco Standard Tuning	GCEAE (G6)
Soprano Akulele Standard Tuning	GCEA (C6)
Soprano Ukulele Standard Tuning	GCEA (C6)
Soprano Ukulele Alternative Tuning	ADF#B (D6)
Sopranino Akulele Standard Tuning	DGBE (G6)
Taropatch Standard Tuning	GCEA (C6)
Tenor Ukulele Standard Tuning	GCEA (C6)
Tenor Ukulele Alternative Tuning	DGBE (G6)
Timple Canario Standard Tuning	ADF#BE (D6/9)
Ukulele-Banjo Standard Tuning	GCEA (C6)
Ukulele-Banjo Alternative Tuning	ADF#B (D6)
Venezuelan Cuatro Standard Tuning	ADF#B (D6)
Venezuelan Cuatro F. Reyna Tuning	EAC#F# (A6)
Walaycho Standard Tuning 1	CFADA (F6)
Walaycho Standard Tuning 2	DGBEB (G6)

ALTERNATIVE CHORD NAMES

C	CM or Cmaj
Cm	Cmin or C-
C-5	C-5 or C(♭5)
C°	Cdim
C4	Csus4(no 5th) or Csus(no 5th)
C5	C Power Chord or C(no 3rd)
Csus2	C(sus2) or C2
Csus4	Csus or C(sus4)
Csus4add9	Csus(add9)
C+	Caug, C+5 or C(♯5)
C6	CM6 or CMaj6
Cadd9	Cadd2
Cm6	C-6 or Cmin6
Cmadd9	Cmadd2 or C-(add9)
C6add9	C6/9, C$^6_9$ or CMaj6(add9)
Cm6add9	Cm6/9 or Cm$^6_9$
C°7	Cdim7
C7	Cdom
C7sus2	C7(sus2)
C7sus4	C7sus, C7(sus4) or Csus11
C7-5	C7♭5
C7+5	C7+ or C7♯5
C7-9	C7♭9 or C7(add♭9)
C7+9	C7♯9 or C7(add♯9)
C7-5-9	C7♭5♭9
C7+5-9	C7♯5♭9
C7+5+9	C7♯5♯9
C7add11	C7/11 or C$^7_{11}$
C7+11	C7♯11
Cm7	C-7, Cmi7 or Cmin7
Cm7-5	Cm7♭5, C-7-5 or C^ø
Cm7-5-9	Cm7♭5♭9
Cm7-9	Cm7♭9
Cm7add11	Cm
Cm(maj7)	Cm♯7, CM7-5, CmM7 or C-△
Cmaj7	CM7 or C△(Delta)
Cmaj7-5	CM7-5, C△♭5 or Cmaj7♭5
Cmaj7+5	CM7+5, C△5+ or Cmaj7♯11
Cmaj7+11	CM7+11, C△+♯11 or Cmaj7♯11
C9	C7(add9)
C9sus4	C9sus or C9(sus4)
C9-5	C9♭5
C9+5	C9♯5
C9+11	C9♯11
Cm9	C-9 or Cmin9
Cm9-5	Cm9♭5
Cm(maj9)	Cm9(maj7), CmM9 or Cm(addM9)
Cmaj9	CM9, Cmaj7(add9), C△9 or CM7(add9)
Cmaj9-5	CM9-5, Cmaj9♭5, C△9♭5 or CM9♭5
Cmaj9+5	CM9+5, Cmaj9♯5, C△9♯5
Cmaj9add6	CM9add6 or C△9add6
Cmaj9+11	CM9+11, Cmaj9♯11, C△9♯11 or CM9♯11
C11	C7(add11)
C11-9	C11♭9
Cm11	C-11 or Cmin11
Cmaj11	CM11, Cmaj7(add11), C△11, CM7(add11)
C13	C7/6(no 9th) or C7(add13)
C13sus4	C13sus or C13(sus4)
C13-5-9	C13♭5♭9
C13-9	C13♭9
C13+9	C13♯9
C13+11	C13♯11 or C13aug11
Cm13	C-13 or Cmin13
Cmaj13	CM13, Cmaj7(add13), C△13 or CM7(add13)

M	major
m	minor
-	minor
dim	diminished
°	diminished
ø	half diminished
sus	suspended
aug	augmented
+	augmented
add	added
dom	dominant
△	delta /major seventh
Q(3)	quartal / double fourth
♯	sharp
×	double sharp
♭	flat
♭♭	double flat

Do	Spanish for C
Dó	Portuguese for C
Re	Spanish for D
Ré	Portuguese for D
Mi	Spanish & Portuguese for E
Fa	Spanish & Portuguese for F
So	Spanish for G
Sol	Portuguese for G
La	Spanish for A
Lá	Portuguese for A
Si	Spanish & Portuguese for B
H	German for B

English Tonic Sol-fa

Do	**C**
Re	**D**
Me	**E**
Fa	**F**
Sol	**G**
La	**A**
Ti	**B**

The majority of music books will use the chords featured in the first column (on the far left and top right), but should you come across alternatives, consult this guide for other naming conventions.

The list above includes most of the symbols and abbreviations that you're likely to encounter in the majority of music books.

NOTES

NOTES

NOTES

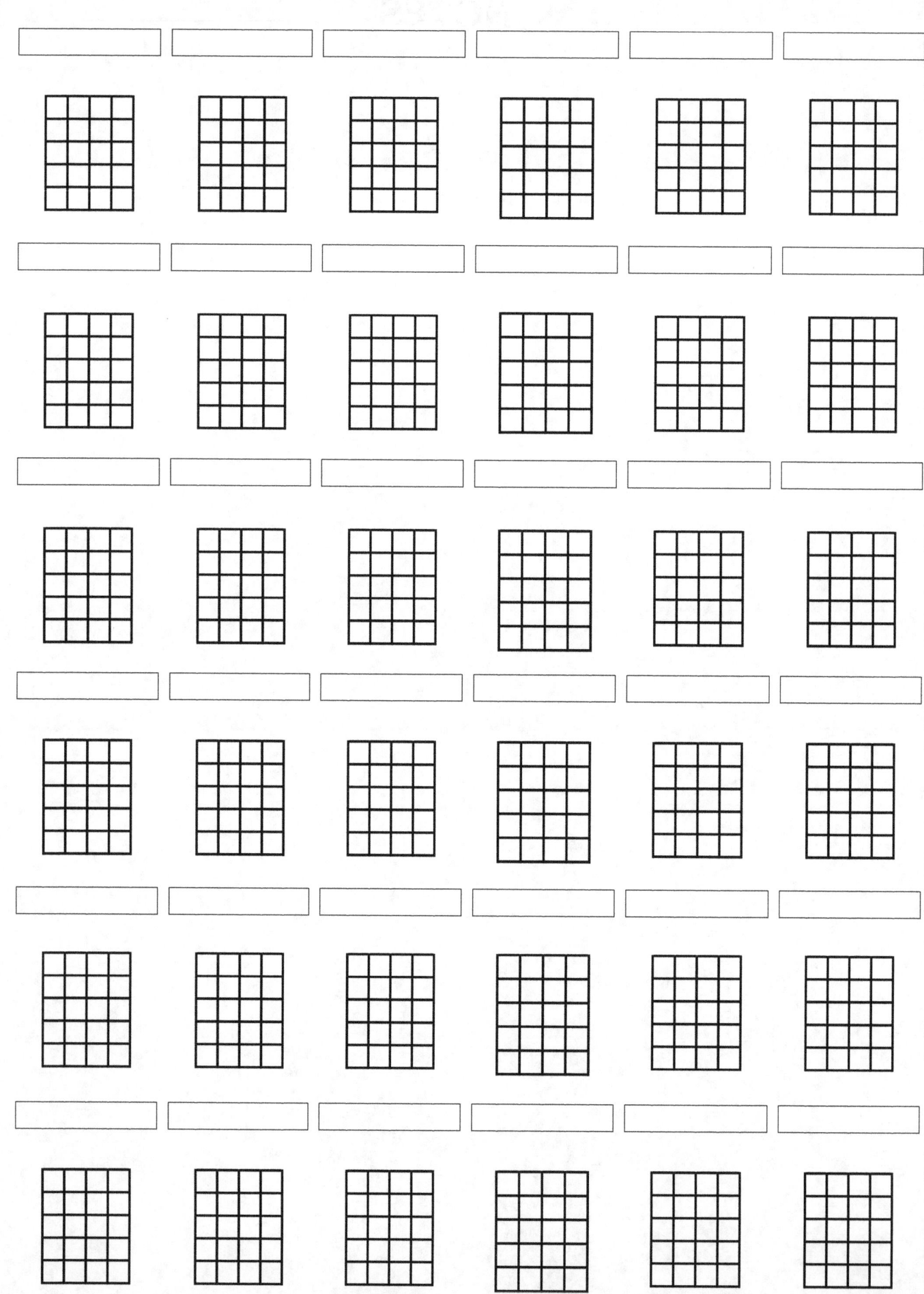

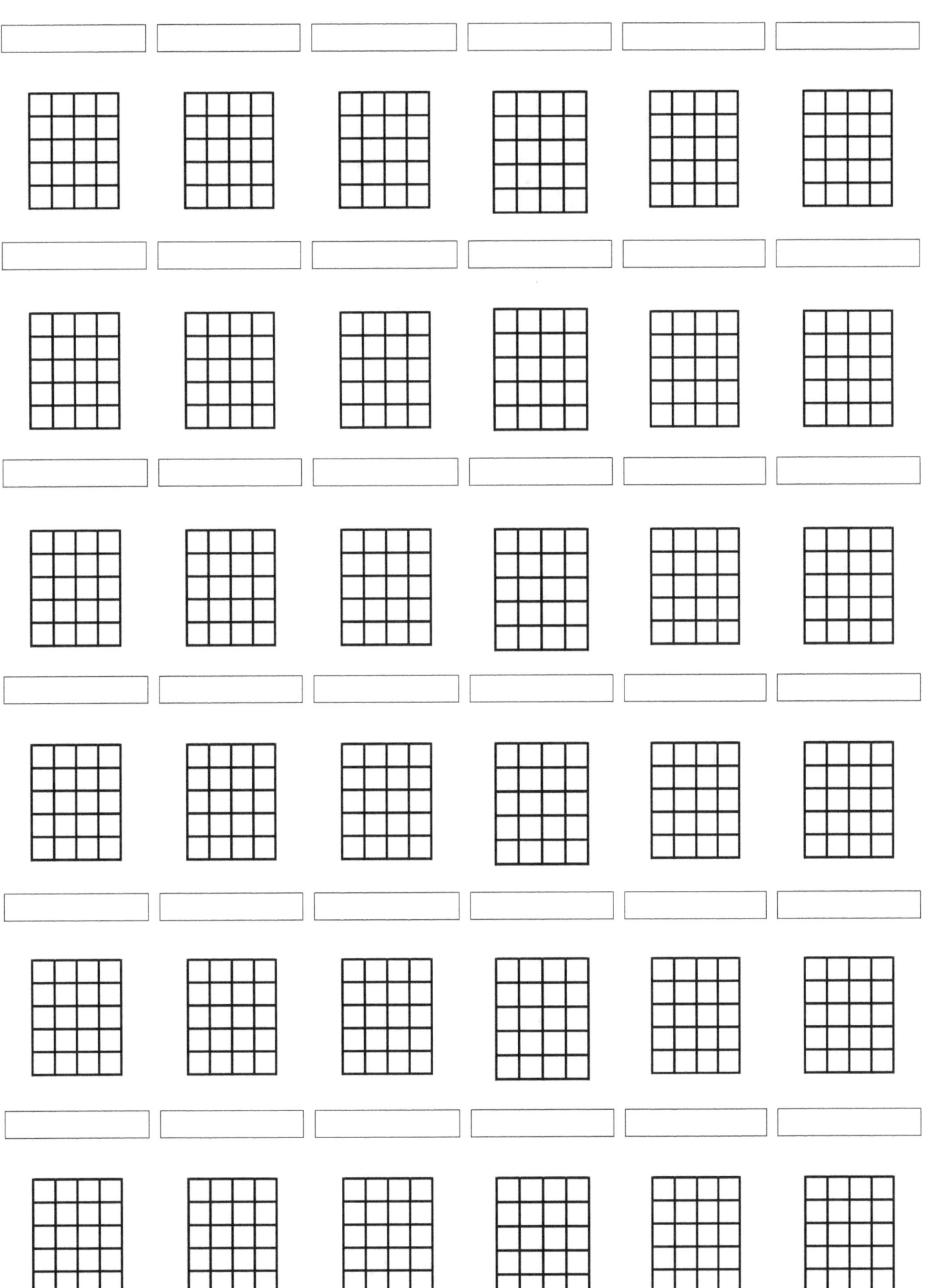

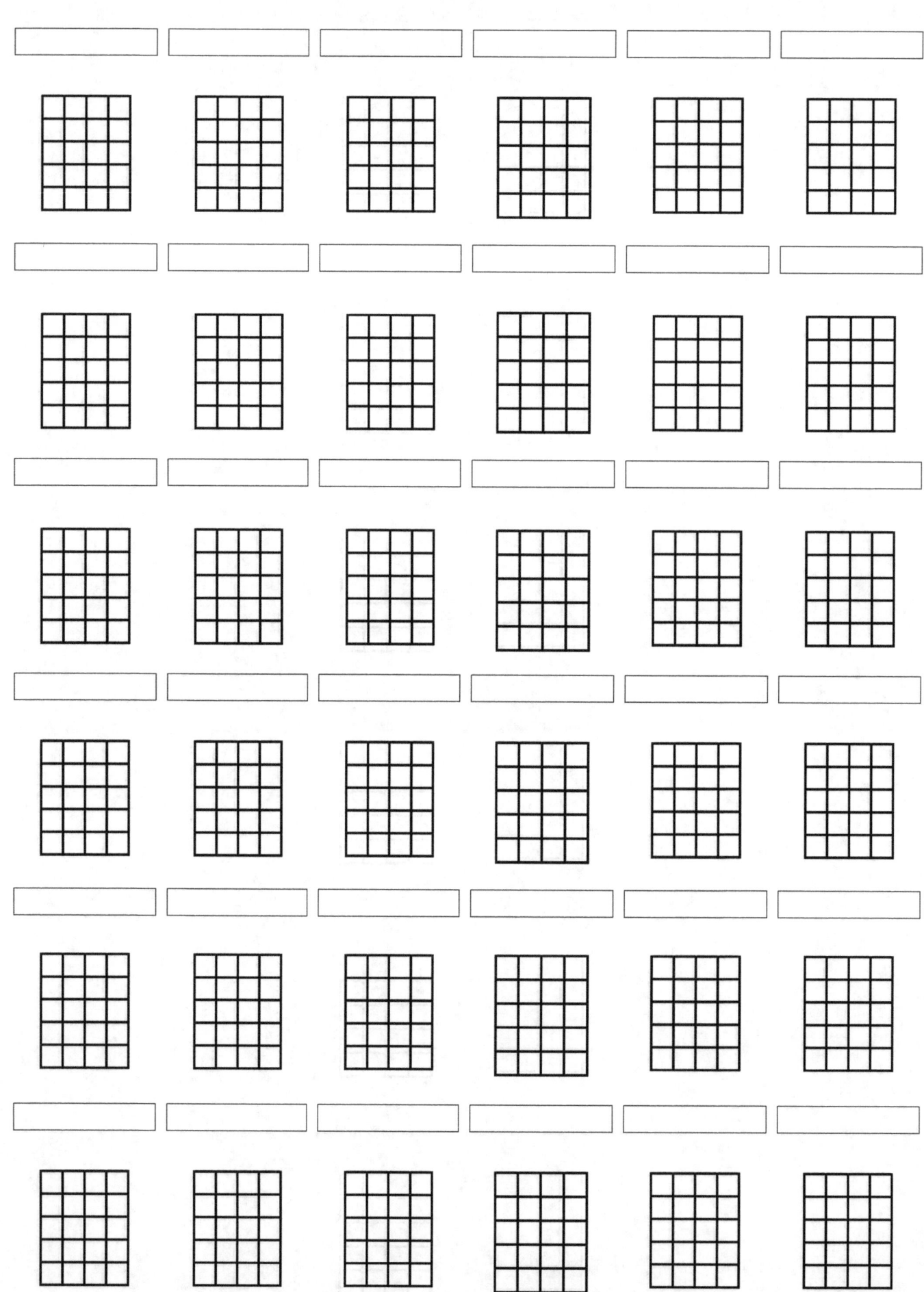

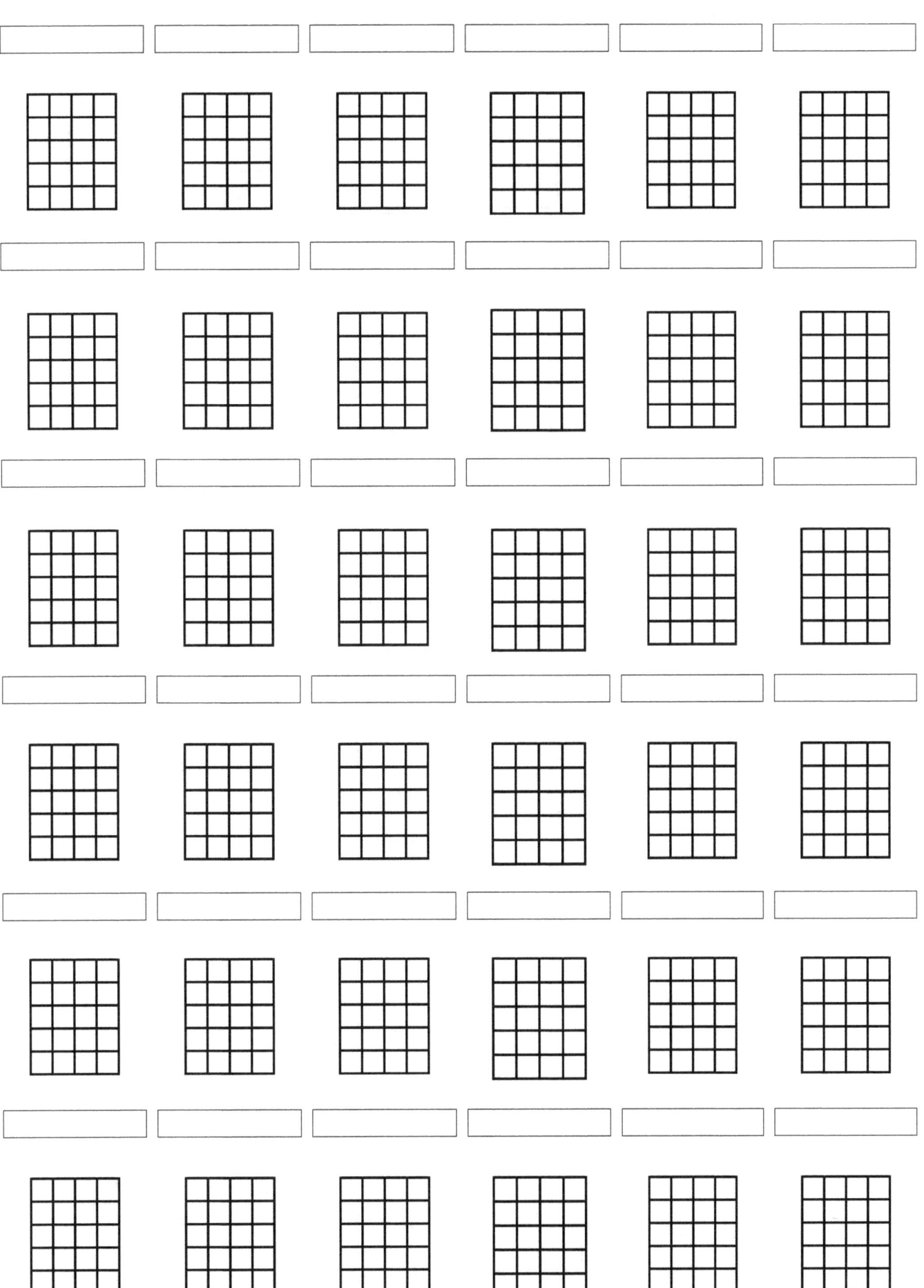

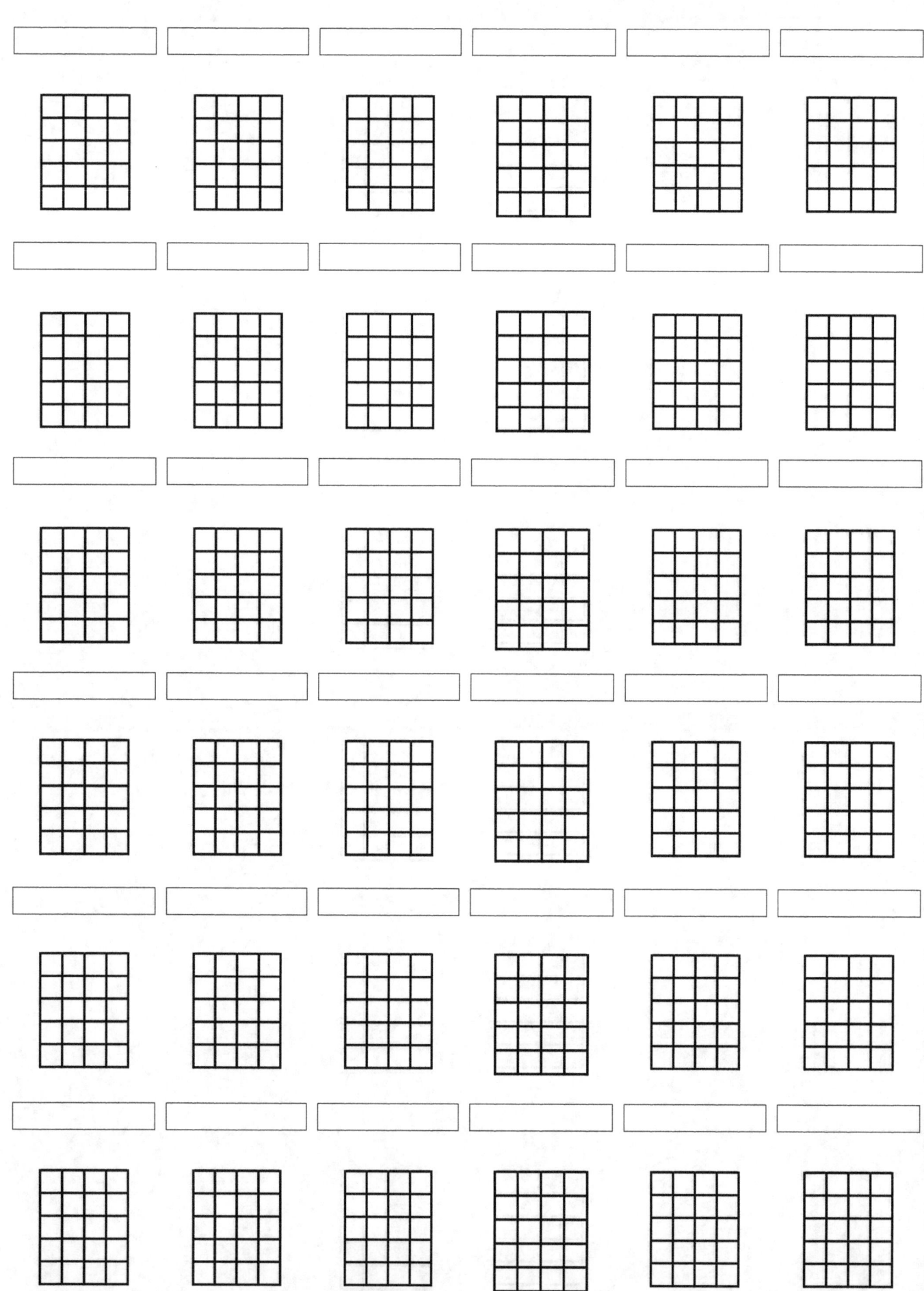

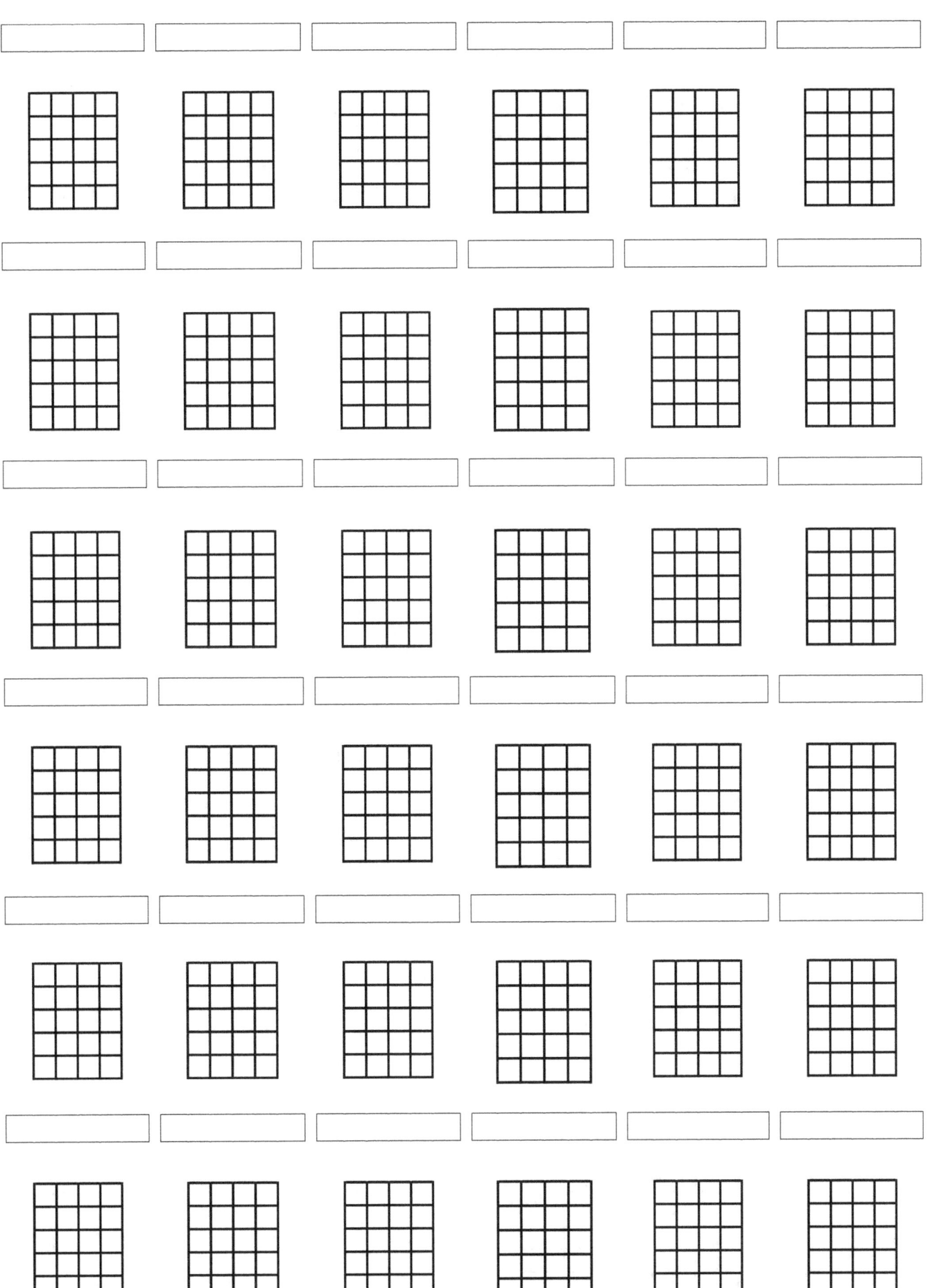

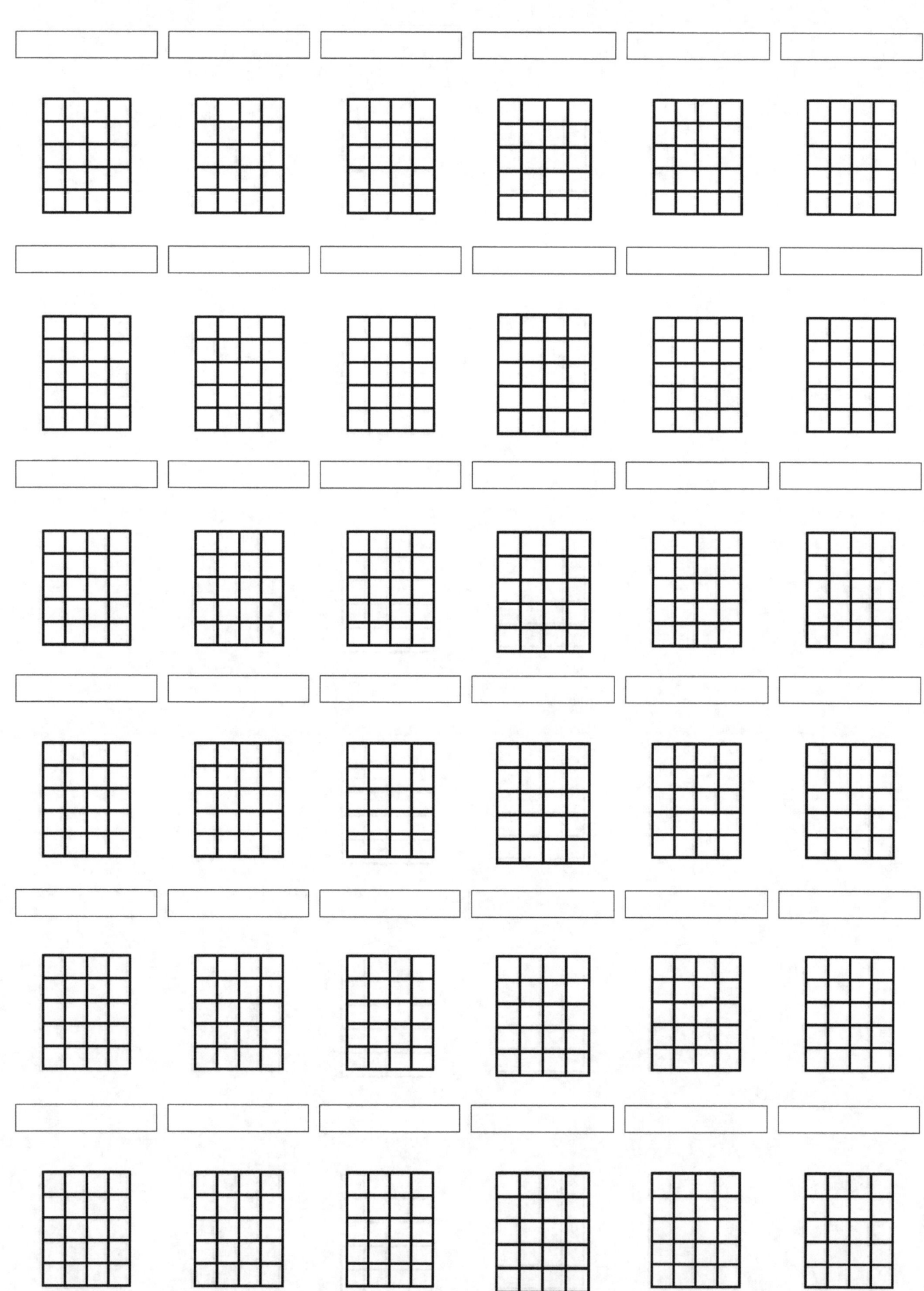

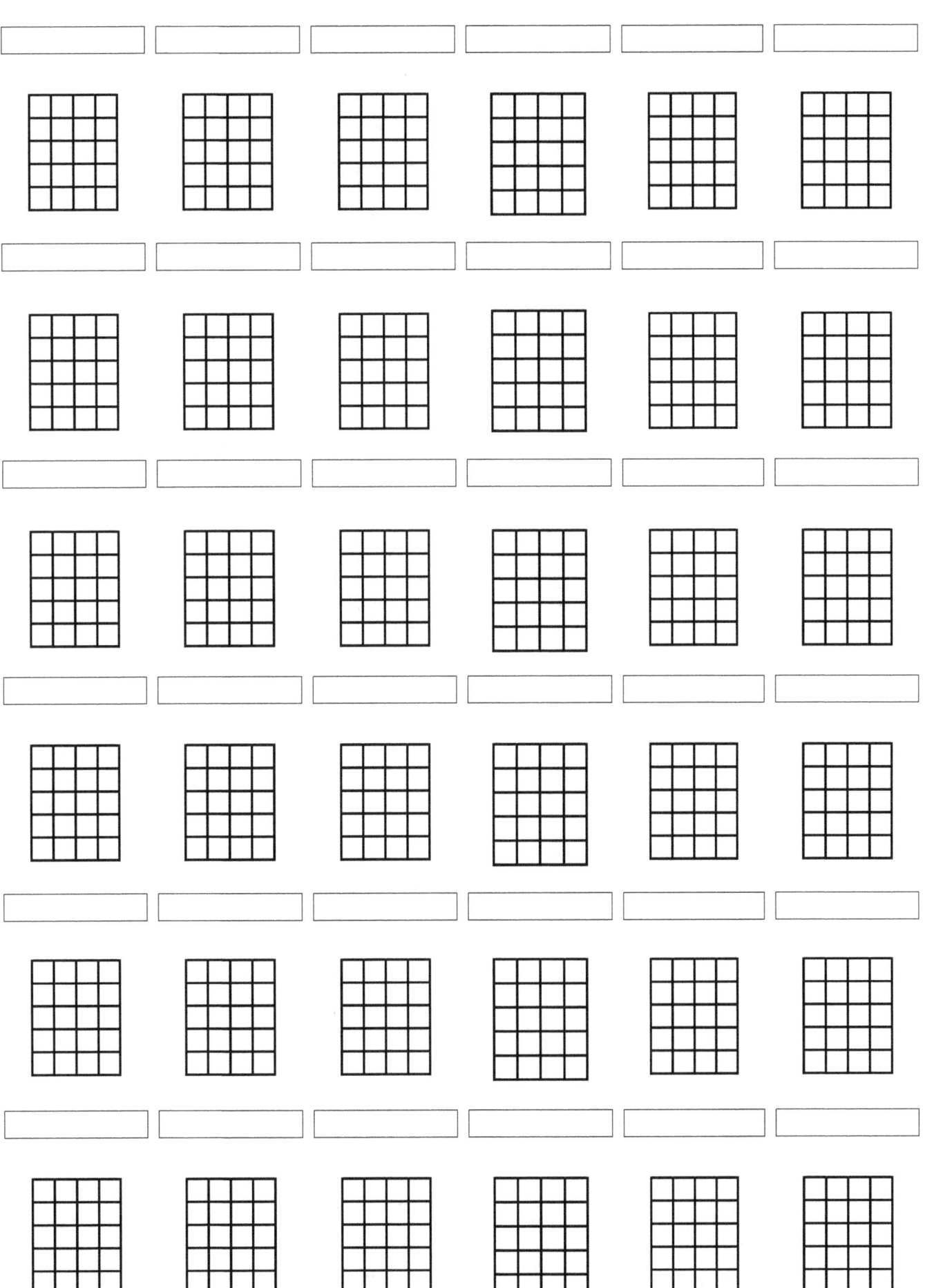

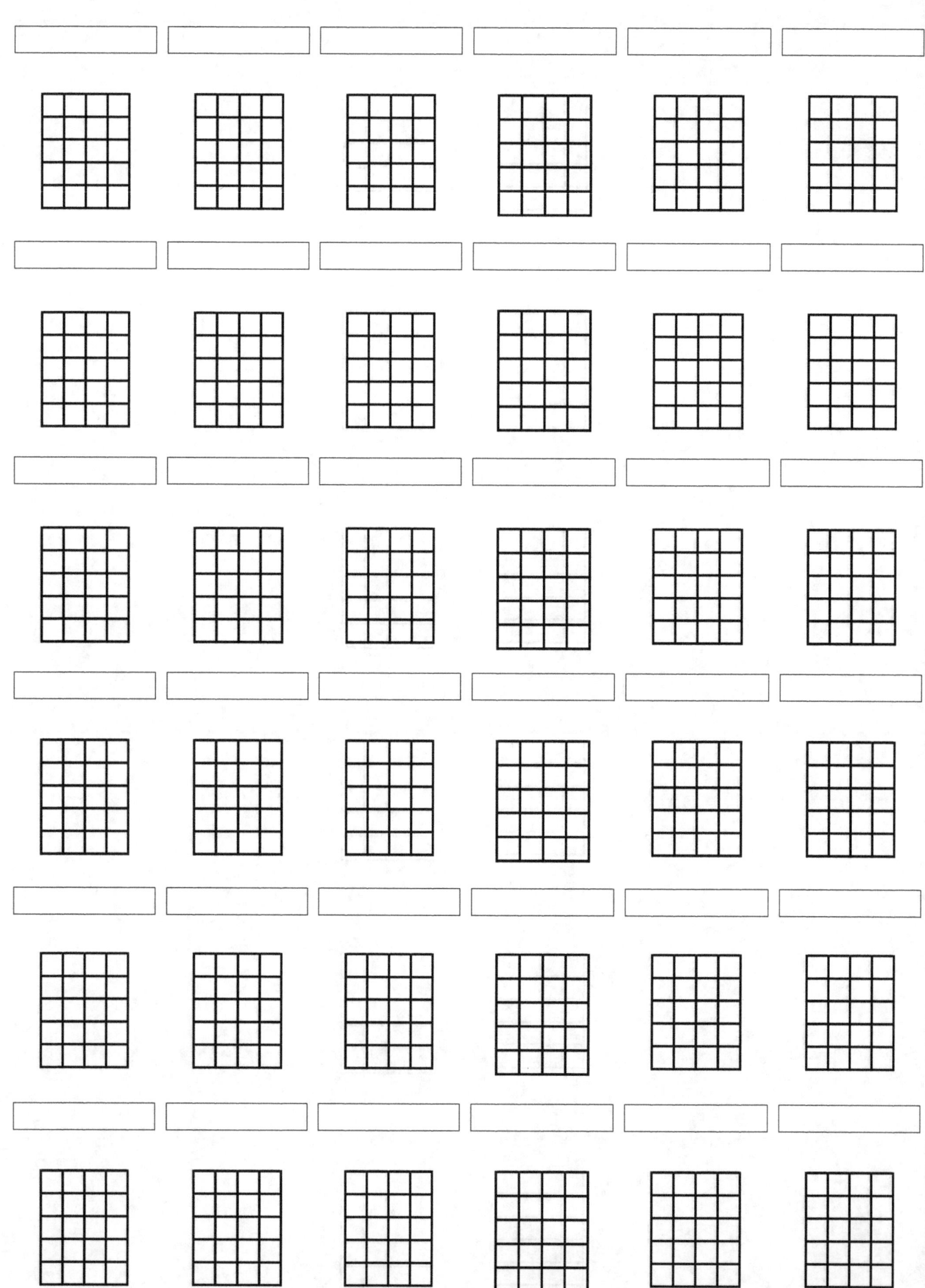

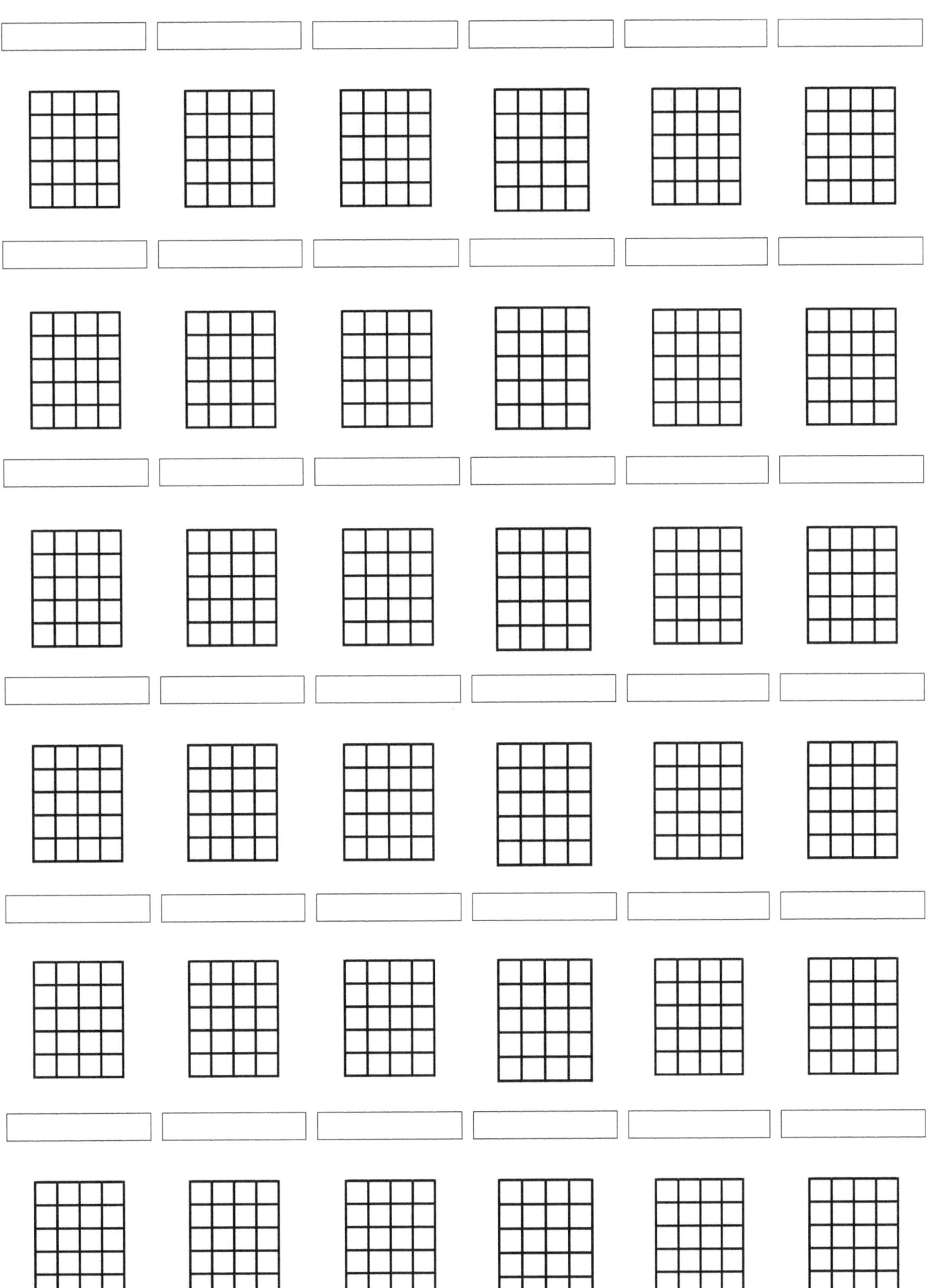

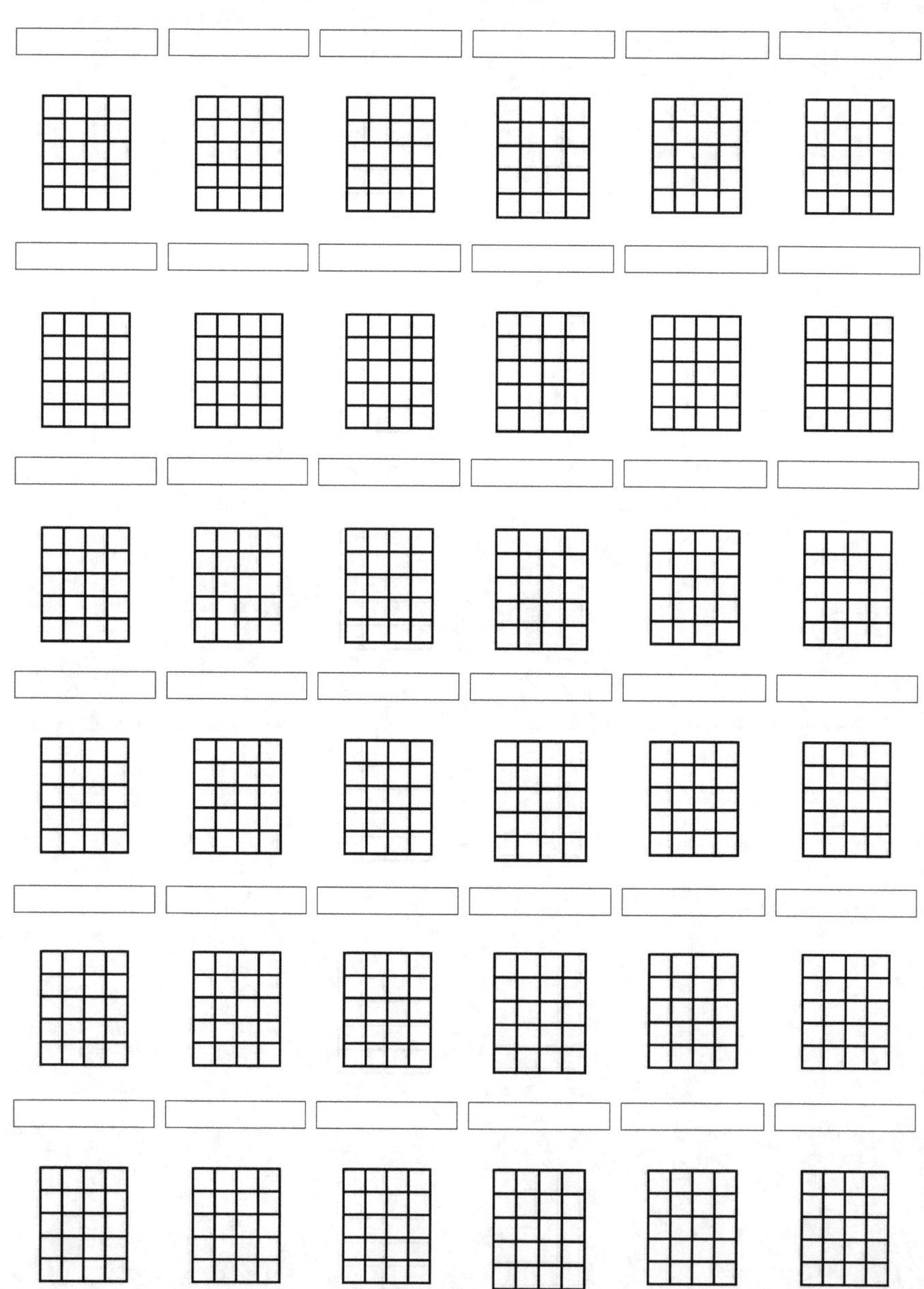

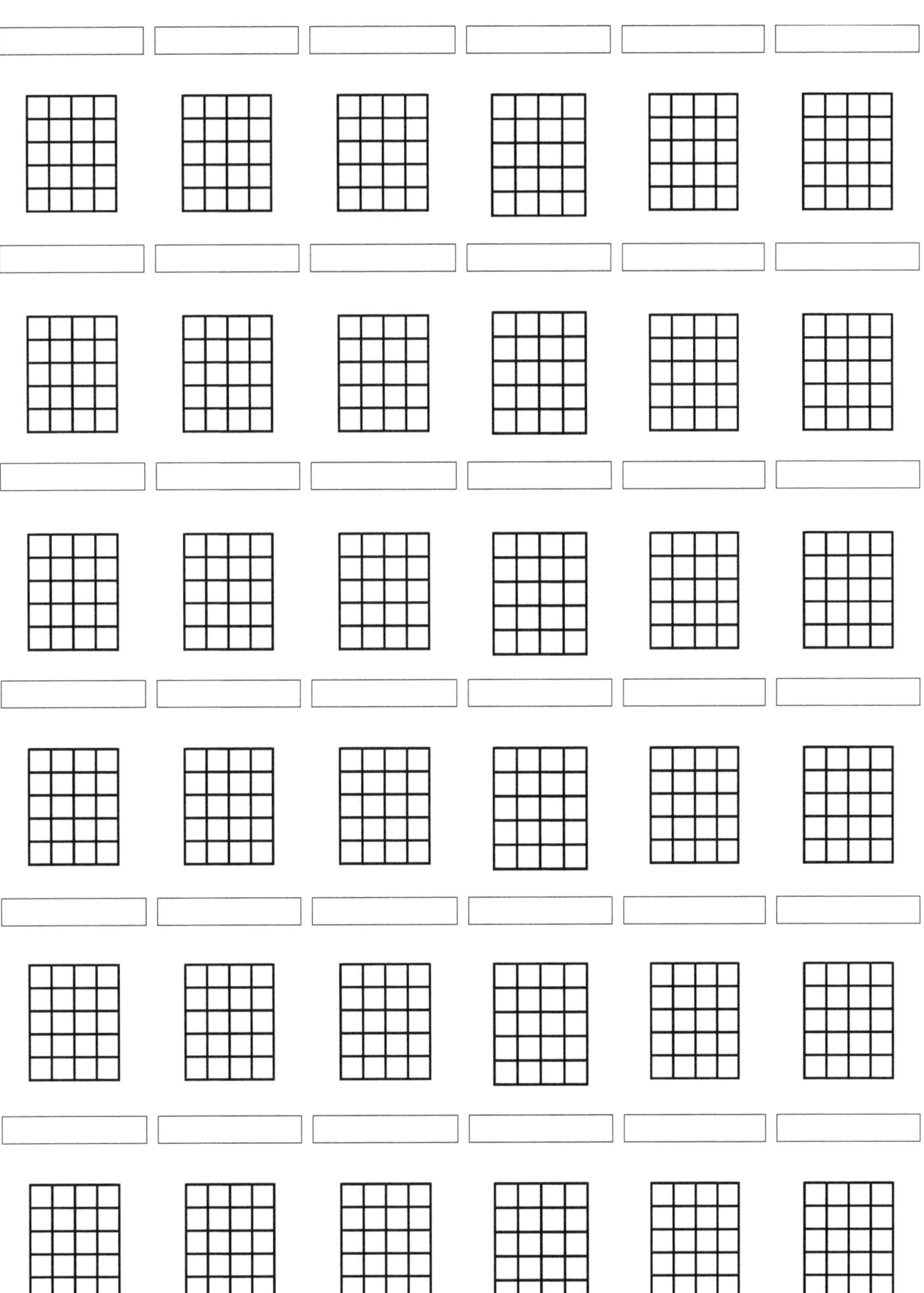

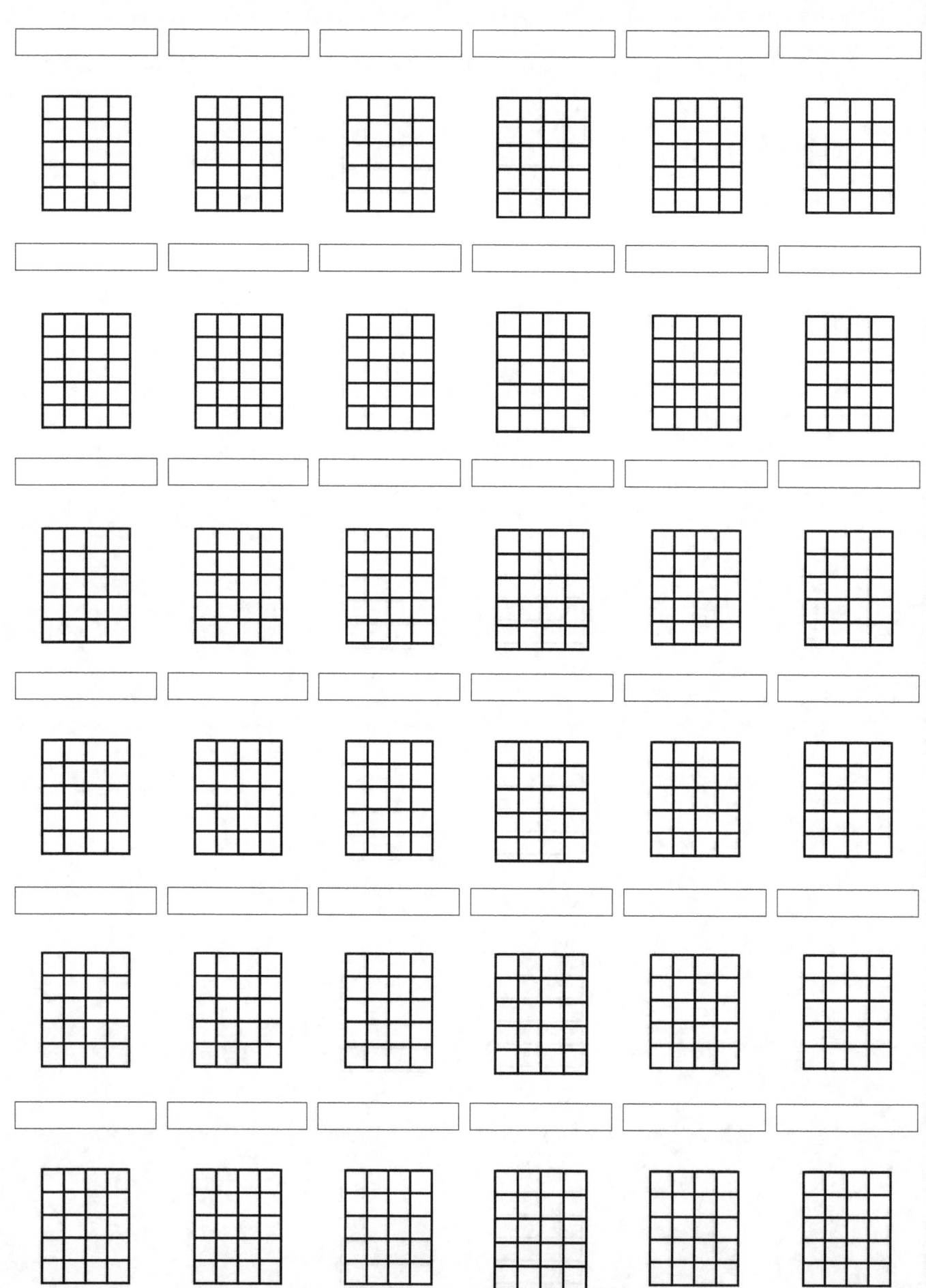

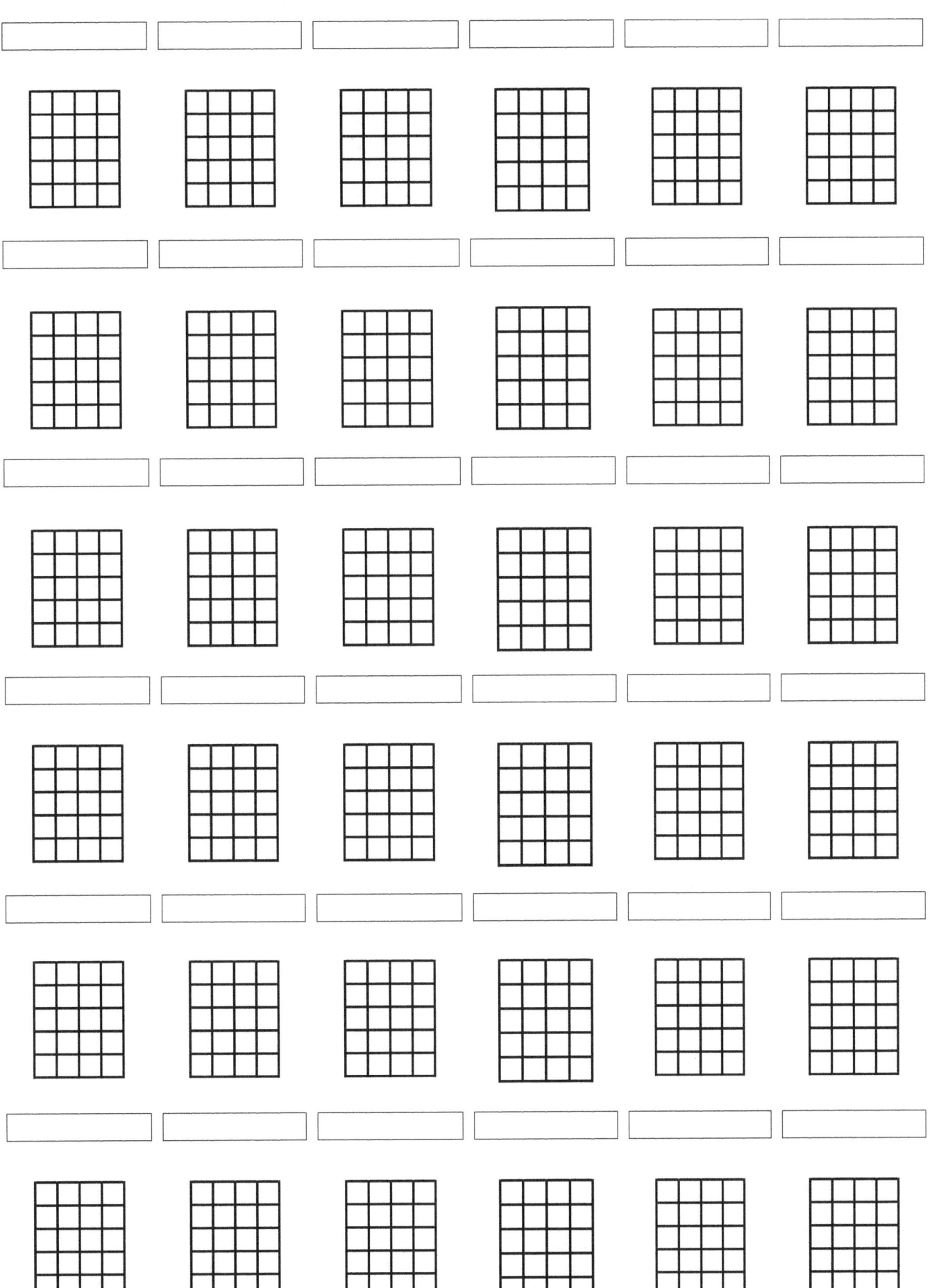

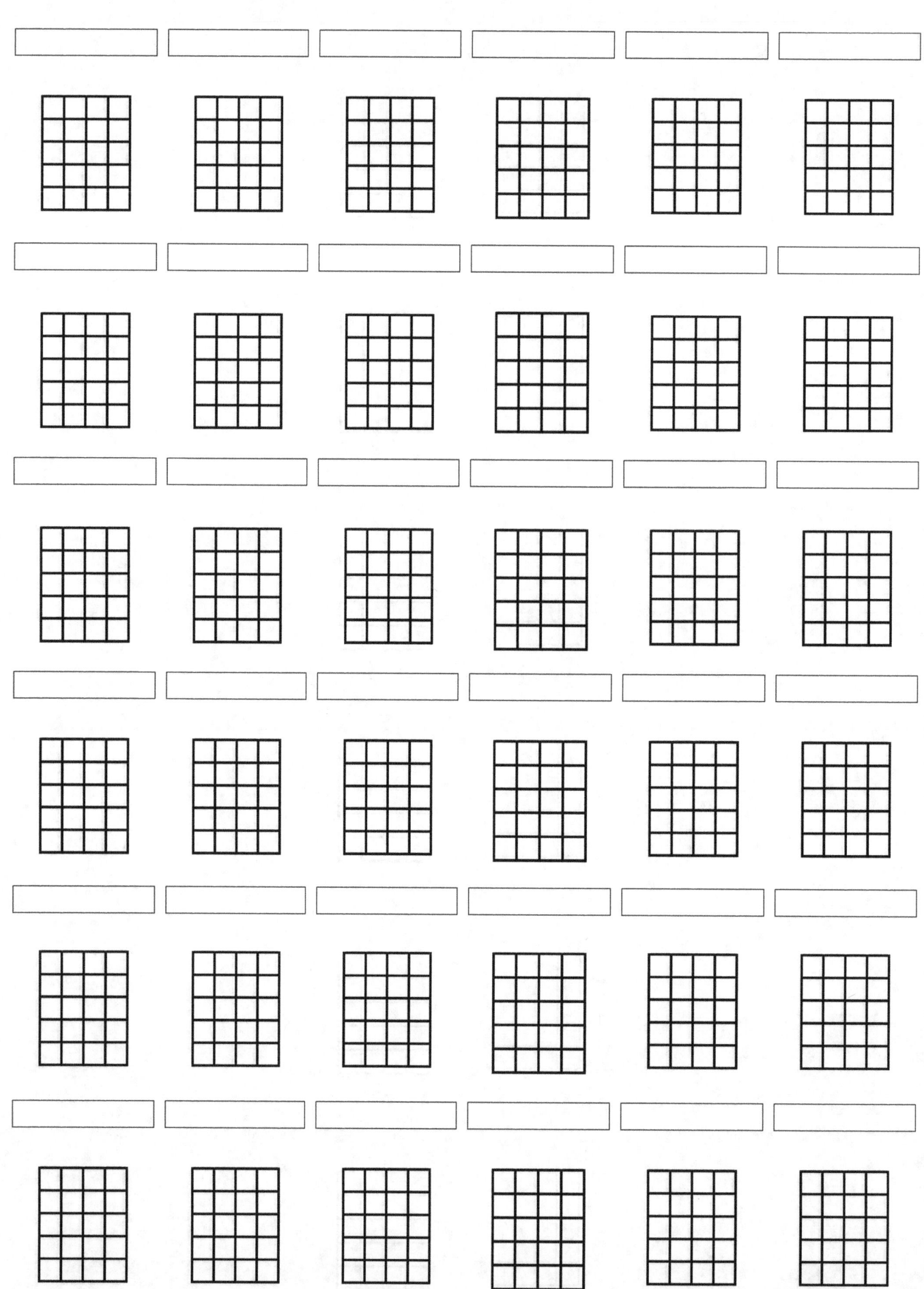

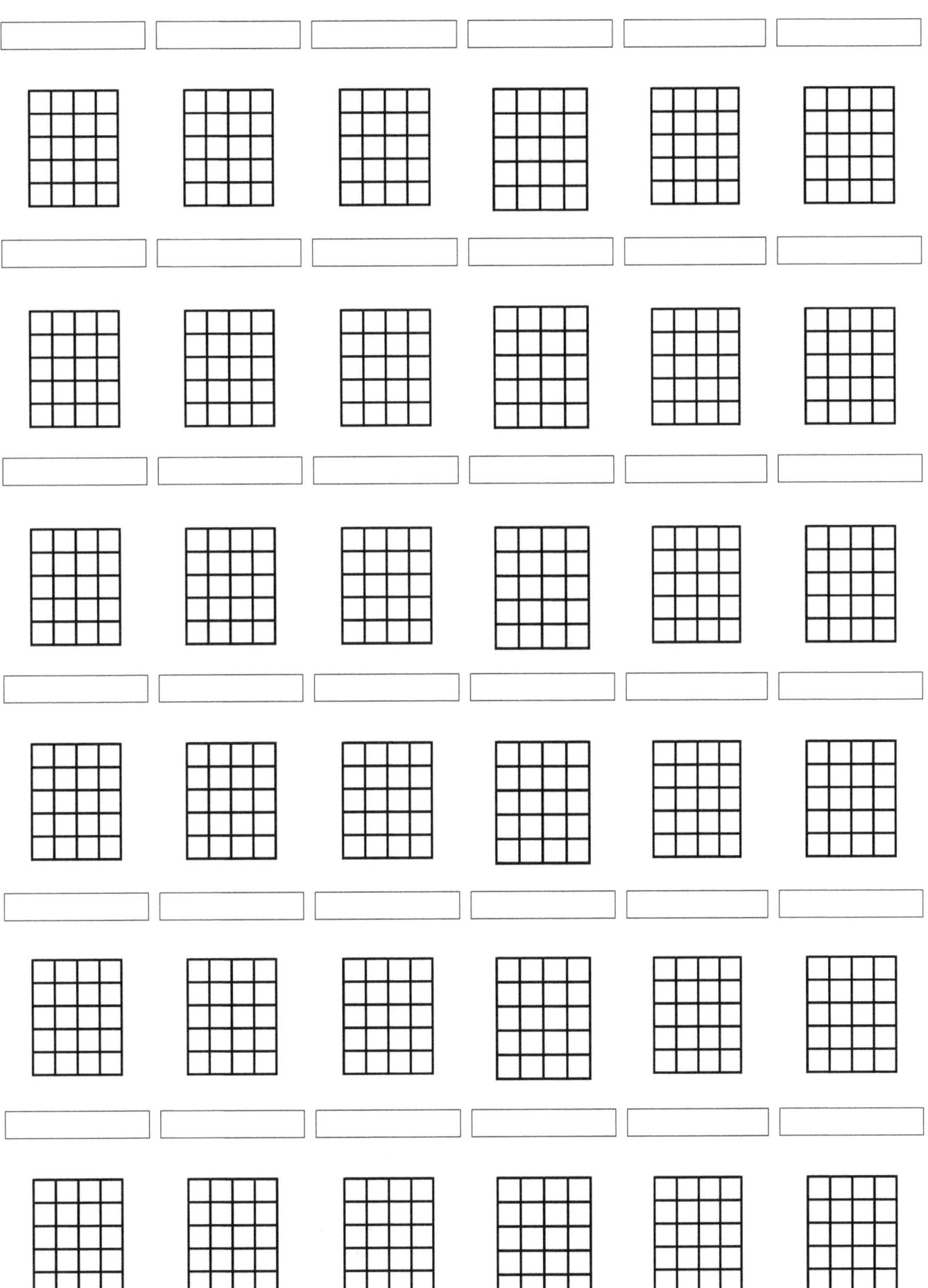

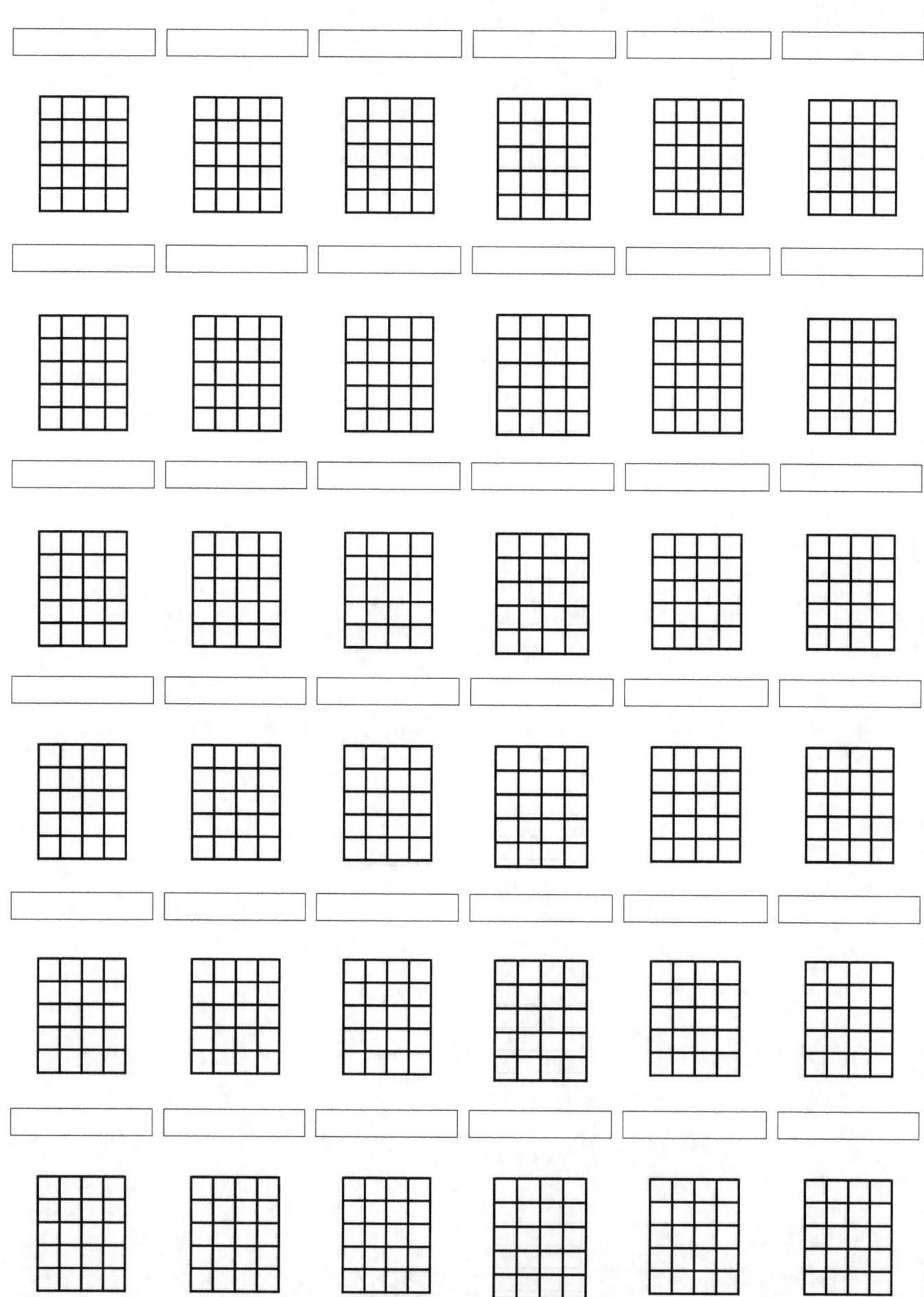

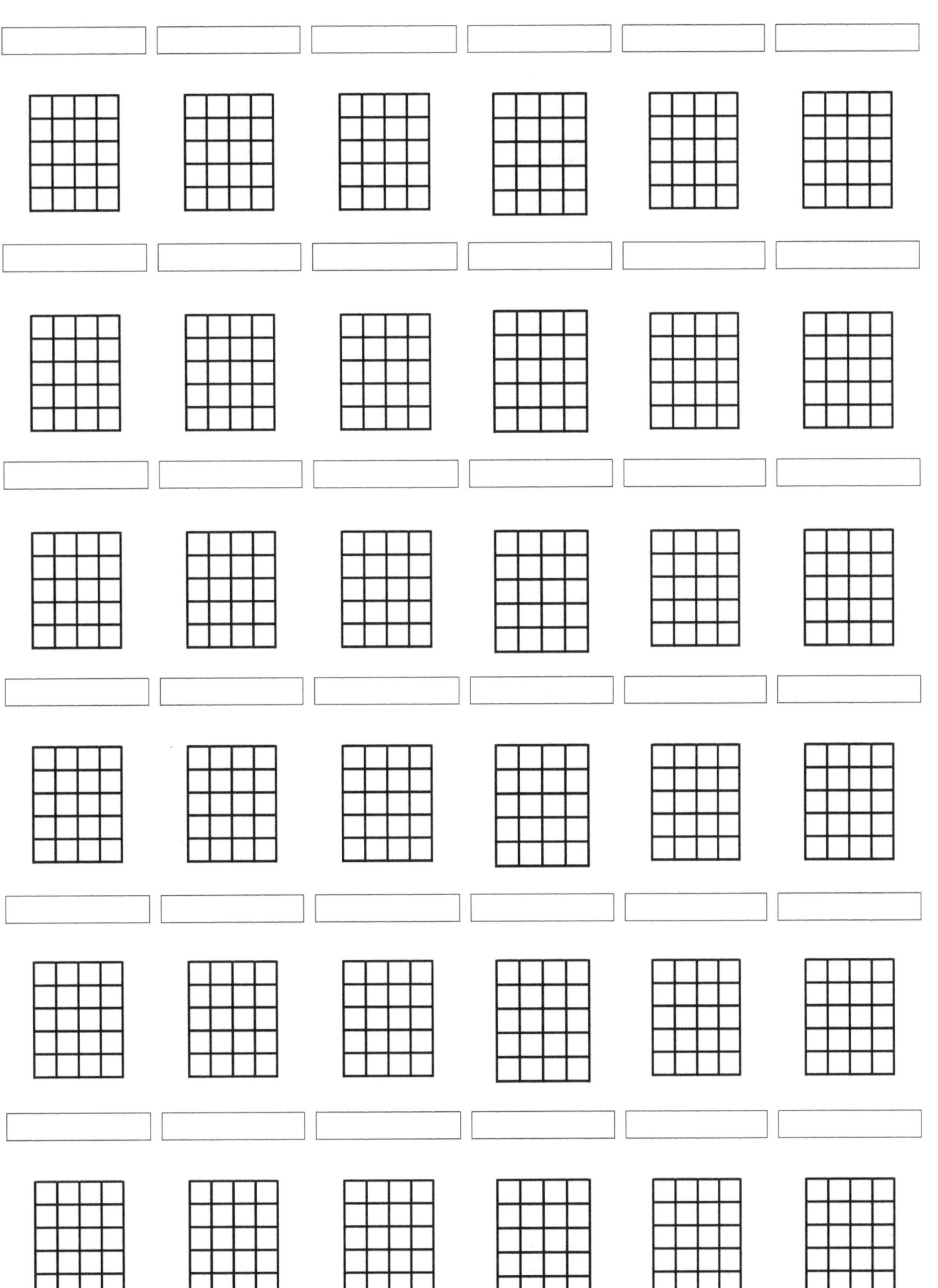

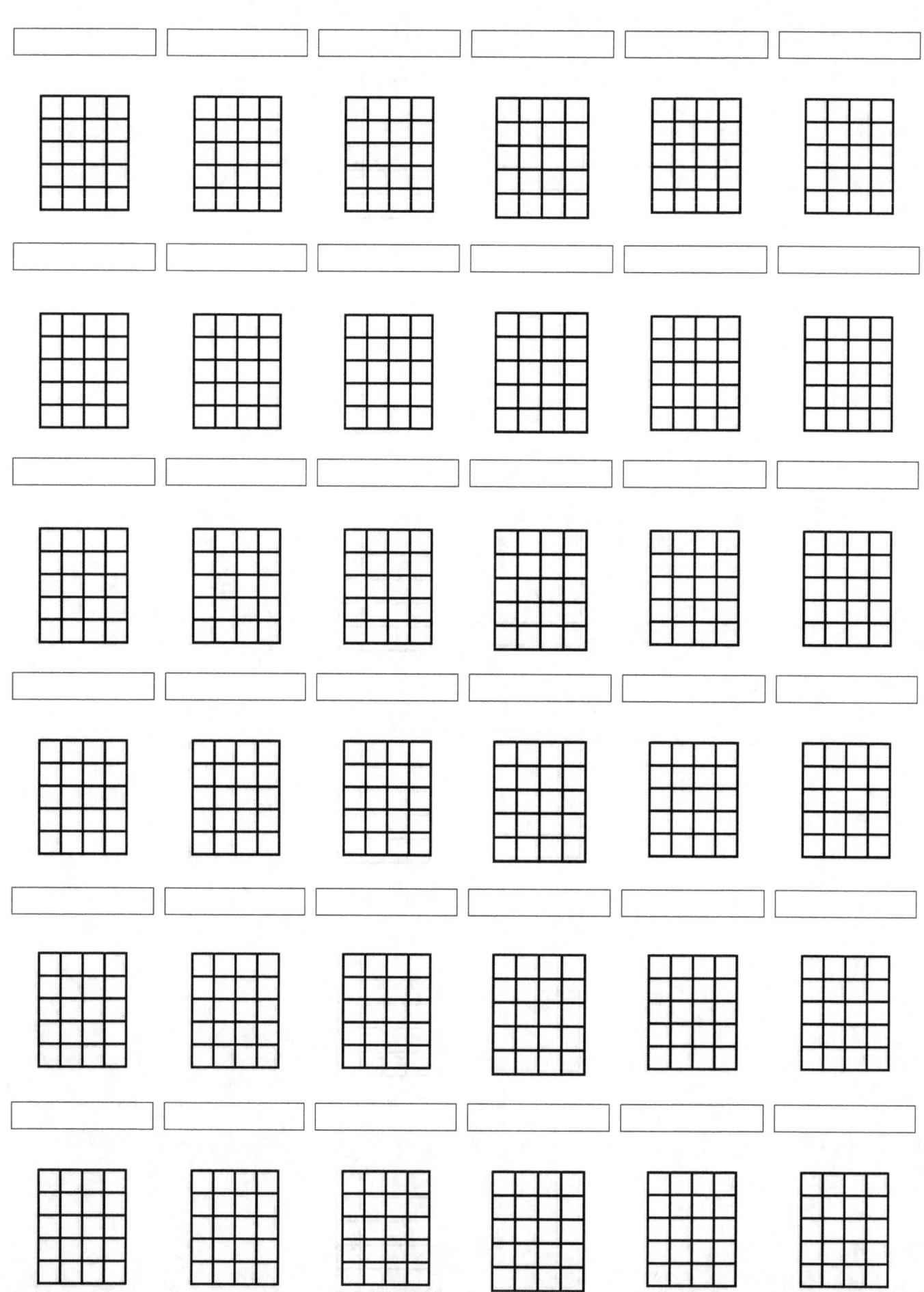

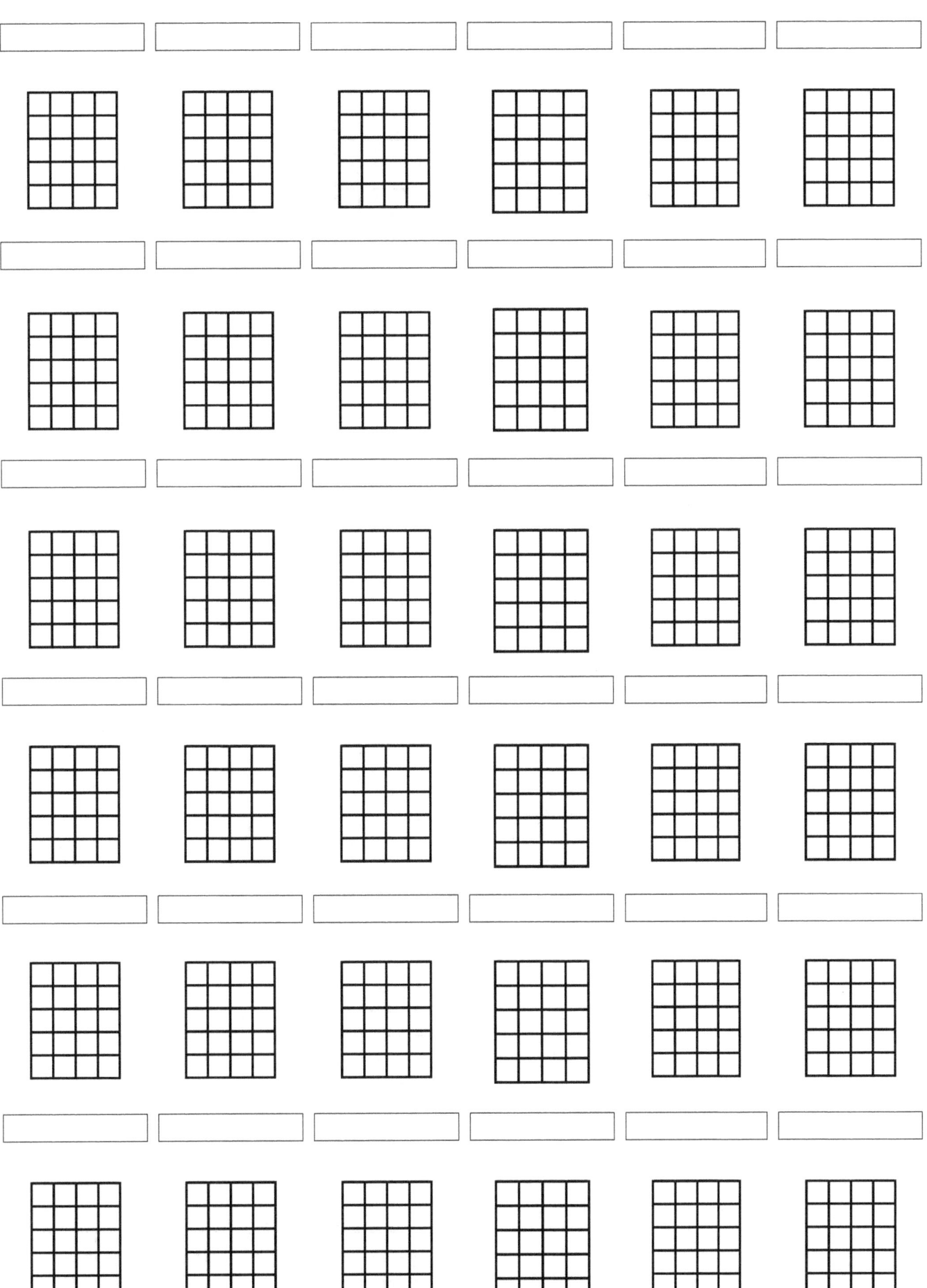

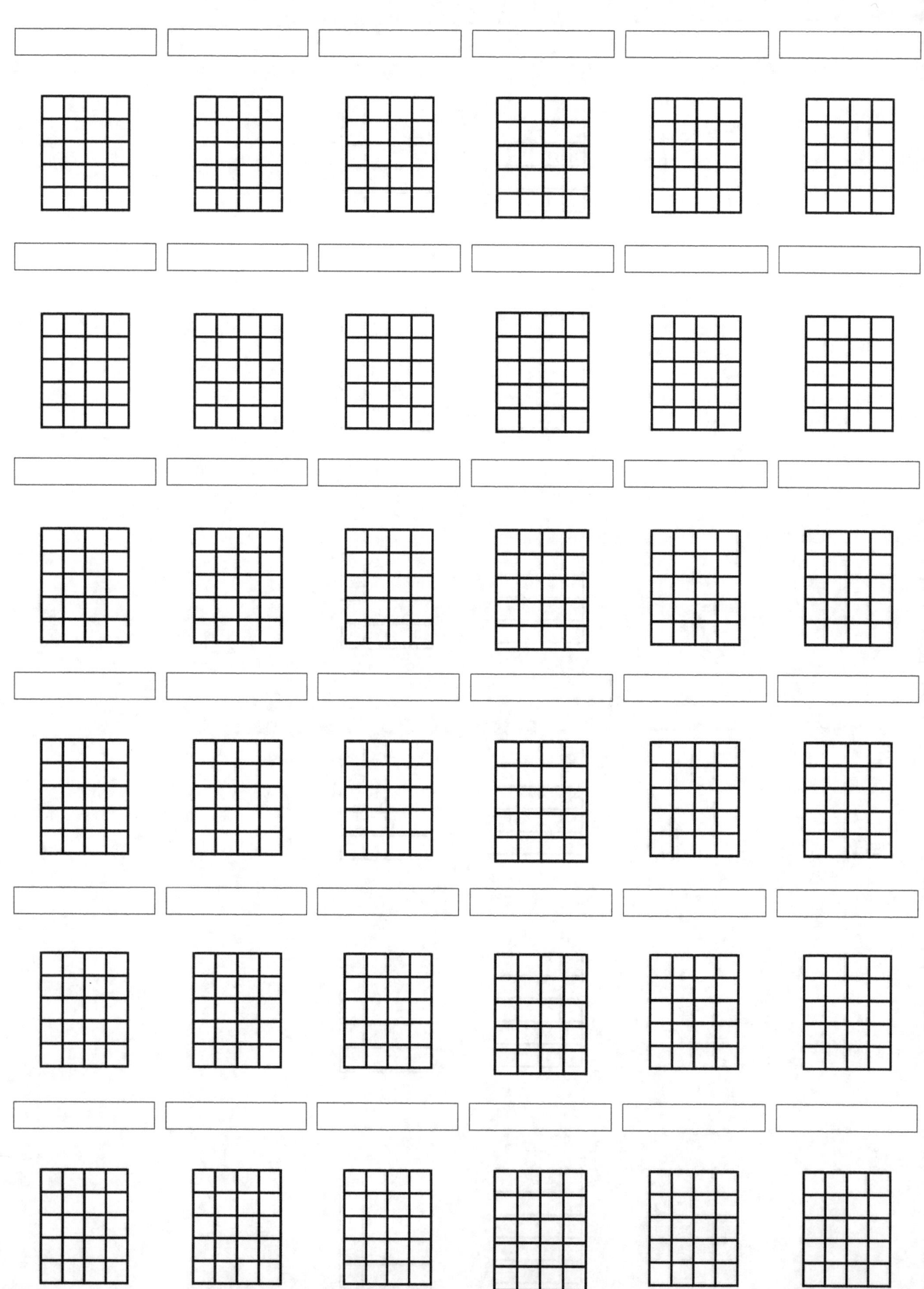

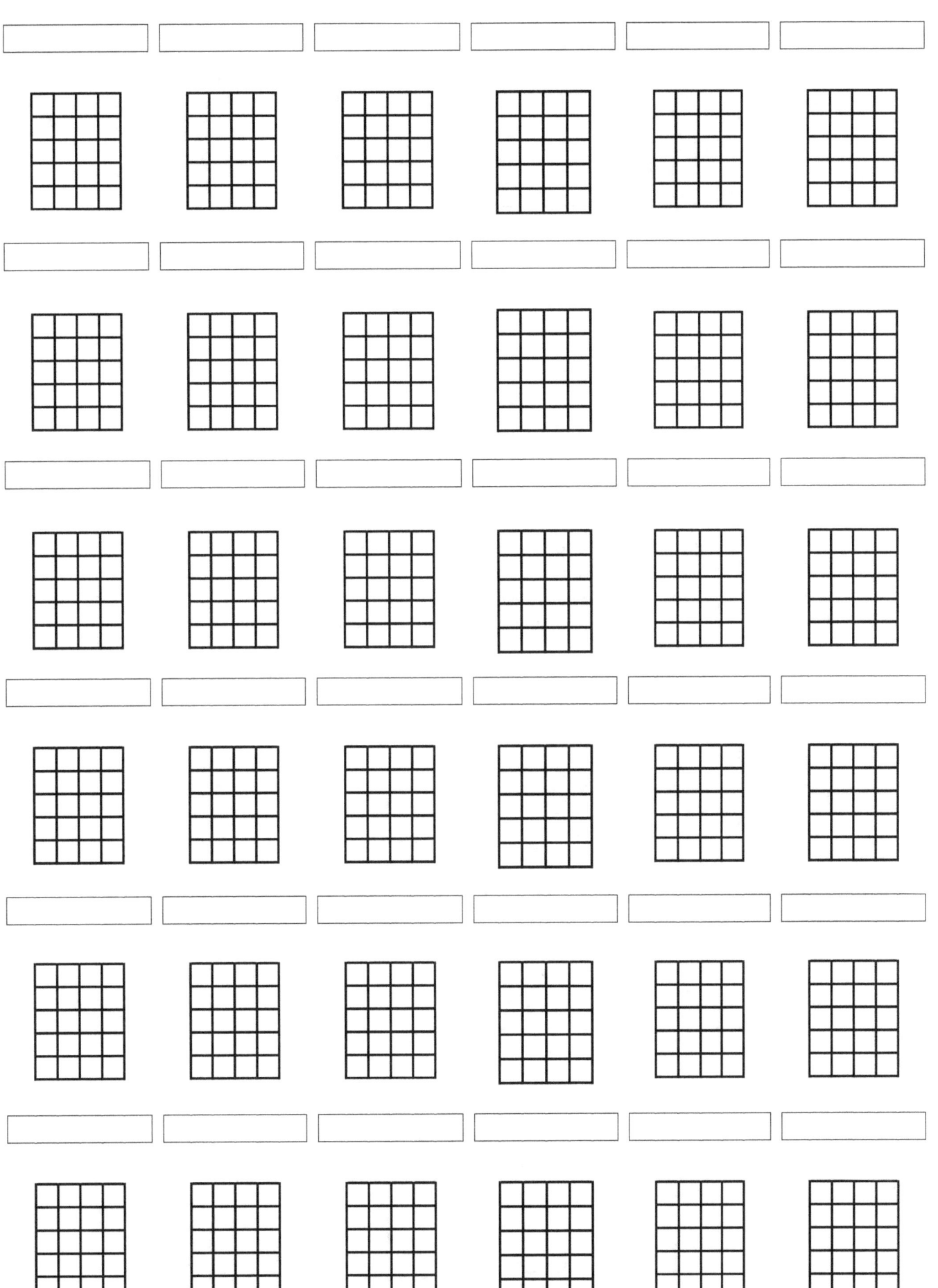

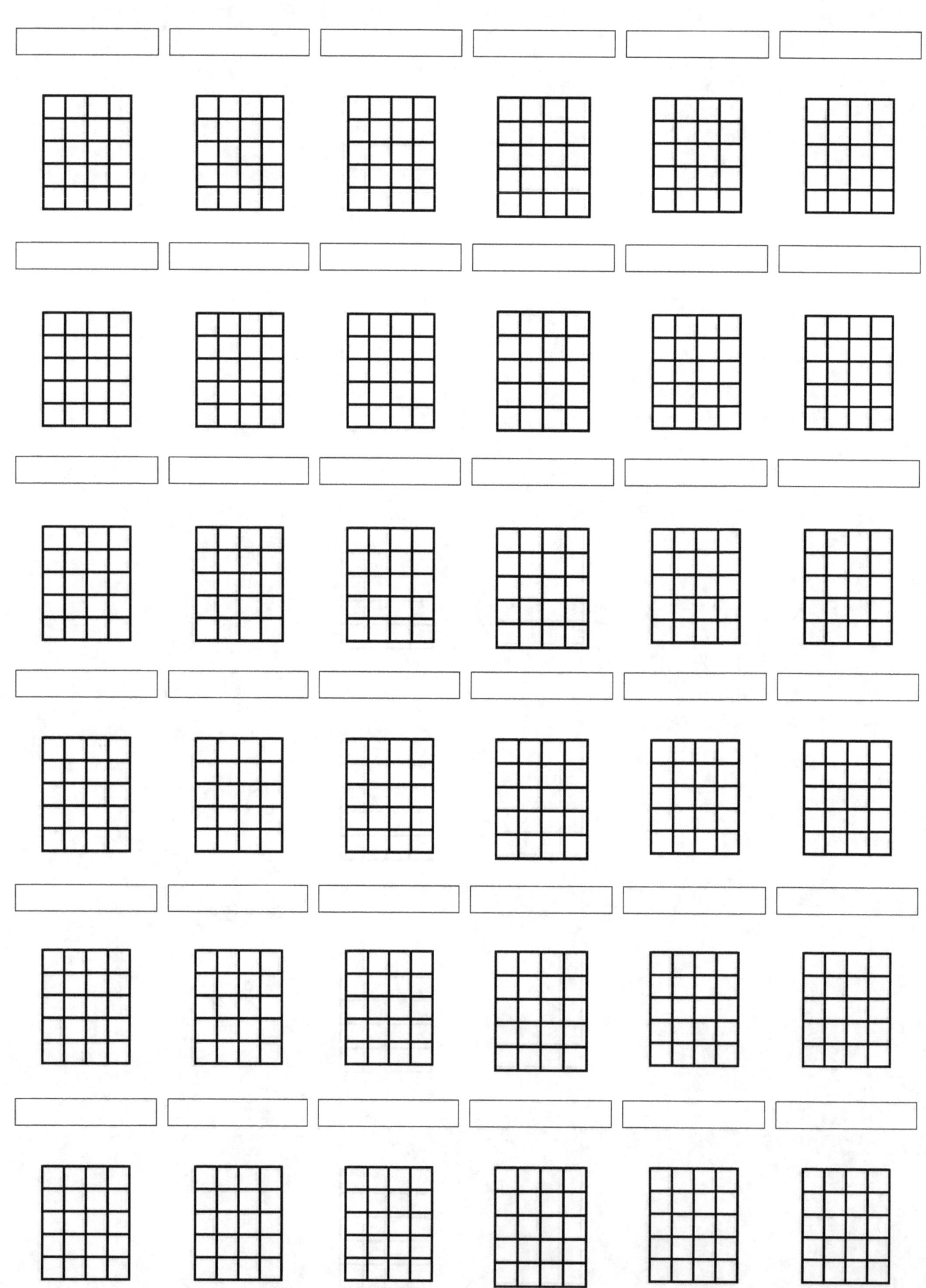

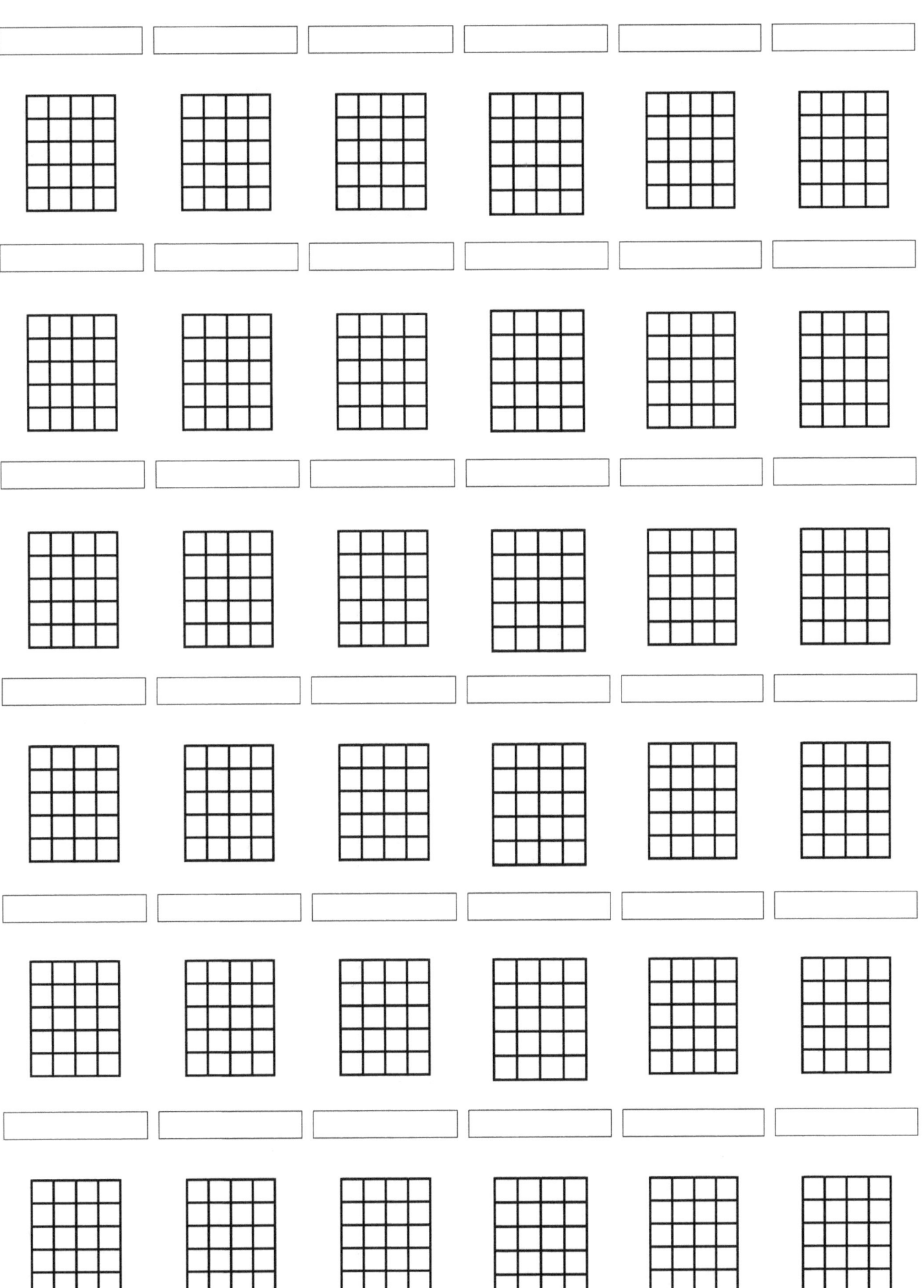

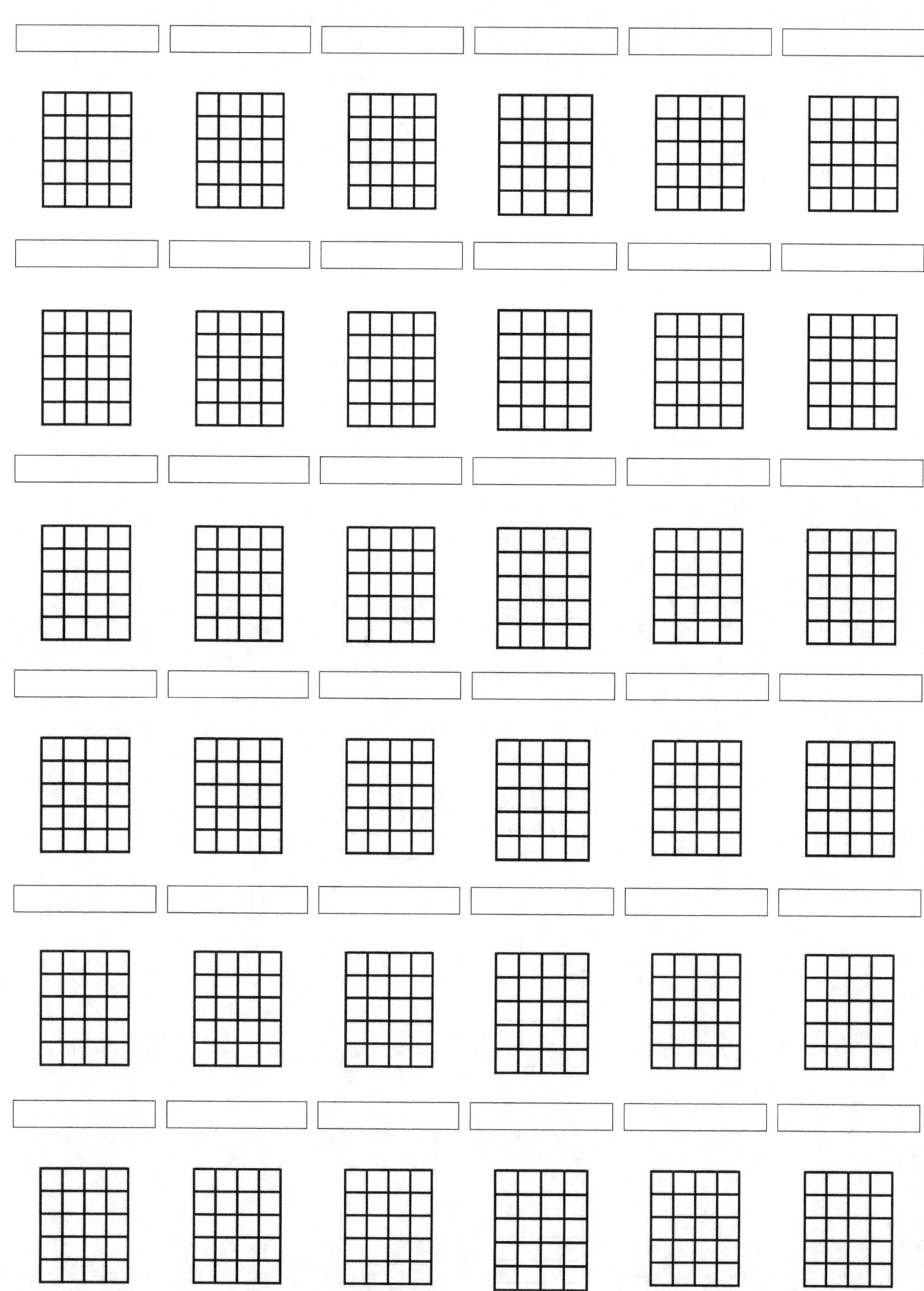